THE

LEMONADE

STAND

A Guide to Encouraging the Entrepreneur in Your Child

THE
LEMONADE
STAND

A Guide to Encouraging the Entrepreneur in Your Child

EMMANUEL MODU

Founder, The Center for Teen Entrepreneurs

GATEWAY PUBLISHERS
Post Office Box 1749
Newark, New Jersey 07101

Published by Gateway Publishers
P.O. Box 1749, Newark, NJ 07101

ISBN: 1–887646–03–5 (formerly 1–55850–058–8)

Printed in the United States of America

This publication is designed to provide accurate and authoritative information with regard to the subject matter covered. It is sold with the understanding that the publisher is not engaged in rendering legal, accounting, or other professional advice. If legal advice or other expert assistance is required, the services of a qualified professional person should be sought.

> —From a *Declaration of Principles* jointly adopted by a
> Committee of the American Bar Association and a
> Committee of Publishers and Associations.

The selection on the back cover by Rush Limbaugh is taken from *The Way Things Ought To Be* (Copyright © 1992 by Rush Limbaugh) and reprinted by permission of Rush Limbaugh and Pocket Books, a division of Simon & Schuster.

The Lemonade Stand is also published in South Korea by: Business Network Co., Suite 401, Sewon Bldg., 92–3, Wonhyoro–2ka, 140–112, Seoul, Korea. Telephone: (82–2) 711–1927–8. Fax: (82–2) 706–5682.

Publisher's Cataloging in Publication Data

Modu, Emmanuel
    The lemonade stand: a guide to encouraging the entrepreneur in your child / by Emmanuel Modu.– [Rev. ed.] – Newark, NJ :
Gateway Publishers, 1996
    p. cm.
    Includes bibliographical references and index.
    Preassigned LCCN: 95–78201
    ISBN: 1–887646–03–5
    1. New business enterprises. 2. Entrepreneurship. 3. Money–making projects for children. 4. Child rearing. 5. Children–Finance, Personal I. Title.
HD62.5.M64   1996   338.7'1'083
                                    QBI95–20330

TABLE OF CONTENTS

ACKNOWLEDGMENTS

This book is dedicated to my wife and friend, Andrea, for her support and encouragement to write it and for taking care of our two beautiful and loving children, Nkem and Amara, while I was completely absorbed in seemingly endless writing marathons. I am also grateful for her help in editing and proofing the various versions of this book.

This book is also dedicated to my father, Dr. Christoper C. Modu for his support and guidance and for setting, by example, high standards for excellence and dedication to any effort; my mother Mrs. Clarice Modu who, through encouragement and by example, showed me the importance of entrepreneurship from a very early age; my sister, Anaezi, who enthusiastically and at all hours of the day or night acted as a sounding board for my ideas; to my other sisters Ijeoma and Enechi for helping with the editing and coming to my rescue when things got tough; and to my brother Chi for his moral support and faith in the "timeliness" of this book.

Acknowledgments also go to my extended family: Dr. Jeanne M. Walker ("Jingle Bells" Grandma), Dr. Arthur D. Walker ("Jingle Bells" Grandpa), Leslie Walker-Naamon, Melissa Walker, Ikenna (thanks for the green!) and Ijeoma Iheoma, Anziya Bundu, and Jeanne Naamon.

A very special "thank-you" to my main editors and proof readers, Arsene Eglis and Euryl December, for their hard work on such short notice. Thanks also to my other editors and proof readers: Lynne Harmacek, Joan DaPonte, and Dr. M.O. Ene.

My deepest thanks to the folks at Junior Achievement—especially, James B. Hayes, Carol Johnson, and Julia Martin.

Finally, many thanks to my agent, Jane Jordan Browne and her former assistant, Matthew Rettenmund, for believing in my book.

FOREWORD

Today's youth face many challenges. Many drop out of school, never reaching their potential. Many never expand upon their own ideas for new services or products. And many never see the career opportunities beyond the traditional workforce. Emmanuel Modu's *The Lemonade Stand* provides a great alternative for every young person.

The Lemonade Stand is written to help students in every grade discover the business person in themselves. It is designed to answer every question they—or their parents—might have regarding turning an idea into a thriving business. And it helps young people realize that their potential is unlimited.

Emmanuel's practical how–to advice and steps provide parents and young people alike with valuable insight on how to turn their ideas into reality. But, most importantly, *The Lemonade Stand* helps students see themselves in a new light—as self–sufficient business people, as entrepreneurs, and as contributing members of their community, their society, and ultimately, of their own families.

Throughout *The Lemonade Stand*, Emmanuel discusses the companies of several young people who saw there was a need for a service or product that wasn't currently available and then developed their ideas into successful businesses. These "success stories" demonstrate the ability in all young people to become self–starters, develop self–confidence and recognize the worth of their ideas.

At Junior Achievement, our mission is to educate and inspire young people to value free enterprise, understand business and economics and to be ready for the workforce of the future. By utilizing real–life business people as classroom volunteers and "hands–on," sequential curriculum materials, Junior Achievement shows students in kindergarten through 12th grade the opportunities to become the business leaders and business owners of the future. *The Lemonade Stand* is a great supplement to the lessons students learn from Junior Achievement volunteers.

With his book, Emmanuel Modu has identified a niche that is just now being addressed—youth entrepreneurship. With sage advice and realistic how–tos, *The Lemonade Stand* provides our youth with the opportunity to be pioneers in tomorrow's workforce. It is truly a book worth owning.

James B. Hayes
President and Chief Executive Officer
Junior Achievement Inc.
(Former Publisher of *Fortune* Magazine)

INTRODUCTION

Child entrepreneurs have come a long way from running lemonade stands and delivering newspapers. Today, kids from 10 to 17 are starting and running full–fledged service and manufacturing businesses.

Consider Larry Villella of Fargo, North Dakota, who at the age of eleven came up with an innovative C–shaped sprinkler that fit around tree trunks and shrubs to make sure that their roots were properly watered. Now 16, Larry has watched his company, Villella's ConServ Products Co., rake in at least $70,000.

When she was 10 years old, environmentalist Melissa Poe of Nashville, Tennessee, was so concerned that pollution was wrecking the environment that she started her own organization called Kids For A Clean Environment (Kids FACE). Kids FACE plants trees and engages in awareness campaigns to show people how they can help clean up the environment. Melissa is now a high school senior and her organization boasts 200,000 young members internationally.

While there are no reliable figures on the number of preteen and teenage entrepreneurs in the United States, all evidence indicates that an increasing number of young people are showing great interest in starting and running their own businesses. *USA Today* had this to say about young entrepreneurs:

Entrepreneurs and executives like these may be leading one of the hottest teen trends of the '90's. No one knows how many of the USA's 27 million teens are in business—big business—for themselves or others. But interest in business workshops, groups and products to help teens start businesses is soaring.

It is no accident that young kids are taking a crack at their own businesses. Their parents are largely responsible for fostering an atmosphere that is receptive to entrepreneurs—no matter how young. These parents have been part of the explosion in entrepreneurship that has gripped America in the past two decades.

The economic realities American corporate employees faced during the 70s and early 80s have contributed to the increased interest in entrepreneurship among parents. During this period, America experienced high interest rates, double–digit inflation, and steep oil prices. Such economic shocks, coupled with intense foreign competition, particularly from Japan, affected the way big corporations conducted business. In this economic environment, corporate downsizing and mergers and acquisitions became the order of the day. Employees could no longer depend on the security of their jobs. Suddenly, corporate giants such as IBM and General Motors no longer guaranteed jobs for life. The massive layoffs that ensued forced employees to reconsider their assumptions about the stability of big–business jobs. Some newly disenfranchised workers, many of whom were parents or were soon–to–be parents, chose to start their own businesses either because they found themselves out of work or because they were unsure of their future in the corporate world. Even those who stayed in their jobs gained an interest in, and a healthy respect for, entrepreneurship.

Today, such parents are increasingly interested in encouraging their kids to become entrepreneurs. More than ever before, they are concerned about their children's future and they realize that reading, writing, and arithmetic are no longer the only skills necessary to guarantee a decent standard of living.

These parents, having witnessed the instability of jobs in the corporate world, are determined to expand their children's career choices beyond the normal professional routes for success, such as engineering, law, medicine, accounting, and teaching. They know that the earlier their kids are exposed to entrepreneurship, the more likely they will be to learn the skills needed to attain economic self–sufficiency.

Thus, the economic realities of the last few decades have fostered a greater appreciation for entrepreneurship among parents and they in turn are passing this appreciation on to their children. As a result, the so called Generation X—those between the ages of 14 and 35—has been dubbed "the most entrepreneurial generation yet" by *Forbes* magazine Indeed, a 1994 Gallup poll commissioned by the Center for Entrepreneurial Leadership Inc. in Kansas City, Missouri, showed that almost 70% of the 602 high school students surveyed wanted to become entrepreneurs. This compares favorably with a survey of 600 adults which revealed that 50% of them wanted to start and run their own businesses.

Not only have many parents recognized the significance of encouraging their kids to become entrepreneurs, but so has the U.S. government. Several years ago, 1,813 small–business owners gathered in Washington, D.C., for The White House Conference on Small Business. The conference provided a forum for small – business owners to discuss issues crucial to America's small–business entrepreneurs. In their final report to the President, the participants made several recommendations concerning small–business owners.

One of the most notable recommendations follows:

The federal government should encourage the advancement of entrepreneurial education and the study of the free enterprise system by promoting an early awareness of the free enterprise system, beginning with primary education and continuing through all levels of education. . . . This training should be taught by small–business people or teachers with hands–on entrepreneurial experience and must include curriculum input from small–business people.

These small–business owners obviously know the value of early entrepreneurial education for children. Many of them have been exposed to entrepreneurs or have been entrepreneurs for most of their lives, and their early business experiences have helped them in running their own businesses. They have made it a priority to get the government to recognize the importance of childhood entrepreneurial education.

Other countries are now recognizing the importance of hands–on business training for kids. Russia, which is now trying to foster a market economy, has been scouting the United States for programs it can adopt to help teach young people about entrepreneurship. The Kirov Institute in St. Petersburg, for example, invited the Volunteers of America (VOA) to help develop a program modeled after VOA's Midas Touch Program, which gives teenagers hands–on business training. In Canada, Projet Entrepreneurship Project (PEP) is one of the most ambitious research projects related to youth entrepreneurship. PEP's mandate is to implement enterprise education across all grade levels. Germany, faced with erasing the vestiges of a planned economy that existed in what was formerly called East Germany, is also showing interest in the topic of youth entrepreneurship. Popular German magazines such as *Stern* and *Der Spiegel* are beginning to feature articles related to youth entrepreneurship. In Korea, the book you are now reading has been translated into the Korean language by a publisher who recognizes the significance of youth entrepreneurship for his country's economic growth.

The great interest in early childhood entrepreneurial education both in the United States and abroad has also come about because entrepreneurship is now being recognized more as a discipline than as an art. In other words, people now believe that entrepreneurs are made, not born. You need only look at the proliferation of courses about entrepreneurship offered in high schools and colleges all over the country to appreciate that people are getting serious about learning what it takes to run their own businesses.

For years, organizations like Junior Achievement, Distributive Educational Clubs of America, and Future Business Leaders of America, have been in the forefront of youth entrepreneurship and business training. But in the past nine years, other organizations have emerged as advocates of entrepreneurial training for young people. Organizations such as The Center for Teen Entrepreneurs, Business Kids, the National Foundation for Teaching Entrepreneurship, and the Institute for Youth Entrepreneurship have all been formed to show kids the benefits of entrepreneurship. In addition, the popularity of new camps such as Teen Business Camp, Camp Entrepreneur, Camp Lemonade at Loyola College, has signaled a new era of entrepreneurship—the era of the child entrepreneur.

1

THE BENEFITS AND MISCONCEPTIONS
OF YOUTH ENTREPRENEURSHIP

Besides the prospect of making extra pocket money, most child entrepreneurs give the following reasons for their decision to start their own businesses: the sense of satisfaction they get from actually putting their ideas into action, and the desire to take control of their own destinies and to express their creative talents. As one young entrepreneur put it, "It's exhilarating to plan something, to watch it grow, and to know you made it happen."

While some parents recognize the importance of encouraging their children to become entrepreneurs, many more are still exposing their children exclusively to the traditional ways of making a living, such as engineering, medicine, law, and the like. Their attitudes are partially shaped by habit. That is, they themselves grew up thinking that a fulfilling life meant finding a stable job after attending high school and college. However, as we all know, stability in the job market is a thing of the past.

Parental attitudes about entrepreneurship are also shaped by parental perception that entrepreneurship and education are incompatible. In addition, some parents mistakenly assume that kids are not capable of understanding business concepts or that child entrepreneurship will turn their kids into materialistic junior yuppies.

In this chapter, I will discuss both the benefits and misconceptions of child entrepreneurship. As you read on, you will see why so many kids are willing to try their hands at real businesses and why their parents are supporting them in their efforts.

BENEFITS

Self–reliance and a feeling of accomplishment

How many of you reading this book can honestly say that you really enjoy your job? A survey conducted by Donald Kanter, professor of marketing at Boston University, and business consultant Philip Mervis reveals some shocking statistics about the job satisfaction levels of workers. Seventy–two percent of the 1,115 people surveyed felt that management treated them unfairly, and 42% said that they hated their jobs and that their hard work was not rewarded. If you happen to love your job, you are among a vanishing breed of workers.

The survey confirms what I have suspected for years—there are a lot of unhappy workers out there who are trapped in jobs they detest and who feel no real sense of accomplishment in their work. What surprises me, however, is that parents with such negative attitudes toward their jobs sell their kids fairy tales about getting a job, working hard, and living the American Dream.

Talk to any number of entrepreneurs, and you will hear the same thing over and over again—the most important benefit of starting and running their own businesses is that they are free to do what they like. For example, I once met a potter in Salt Springs (one of the islands near Vancouver, British Columbia, Canada). As I walked into his pottery store, I noticed that his shelves were bare. There was a sign on one of the tables that read, "I am currently low on inventory. Please bear with me." As I chatted with him, I asked him how much time he spent on his business. He responded that he spent enough time to enjoy his creations, but not so much time that his pottery business would become an annoying chore. This explained why his shelves were empty! He was quite happy doing what he was doing at his own pace, and he did not want to turn it into drudgery. To me, this is the essence of entrepreneurship—the freedom to do what you like. Some entrepreneurs may spend 30 hours a week, while others may spend 100 hours. The bottom line is that no matter how much time they spend on their businesses, they feel a sense of pride in operating them. This sense of fulfillment is more rewarding than money.

I conducted a survey of 160 teenagers (ages 16 to 18) who attended Entrecon, a high school conference on entrepreneurship at the University of Pennsylvania. I asked the participants why they were interested in starting their own businesses. These young people expressed their motivation for becoming entrepreneurs in terms of the sense of satisfaction that entrepreneurship gave them as well as the sense of being in control of their own destinies. A statistic that may surprise you is that only 15% of the students were interested in entrepreneurship solely as a way to earn money. I will discuss the survey in its entirety in a later chapter.

When one of the kids at Entrecon was asked what got her interested in entrepreneurship, she said, "security—happiness that I will be working at something I created. As an entrepreneur, you don't have limits unless you limit yourself."

A 1994 Gallup poll commissioned by the Center for Entrepreneurial Leadership Inc. in Kansas City, Missouri, showed that 43% of the 602 high school students surveyed wanted to become entrepreneurs so they could work for themselves (and thus control their own destinies), and that only 18% of them wanted to start a business solely to make money.

The results of the Gallup survey correlate well with my own unscientific poll taken in 1991. Chapter 17 will give you more details about my survey. You will see that young people do indeed feel that the ability to control their destinies is one of the most important benefits of becoming an entrepreneur.

Freedom of choice

Anyone who spends enough time around children quickly learns how impressionable they are. One often hears children talking about the types of careers they would like to have when they grow up. Some may want to be firefighters, others police officers, and still others may want to be pilots or nurses. Chances are that if you talk to kids long enough to find out why they are interested in these occupations, you will find that perhaps firefighters, police officers or pilots visited their schools, or that they have had some contact with the school nurse. If they have not been influenced by these role models in person, they may have chosen their role models straight from the television set.

There is nothing wrong with these professions. However, to help your kids reach their full potential and to truly give them the freedom to determine their own destinies, you should expose them to entrepreneurship.

While outsiders can influence children's goals and aspirations, children are more influenced by their parents' likes and dislikes, habits, attitudes, and occupations. Unfortunately, the traditional ways of making a decent living are still the only games in town for many well–meaning parents. They cling to the hope that when their kids grow up they will work for prestigious companies and, thus, lead fulfilling lives. These parents hang their hats on corporate benevolence to provide their kids with a decent standard of living in the years ahead. But things have changed in the past twenty years.

In the good old days, the unwritten corporate rule went like this: *get a job with a large corporation and demonstrate total loyalty to the company for a successful career.* This philosophy about work and loyalty to the employer may have come about because of the social turmoil created by the Great Depression. American workers learned that the key to job security was an unwavering allegiance to the almighty company. As the years went by, the loyal workers collected watches, gold badges and tie clips in commemoration of their fifth, tenth, fifteenth, and twentieth year of service. When retirement time came around, the workers looked forward to collecting their pensions.

All of this has changed. Those parents who cling to the out-dated notion of corporate benevolence are living in the past. In the past few decades, the fragility of the economy and foreign competition have made the implicit corporate guarantee of lifetime jobs null and void. *Inc.* magazine said this of the changing employment outlook for young people:

> *Like it or not, this generation of students and the ones to come are going to have to take care of themselves economically—and they're not being prepared to do it . . . . Instead, at our best, we are teaching them to be loyal employees and dutiful consumers, preparing them for a world that no longer exists.*

In the 90s, as in the 80s and 70s, the economy is once again unstable. At the height of the 1990–1991 recession, a survey conducted by *The New York Times* and *CBS News* revealed that 58% of the people responding said they "knew someone well who was currently out of work." About half said they were finding it harder to make ends meet. These statistics tell a grim tale of uncertainties and hard luck that workers are increasingly facing.

Lest you think that job instability is caused solely by periodic recessions, a 1995 *Wall Street Journal* article points out that corporations are laying people off even in the midst of record profits:

> *While corporate profits were surging to record levels last year, the number of job cuts approached those seen at the height of the (1990–1991) recession. Corporate profits rose 11% in 1994, after a 13% rise in 1993, according to DRI/McGraw Hill, a Lexington, Mass., economic consultant. Meanwhile, corporate America cut 516,069 jobs in 1994, according to outplacement firm Challenger, Gray & Christmas in Chicago. That is far more than in the recession year of 1990, when 316,047 jobs were eliminated, and close to the 1991 total of 552,292 jobs.*

As unstable as the economic environment is now, some economists are predicting that the business climate in America will become more volatile in the future. These individuals are saying that the North American Free Trade Agreement (NAFTA) and the General Agreement on Tariffs and Trade (GATT) may make it easier for corporations to pick up and move to cheaper–labor sites. This may ultimately mean fiercer competition in the global economy, thus leading to more layoffs. Furthermore, new trade arrangements such as the European Economic Community and the Asian–Pacific trade bloc may further erode the global position of the United States.

Besides depending on the stability of jobs in the corporate world to provide gainful employment for their children, some parents also let their egos get in the way of encouraging the entrepreneurial activities of their kids. Most parents would rather tell their friends that after their kids graduate from college they will work as programmers for IBM than tell them that their kids will start a word–processing business. They are mainly concerned about the prestige quotient of their children's occupations.

Parents who raise their children without opening their minds to the possibility of running their own businesses or organizations are sentencing their kids to a life of what I call "corporate bondage." A person is a victim of corporate bondage when he or she has swallowed the idea that working for someone else until retirement is the only option. This victim is conditioned to think this way by a combination of parents, friends, the victim's educational institutions, and society in general.

As parents, we all want the best for our children. We want them to be happy and financially secure when they grow up. We also want them to avoid unnecessary risks that could leave them financially unstable. However, this is no excuse for neglecting to show kids the entrepreneurial alternatives that are around them.

As guardians and role models for your children, you owe it to them to expose them to alternative ways of leading satisfying lives. Specifically, you must expose them not only to the traditional professional occupations in banking, engineering, and law, but also to the possibility of actually starting and running their own businesses. In this way, you will be giving them true freedom of choice in deciding what to do with their lives.

The earlier the better

By age 14, Bob Wilson of Los Angeles, California, had started his third business. His first two attempts failed miserably. Nevertheless, he took a stab at a third business—lawn mowing. I was impressed by Bob's perseverance so I asked him whether he was ever discouraged because of the failure of his first two businesses. He answered, "I learned from my mistakes in my first two businesses. Now I feel like a really experienced entrepreneur. I am not making much money now, but I am learning a lot about what it takes to run a business without losing all my money."

Bob believes that he learned more about entrepreneurship with each business failure. He more or less used these failures as training ground for a successful business in the future.

Although it is rare for kids to be this philosophical about their failures, Bob is on the right track. If your kids start their own businesses, even their failures can teach them about the kind of qualities and skills it takes to become entrepreneurs. What's more, your young entrepreneurs will be risking relatively little money. They have no family to support, no mortgage or car payments. In short, business failures are not as disastrous at a young age as they can be as an adult when one is burdened by other responsibilities and obligations.

Starting kids young also has another big advantage. In general, people pick up skills faster when they are young than when they are adults. For example, kids pick up languages faster than adults. *Maybe they just have less clutter in their minds*. But this same reasoning applies to other disciplines as well as to entrepreneurship. Starting your kids at a young age on the road to entrepreneurship gives them a head start over their peers. With business experience under their belts, they will be better able to start and run successful businesses as adults. By the age of sixteen, Morris Beyda of Dix Hill, New York, was running his own computer consulting firm called Computers Simplified. Morris had this to say about his early entry into the world of entrepreneurship: "I feel that I will have a large advantage over others of my age when I finally reach the real world as a result of my experiences."

A number of studies have been conducted establishing that children acquire entrepreneurial skills more easily than adults, and that as children grow older, the traits that are necessary for becoming an entrepreneur begin to diminish if they are not nurtured. Marilyn Kourilsky, former dean of teacher education at UCLA's Graduate School of Education (and current Vice President of the Ewing Marion Kauffman Foundation's Center for Entrepreneurial Leadership Inc.), found that 25% of kindergarten children show characteristics such as risk taking and high achievement motivation that are usually associated with business success. She also found that by high school, only about 3% of students show these same qualities. From her research she concluded that parental and societal influences help encourage kids to conform to non–entrepreneurial behavior.

Teaching them how to make money on their own

Every summer, millions of kids go through the ritual of trying to find employment. Some are fortunate enough to find challenging employment that provide them with the opportunity to develop skills that they can use later in starting their own businesses. However, the vast majority of kids end up working at the local hamburger joint or the local grocery store, making minimum wage. If your children are fortunate enough to get jobs that pay the minimum wage of $4.25 per hour, they won't even net enough money in one hour to afford movie tickets. Moreover, such jobs do not contribute much to your children's entrepreneurial development. Sure, they can make a few dollars, but these jobs are not meant to encourage any creative behavior. Rather than working in these types of jobs, your kids are better off starting their own businesses.

One summer, 17–year–old Ronald Silver decided that he was not going to accept his usual summer job at a hardware store. During the previous summers, while Ronald was working at the store, the owner had shown him how to strip and finish wood furniture. Instead of taking the same job for the third summer in a row, he decided to start his own business as a furniture stripper and finisher. By his calculation, he made about $7 per hour that summer—nearly twice as much as the minimum wage at that time. Ronald says, "Kids don't have to settle for minimum wage if they have special skills people want." Ronald was fortunate enough to pick up the skills he needed for his furniture–stripping business. Kids who do not have skills that can be turned into cash should follow Ronald's example and try to obtain apprenticeships so they can pick up skills they can use in their future business ventures. One teen entrepreneur took a summer job at a print shop with a desk–top publishing facility so that he could learn how to use popular desk–top publishing software. One year later, he started a business helping companies create in–house newsletters and advertising brochures.

Not only does running a business enable kids to make extra money, but it also teaches them sound money management skills. When kids make their own money, they have a greater appreciation for the value of a dollar. For parents, who have a hard time teaching their kids that money does not grow on trees, allowing their kids to start businesses will help them convince these kids that it takes sweat to make a dollar.

Self–help for the economically disadvantaged

As far as I am concerned, education is still the best way economically disadvantaged kids can pull themselves out of poverty. However, a good education coupled with entrepreneurship is the most potent combination for achieving that purpose.

Many kids growing up in poor areas face seemingly insurmountable obstacles. Generally, the schools they attend do not prepare them to join the work force when and if they finish high school. Furthermore, many see little chance of escaping the poverty that surrounds them. In this environment, it takes an extraordinary youngster to acquire the vision to change his meager existence and bleak future. For this reason, teaching these kids about entrepreneurship is one way to show them that they can in fact help themselves by starting and running their own businesses.

At the risk of oversimplifying a very complex problem, what many disadvantaged kids have in common is that they typically don't think about entrepreneurship as a way out of poverty. This is understandable. They may be too busy trying to acquire the necessities of life to worry about such things as starting and running businesses. Perhaps more important, unlike some middle–class children, they lack ethical entrepreneurial role models at home or in their immediate environment to inspire them. Indeed, the entrepreneurial role models of many economically disadvantaged youngsters are drug dealers and pimps, people who without a doubt have cast aside moral values in their quest to escape poverty. Furthermore, in many cases these kids come from one–parent households in which the single parents are busy struggling to make a living. Oftentimes, these parents themselves have never thought about entrepreneurship. In short, economically disadvantaged kids frequently grow up in environments that stifle the possibility of ethical entrepreneurship. And yet, these youngsters have the most to gain from exposure to entrepreneurship.

Fortunately, there are organizations formed especially to teach these kids how to start and run their own businesses. Over the past few years, these organizations have shown that teaching kids about business helps them in several ways. For one thing, it shows them that they are capable of creating their own jobs. Second, it boosts their self–esteem. Third, it has the surprising effect of encouraging them to continue their education.

An example of an organization that encourages urban (and often economically disadvantaged) youngsters to embrace entrepreneurship is the Center for Teen Entrepreneurs, which runs Teen Business Camp—a two–week overnight entrepreneurship and business camp held at the New Jersey Institute of Technology and Rutgers University campuses.

Another organization that focuses on economically disadvantaged kids is the National Foundation for Teaching Entrepreneurship (NFTE). NFTE was founded "for the purpose of making Black and Hispanic inner–city youth economically and entrepreneurially literate."

Kim McCombs, a young entrepreneur participating in a program at the University of California at Berkley for inner city kids called the Young Entrepreneurs, sums up her experience this way: "The program has changed my life. It takes inner–city minority children who have been told by society that they would never amount to anything, gives them goals, and the opportunity to make something of themselves."

An outlet for children's creative talents or hobbies

Quite often, child entrepreneurs start their businesses because they have talents or hobbies they want to share with other people. Sixteen–year–old Mark Andelbrandt of Hinsdale, Illinois, began his catering service for school events because he loved to prepare delicious pastries. Mark's dishes were so delectable that he won Hinsdale Central High School's Culinary Arts festival competition. Mark plans to open his own restaurant after attending the Culinary Institute.

If your children have special talents and abilities like Mark, starting and running their own businesses provides them with an excellent opportunity to foster and develop these skills. Unused, these special abilities just wither away.

Breaking the glass ceiling

Increasingly more women are starting and running their own businesses. Women are becoming entrepreneurs at a faster rate than men. For some women, starting their own businesses from home is one way they can earn money as they raise young children. Many women, motivated by the limitations they face in the corporate world, decide to try their hands at their own businesses.

In 1995, the Labor Department released a 3–year study called the Glass Ceiling Commission report, which, for the first time, quantified the realities of the "glass ceiling" women face as they climb the corporate ladder. The term "glass ceiling" is used to describe a barrier that allows women to see the higher–level positions in the corporate world but does not allow them to enter into the higher echelons of management. Although equal employment opportunity programs have benefited some women, the senior and executive level positions in the corporate world are still heavily dominated by men. The report showed that white men hold 97% of senior management positions in the *Fortune* 1,000 industrial corporations. The apparent lack of women in corporate America's senior management ranks is probably one of the reasons why women have one of the highest entrepreneurship growth rates in the country.

If you have daughters, you should encourage them to become entrepreneurs to prepare them for the realities of the glass ceiling. Your daughters should grow up with the skills they need to start and run their own businesses if they choose to do so. They don't have to be limited by the glass ceiling. There are viable alternatives to making it in the corporate world.

Breaking the acrylic ceiling

If women face a glass ceiling, minorities face an acrylic ceiling. Acrylic is nearly as transparent as glass, but even tougher to break. Once again, as in the case of women, some minorities have benefited from equal employment opportunity programs. In the past 20 years, an increasing number have been creeping into the middle class. However, minorities still find themselves locked out of certain positions, regardless of their qualifications.

Parents of minority children should be particularly interested in teaching their kids about entrepreneurship. Respected African–American scholar Dr. Carter Woodson has said, "Those who have not learned to do for themselves and have to depend solely on others never obtain any more rights or privileges in the end than they had in the beginning." The limited opportunities that many minority children will face when they become adults make it imperative that parents provide them with the skills they need to become entrepreneurs. This will present them with viable alternatives to the prospect of working for companies that may stunt their professional growth.

MISCONCEPTIONS

Incompatibility of education and entrepreneurship

One misconception that turns parents away from exposing their children to entrepreneurship is that entrepreneurship is incompatible with education. This is simply not true. My contact with young entrepreneurs has shown me that they are keenly aware of the importance of a solid education.

I spent some time with teenagers who attended the Young Entrepreneurs at Wharton Program—a program offered by the West Philadelphia Project at the University of Pennsylvania's Wharton School of Business. Out of about forty students, I met only one young person who was considering foregoing college—she was considering joining the Air Force after graduating from high school.

In a survey I conducted with 160 young people who attended Entrecon, the high–school conference for young entrepreneurs, all of them said they were going to college. One of these kids, a young entrepreneur, who was grossing $500,000 in his own ski shop, was a sophomore at Villanova University in Pennsylvania. Many of these young enterprisers recognize that going to college will help them even more in business and that it will make them well–rounded entrepreneurs.

As someone with degrees from Princeton University and University of Pennsylvania's Wharton School of Business, two highly regarded schools, I certainly recognize the importance of a good education. In my opinion, a good education can provide your children with the safety net they need in life, and it can make them well–rounded adults. It is an asset that cannot be taken away from them. Obviously, the fact that a good education makes it easier for your kids to find a job—until they can strike out on their own as entrepreneurs—is another benefit.

Entrepreneurship breeds greed and materialism

During the 80s, a popular movie, *Wall Street*, popularized the phrase "greed is good." This phrase probably summarizes some of the excesses in the corporate world during the financial boom periods of the 80s. As things turned out, greed was not so good. In the second half of the 80s and the early 90s, a steady stream of revelations of insider trading activities landed some high–profile executives in jail. These convictions highlighted the worst aspects of the corporate world.

Some parents believe that advocating entrepreneurship will ultimately lead their children to the same type of greed mentality and materialism as in the past decade. Not only have these parents been turned off by Wall Street greed, but they also have an aversion to the conspicuous consumption that characterized the 1980s. Equating entrepreneurship with greed and materialism is a knee–jerk reaction that is based on anecdotal examples of financial skull-duggery. Parents who harbor this misconception believe that the only reason someone would want to become an entrepreneur is for money. These parents are afraid to encourage their kids to start and run their own businesses for fear that they would be pushing profits ahead of other important things in life.

Of course, this is just not so. For one thing, not all entrepreneurs start businesses to make money for themselves. Many entrepreneurial ventures are actually nonprofit businesses. For example, eleven years ago at the age of twelve, Trevor Ferrel started a homeless shelter in Philadelphia called Trevor's Place, which at one point operated on a $20,000 monthly budget. Clearly, Trevor did not start his homeless shelter out of a love for money.

Even for those who operate for–profit businesses, the main motivation for starting the business is not purely financial. As with most adult entrepreneurs, child entrepreneurs start businesses because they have an interest in a particular area or because they want more control of their lives. The key is the sense of satisfaction that operating their own business can bring them. Whether the businesses are highly profitable or not, entrepreneurs find that their businesses bring a sense of satisfaction that cannot be obtained by working for someone else.

It is important to bear in mind that the question of materialism in our society is a moral issue. It is an important issue regardless of whether you encourage your kids to become entrepreneurs or whether you encourage them to pursue more traditional careers. Materialism is a societal problem that transcends socioeconomic boundaries.

It is your responsibility to teach your kids moral values—this is true in the context of entrepreneurship or other pursuits. The moral values you have taught your children are the same values they will apply to any activities in which they choose to participate. This is true whether they decide to become employees or employers.

Kids don't have the mental capacity to learn about business

If college students can be taught the basics of becoming business owners, why can't kids learn the principles of running their own businesses? The reason you are likely to hear is that teaching kids economic principles at a young age is difficult. But this has been proven wrong time and again. Educators have shown that children can learn economic principles if they are properly presented to them.

When you think about it, this is really a revolution in education because economists have traditionally made their discipline seem so difficult or esoteric that even adults are intimidated by the jargon. There are several programs that are breaking this educational barrier.

Most of you have probably heard of Junior Achievement—the largest, oldest, and fastest–growing, nonprofit economic education organization in the world. Junior Achievement has indeed devised innovative ways to teach kids basic economics for the past 70 years. Other organizations and programs have cropped up in the past few years to teach kids about economics and business. For example, Camp Lemonade (at Loyola College in Baltimore) is one of several programs that teaches kids the basics of entrepreneurship and economics.

Two other examples of programs that teach children about the basics of economics and entrepreneurship is Kinder–Economy and Mini–Society. Kinder–Economy is aimed at kids in the first and second grade, and Mini–Society is for children in grades three to six. These two programs are the brain–child of Dr. Marilyn L. Kourilsky, formerly of UCLA's Graduate School of Education.

In Kinder–Economy and Mini–Society, children as young as 5 years old set up tiny societies that are modeled after the real world. These societies are complete with businesses and governments. The children in these tiny societies eventually learn to discuss topics such as supply and demand, scarcity, opportunity cost, monopoly, and other economic concepts. By Dr. Kourilsky's estimate, her system is being taught in at least 40 states.

Dr. Kourilsky and her associates have given true–false tests to graduates of Mini–Society and to college sophomores who are taking their first college–level economics course. Their results showed that both groups were equal in economic literacy.

There are other programs, described in greater detail in Chapter 18, that have proven that kids can learn economics and entrepreneurship principles if properly presented through the use of current events, real–life situations, and other innovative methods.

If organizations can instill entrepreneurial qualities in kids, then parents can certainly do the same at home by:

1. Instilling qualities such as independence and determination in their children.

2. Communicating business concepts to their kids.

3. Advising their kids on how to start and operate their own businesses.

Children are being manipulated

What happens to a child's free choice in choosing her or his own path in life? Are parents to force their kids to live entrepreneurial lives? Let me answer these questions this way. Free choice is not only preserved by teaching children entrepreneurship but it is also enhanced because, instead of presenting children with just the professional options for living a fulfilling life, parents also present them with entrepreneurial options.

No one who is genuinely interested in early entrepreneurial education for kids in the home environment will advocate the manipulation of children against their will. But this does not mean that parents should not help their children decide how to lead their lives. This is the essence of parenthood—to help kids make choices in life.

Unfortunately, some parents neglect their responsibility to help with these choices. For example, some parents may feel that by ignoring topics such as sex, religion, and money their kids can learn about them on their own. But what kids discover on their own, outside of the home, are generally not their parents' philosophies and values.

As a parent you cannot escape your responsibilities so easily when it comes to your children's values, and their preparation for successful lives. You have to play a more active role. This philosophy is rooted in the fact that parental duties involve guiding children to gain skills in life that will help them lead a better life in the long run. If this is manipulation, then one can say that encouraging kids to take piano lessons, to get involved in sports, to participate in any recreational activity, and to follow organized religion is also manipulation.

2

ASSESSING YOUR LIKELIHOOD OF RAISING ENTREPRENEURIAL CHILDREN

It should be no surprise to you that the way you bring up your children affects their likelihood of becoming entrepreneurs. Your parenting style affects components of entrepreneurship such as self–esteem, creativity, problem–solving skills, money–management skills, and achievement–motivation—all aspects of entrepreneurship I measure in the questionnaire in this chapter.

Through some questions, I measure your interactions with your children, and through others I measure your personality. Either way, I am searching for information that will help me gauge how you are currently raising your children and how your personality and attitudes can influence their entrepreneurial potential.

The answers I have given below to these questions are the answers I expect if you are likely to encourage entrepreneurship in your children. Although it may not be immediately clear to you what some of these answers have to do with entrepreneurship, the details will be revealed later in this book.

Answer the questions according to the way you currently behave, not the way you think you should respond. For now, sit back, take the test, and grade yourself. Give yourself 1 point for every answer that matches mine, and 0 for every answer that does not match mine. Please answer each question as honestly as you can.

Questionnaire on Raising Entrepreneurial Children

SELF–ESTEEM, CREATIVITY, AND PROBLEM–SOLVING

1. You had a fight with your boss today. As you walk into the house after a hard day your 8–year–old daughter greets you with open arms but immediately notices that you are not your usual self. She asks you, "What's the matter?" Which one of these answers are you most likely to give.

    a)   Nothing. Everything is fine.

    b)   I don't want to talk about it.

    c)   I had a hard day at the office. It's a grown–up problem I'll have to resolve myself.

2. You have just stopped your son from doing something naughty he has never done before. You are quite angry. Which one of these actions are you most likely to take?

    a)   Tell him to refrain from the mischief in the future.

    b)   Tell him to refrain from the mischief and explain why it was wrong.

    c)   Punish him immediately without explaining why he is being punished.

3. You have a 15–year–old son who has decided that he wants to be a vegetarian. Which one of these attitudes are you most likely to have about his new eating habit?

    a)   He has to eat what the rest of the family eats or he goes hungry.

    b)   I will try to make sure that there is a vegetarian dish available for him when we have our meals.

    c)   The whole family will go vegetarian.

    d)   I won't allow him to be a vegetarian.

4. You come home from work and you are exhausted. You also want to spend some time with your kids. Which one of these conditions exists when you are spending time with them?

    a)   The television is on.

    b)   The radio is on.

    c)   I am reading the newspaper, but my kids are around me.

    d)   Everything is turned off and I am focused on them.

5. You are getting ready to plan your vacation for next summer. Your high–school daughter is excited. Which one of these actions are you most likely to take?

    a)   I will give her some choices as to where we should go and then ask her to choose one. We will then all take a vote.

    b)   My spouse and I will make the decision on where the whole family would like to go. After we make our decision, we will tell our daughter.

6. Do you sometimes avoid confronting your children when they have done something mischievous?

    YES   NO

7. Your son asks your permission to do something. Do you tell him to ask your spouse instead?

    YES   NO

8. Do you sometimes waver on decisions you make about your children's requests?

    YES   NO

9. You disapprove of your high school daughter's recreational activity because it is dangerous. Which one of these actions are you most likely to take?

   a)   Tell her to stop it because you think it's dangerous.

   b)   Tell her to stop, tell her the reasons you object to it, and give her alternatives.

   c)   Give her alternative activities, but don't force her to stop her current activity.

   d)   Let her discover for herself that it is dangerous.

10. If you can afford it, do you try to meet all of your children's purchasing requests?

   YES   NO

11. Even after disciplining your children, do you sometimes hold a grudge for a while?

   YES   NO

12. When your children can't do something on their own, do you usually do it for them?

   YES   NO

13. Your son fails to reach one of his own academic or athletic goals. Which one of these choices best describes how you handle the failure?

   a)   I don't mention the failure. I totally ignore it.

   b)   I talk to him about it to get him ready for his next challenge.

   c)   I come down hard on him.

14. Do you feel that you should be able to look through your children's belongings anytime you want?

     YES   NO

15. Do you let your children question or criticize your decisions?

     YES   NO

16. Are your children aware of your standards when it comes to their performance in school?

     YES   NO

17. Do you let your children know that you trust their ability to handle difficult situations?

     YES   NO

18. Does how you feel about yourself depend on how successful your children are in their endeavors?

     YES   NO

19. Do you feel that your children trust you?

     YES   NO

20. Do you feel that your children's personal worth is dependent upon performance?

     YES   NO

21. Do you sometimes curse at your children when they are mischievous?

     YES   NO

22. Do you encourage your children to try things on their own?

    YES   NO

23. Do you consciously encourage your children to think of different solutions to problems that face them?

    YES   NO

24. Do you sometimes solicit advice from your children?

    YES   NO

25. Do you encourage your children to be imaginative?

    YES   NO

26. Do you like the curiosity of your children?

    YES   NO

27. Do you believe toys help children develop their creative talents?

    YES   NO

28. Do you like to have your children explain things to you just to see their perspective?

    YES   NO

MONEY MANAGEMENT

1. Which one of the following choices best describes the way you dispense money to your child?

    a)   I give a regular allowance with few or no strings attached.

    b)   I pay for the chores completed.

    c)   I give a regular allowance and I control how it is spent.

    d)   I give money on an as–needed basis.

2. Do you decide how big an allowance to give your children by sitting down with them and discussing their financial needs?

    YES   NO

3. Do you try to encourage your children to save their money?

    YES   NO

4. Do you actively try to teach your children to spend their money wisely?

    YES   NO

5. Do you give your children money for good behavior?

    YES   NO

6. Do you involve your children in the family budget?

    YES   NO

7. When your children use up their allowance money too fast, do you give them more?

    YES   NO

ATTITUDES TOWARDS ENTREPRENEURSHIP

1. What do you consider most important about becoming an entrepreneur?

   a)   Entrepreneurs make lots of money.

   b)   Entrepreneurs do not have to answer to anyone but themselves.

   c)   Entrepreneurs can be as creative as they want.

   d)   Entrepreneurs do not have to work as hard as people who have regular jobs.

2. Do you believe that entrepreneurs are born rather than made?

   YES   NO

3. You prefer tasks that are

   a)   very easy to accomplish.

   b)   moderately difficult to accomplish.

   c)   almost impossible to accomplish.

4. Do you respect people who start their own businesses even if they are small–time entrepreneurs?

   YES   NO

5. Do you feel that a college education can help a person become an entrepreneur?

   YES   NO

6. Do you make an effort to expose your children to entrepreneurs you know?

   YES   NO

7. Do you set goals for yourself?

    YES   NO

8. Are you the type that does not like to worry about small details?

    YES   NO

9. Are you most comfortable working by yourself?

    YES   NO

10. Do you prefer to undertake projects that can be accomplished in
    a short time?

    YES   NO

ACHIEVEMENT MOTIVATION

1. Do you like to take risks?

    YES   NO

2. Do you feel that you can control your destiny?

    YES   NO

3. Do you like an objective measure of your performance?

    YES   NO

4. Do you encourage your children in their interests, no matter
    how insignificant?

    YES   NO

Answers to Questionnaire on Raising Entrepreneurs

For each question, if your answer matches mine, give yourself 1 point. If it doesn't, give yourself 0 points.

SELF–ESTEEM, CREATIVITY, AND PROBLEM–SOLVING

1. *C.* The experts say that honesty is important to establish trust between you and your kids. Trust is fundamental to the acquisition of a high self–esteem. Admit something is wrong and if you choose to, discuss it. If not, keep it to yourself.

2. *B.* Explaining why you disapprove of your kids' behavior reinforces the fact that you have rules and guidelines they must follow. It helps them make their own informed decisions about how to refrain from such behavior when you are not around to hold them back. By explaining the reasons for your dissatisfaction, you are helping them become better decision–makers when they are faced with the same opportunities to involve themselves in the mischief. As you will see later on, the decision–making skills relate to problem–solving (an important component of the entrepreneurial process) and affect a child's self–esteem.

3. *B.* Respecting your children's separateness lets them know that you recognize that they are individuals with their own likes and dislikes. This helps them feel cherished and boosts their self–esteem.

4. *D.* If you want to spend quality time with your kids, you should do it with no distractions.

5. *A.* Getting your children to participate in the family's decision–making process helps them understand that their opinion is important to you. This helps them in developing the self–esteem they need to lead an entrepreneurial life.

6. *NO*. Parents have the responsibility to set guidelines for their children's behavior. If you are not consistent when your kids have been mischievous, you leave them wondering if and when you will express disapproval of their behavior. This unpredictability causes anxiety in kids and lowers self–esteem.

7. *NO*. Referring them to your spouse will give them the impression that you cannot make your own decisions.

8. *NO*. Mixing signals about what you allow and disallow makes your children unsure about what you consider to be acceptable. This uncertainty leaves your children unsure about what action to take when they are not under your watchful eyes, and this in turn means that they can't properly exercise their decision–making skills—a crucial aspect of entrepreneurial behavior.

9. *B*. Giving children alternatives helps them exercise decision–making skills that are necessary for creative problem solving.

10. *NO*. Spoiled children have everything they need, therefore they have no need to set and achieve goals.

11. *NO*. If you hold a grudge even after letting them know how you are displeased with their actions, they may think that you are angry with them and not over their actions. This of course diminishes their self–esteem and discourages the acquisition of entrepreneurial qualities.

12. *NO*. Parents who give a helping hand to their children by actually performing the tasks for them do their children a disservice. These parents do not really teach their children how to walk through problems or tasks on their own. A result is that these children may forever depend on other people to do things for them. Such a dependency does not build self–esteem.

13. *B.* When your children don't meet their objectives, it is best to talk it over with them so you can show them how they can do better the next time. By so doing, you make them realize that it is natural to fail, and more important, that there are usually remedies for failures. When children learn that failure is not fatal, they are more likely to maintain their self–esteem and to have the courage to try again and again.

14. *NO.* Like you, your children need their privacy. If you invade this privacy too much, your actions suggest that you don't really trust them and that you are always watching them. Many children in this situation will feel that in your eyes, they cannot do anything right. This of course undermines their self–esteem.

15. *YES.* It is best to allow room for discussion of your decisions because this shows your children that you are not a dictator. This is not to say that you will necessarily change your mind, but that you will give them a chance to express their opinion.

16. *YES.* One of the basics in proper parenting techniques is to set limits of behavior. You will see later on in this book how important this is for entrepreneurship.

17. *YES.* When your children know that you trust them, they feel good about themselves and their self–esteem is increased.

18. *NO.* When you tie your self–esteem to your children's success, you are likely to push them into doing things that will enhance how you feel about yourself without regard to their mental and physical capabilities or their own needs.

19. *YES.* The experts say that children must first trust their parents before they can achieve a high level of self–esteem.

20. *NO.* You should not decide how important your children are to you by their accomplishments. If you do, you are destroying their self–esteem because they will quickly learn that the only time they please you is when they do well in their activities.

21. *NO.* By cursing at your children, you are telling them that you disapprove of them, not their actions. Cursing generally aims straight at the very existence of the person to whom it is directed.

22. *YES.* Encouraging your children to explore new and different opportunities and activities helps them to become more creative and adventurous. Their willingness to explore these different activities gives them the self–confidence they need to lead healthy entrepreneurial lives.

23. *YES.* This encourages creativity and nurtures problem–solving skills.

24. *YES.* Asking their advice helps them think through situations and also prompts them to give suggestions. This nurtures problem–solving skills.

25. *YES.* Many parents don't know that they can play an active role in stretching their children's imagination. An active imagination can help in the development of entrepreneurial creativity.

26. *YES.* Some parents are pestered by the avalanche of questions asked by their children. But children's brains are like blank tapes. The children are anxious for their tapes to be filled with information. Just think back to when you were a child. You probably wanted to know everything there was to know in the world in one day. If you squelch your children's curiosity, you are also putting an end to the development of their problem–solving skills.

27. *YES.* Toys and games help kids develop their creative and problem–solving talents. Do not deprive them of these simple, fun, and educational pleasures.

28. *YES.* Having your kids explain things to you helps them think logically. When you think about it, logical reasoning is essential to problem solving.

MONEY MANAGEMENT

1. *A.* The experts say that giving your children a regular allowance with few or no strings attached is the best way to teach money management skills. Your kids can use their discretion to save and plan for the use of their money.

2. *YES.* Of course just because you discuss their financial needs with them does not mean that you should give them money for ridiculous expenses. Talk things over with them, veto some items on their list, and compromise on others.

3. *YES.* Teaching your children to save their money is one of the basics in showing them how to manage their money.

4. *YES.* It is better for them to learn the fundamentals of money management at a young age.

5. *NO.* Now this is a big no–no. Do not confuse teaching your kids to behave themselves with teaching them about money. They should not be paid for things they should be doing on their own anyway.

6. *YES.* The experts agree that letting children participate in the family budgeting process is a good way to teach them about money matters.

7. *NO.* If you supply them with more money when their allowance runs out, why give the allowance in the first place? Why not just have them come to you when they need money? The bottom line is that when you supply them with more money because they have used their allowance money unwisely, you are encouraging poor money management.

ATTITUDES TOWARDS ENTREPRENEURSHIP

1. *B.* I have found that for many entrepreneurs, the most exciting thing about starting their own businesses is that they are autonomous. Money is not usually their motivation because many of them can probably make more money as employees. Besides, it is the exceptional entrepreneur who strikes it rich.

2. *NO.* The proliferation of high school programs and college classes on entrepreneurship should help convince you that there are aspects of business start–ups that can be taught.

3. *B.* Entrepreneurs like difficult challenges, but they also like the satisfaction of accomplishing their tasks successfully.

4. *YES.* Your attitude towards entrepreneurs can influence what your children think about starting their own business. Transmitting positive images about entrepreneurs to your children can help them become enthusiastic about entrepreneurship.

5. *YES.* Today's high–tech entrepreneurs certainly have to be technically competent. But even low–tech entrepreneurs can use the basic business skills acquired in college.

6. *YES.* These entrepreneurs can be role models for your children.

7. *YES.* If you set goals for yourself, you are probably the kind that takes action to make changes instead of just sitting around and wishing for things to get better.

8. *NO.* Business owners often have to take care of the smallest details, especially when their businesses are new. If you are the type that is concerned only with the big picture, chances are you are not entrepreneurially inclined and you are also not likely to encourage entrepreneurship in your children without this book.

9. *NO*. Cooperation is important for entrepreneurship. You may need other people's expertise and money to run a business. If you prefer to do everything on your own, you may never maximize the use of the resources around you.

10. *NO*. Entrepreneurs are typically not interested in get–rich–quick schemes. This means that they are willing to put the time and effort into starting a new business. They are not looking for instant gratification.

ACHIEVEMENT MOTIVATION

1. *YES*. Entrepreneurs like to take some calculated risks. I am not saying that they are outright gamblers, but they will tread in areas many people avoid.

2. *YES*. This is a basic characteristic found in entrepreneurs. If they feel that they can control their destiny, they are more likely to find the motivation to start their own business.

3. *YES*. Entrepreneurs typically like to be measured objectively. They like their performance assessed by impartial judges.

4. *YES*. Parents' interest in their children's hobbies or interests is really very important in helping them do well in these areas. When I was competing in athletics in high school, nothing made me feel better than seeing my parents in the stands.

Scoring

45–49	excellent
40–44	good
30–39	fair
25–29	poor
0–24	terrible

3

A SHORT COURSE IN DEVELOPMENTAL PSYCHOLOGY

Developmental psychology is important for understanding how children acquire their self–esteem and their cognitive or problem–solving skills—important components of the entrepreneurial process.

As adults, we take it for granted that wood can burn, balls roll, and birds that fly out of sight still exist. But to the child these observations are not so apparent. His new world gradually reveals these unfamiliar properties. Understanding how these unfamiliar properties unfold for young children can help us in looking at things adults can do to help children acquire entrepreneurial skills.

HOW CHILDREN LEARN THROUGH ASSIMILATION AND ACCOMMODATION

One of the most popular views of developmental psychology is called cognitive–structuralism. The most respected school from this school, Jean Piaget (1918–1980), conducted several psychological experiments with his two children. Although some may argue that his research lacked thorough scientific controls, his work has become the standard for many developmental psychologists.

The cognitive–structuralists' view of psychology focuses on how children view the physical world. More specifically, how they understand the existence of objects, the concepts of cause and effect, time and space.

Piaget showed that from birth a child begins to create models for his activities and all the ways he interacts with the world. These models, or schemes, as Piaget called them, are the child's reference points for a variety of activities. You can think of schemes as road maps the child creates for himself for performing some tasks or activities. For example, an infant builds a scheme for sucking his mother's nipple. He knows exactly how wide to open his mouth and how hard to suck to draw milk. This scheme for sucking the nipple can be transferred to sucking a thumb, a feeding bottle, or to any number of activities where the mouth is used to manipulate objects. According to Piaget, schemes are very dynamic, and the infant is constantly revising them. Children update their schemes through assimilation and accommodation.

Assimilation is the process whereby the child interacts with the world by virtue of his already existing schemes. For example, he assimilates everything near his mouth into the sucking scheme. The child reasons that all objects that come close to his mouth are meant to be sucked. Now suppose the child is confronted with the problem of getting milk out of a feeding bottle. He can position the bottle so that it approximates the angle of his mother's breast. By so doing, he has assimilated the bottle into his sucking scheme.

Accommodation, the other way infants revise their schemes, refers to modification of the scheme to fit the present activity. For example, instead of changing the angle of the feeding bottle, as in assimilation, the infant can change the shape of his mouth to be able to suck more effectively from the bottle. In this case, the child's sucking scheme has been slightly altered to accommodate the bottle. In short, assimilation requires a change in the child's environment, whereas accommodation requires the child to change to handle different situations.

Through assimilation and accommodation, the child is not only learning about the world but, more important, is also building his cognitive or problem–solving skills. This happens as the schemes become more complicated and as they are applied to a wider variety of situations.

The proper development of problem–solving skills is important if a child is going to develop entrepreneurial skills. As a child thinks of ways to solve the different problems that face him, he also becomes more and more creative. The increased creativity means that his mind is more open to trying innovative solutions, and this is one of the many characteristics of successful entrepreneurs. The sooner these skills are developed and encouraged, the better the chances the child will lead an entrepreneurial life.

THE STAGES OF DEVELOPMENT OF PROBLEM–SOLVING SKILLS

Piaget clearly defined four stages in life in the development of problem–solving skills:

1. Sensory–motor stage (0–2 years).

2. Symbolic or preoperational stage (2–7 years).

3. Concrete operational stage (7–11 years).

4. Formal operational stage (11–15 years).

The sensory–motor stage (birth to 2 years)

In the sensory–motor stage, Piaget proposed that the child interacts with the world only by motor and other sensory activities. For example, he might grasp objects close to his hands or he might look at the shadow his hand casts on a nearby wall. In this stage, the child develops reflexes such as waving his hand, crying, and sucking. In the early part of the sensory–motor stage, the infant doesn't realize that an object exists when that object is out of sight. For example, if he is playing with a ball and you take it away, to him that ball no longer exists. He cannot imagine the ball's permanence in space. At about one and a half years of age, the child begins to represent objects through the use of mental imagery. As the child perfects this technique of symbolic representation, he moves into the next critical stage in cognitive development: the symbolic stage.

The symbolic, or preoperational, stage (2 – 7 years)

In the preoperational stage, as symbolic representation skills grow, the child begins to see himself as an entity separate from others around him. In this stage, however, Piaget considers the child to be egocentric. In this context, egocentricism merely means that the child cannot see things from another person's point of view. It does not mean that he is selfish or self–centered. He just believes that everyone knows what he knows and sees what he sees. This belief is evident when a child is describing some recent experience. He does not give all the details of the story because he assumes that the person he is talking to is aware of the setting of his story. The ability to see other people's viewpoint and the ability to show logical consistency in reasoning are learned in this stage. These cognitive skills can be acquired by children through their interaction with other kids in the playground as well as in the classroom.

The concrete operational stage (7 – 11 years)

In the concrete operational stage, children continue to build their problem–solving and reasoning skills. In this stage, they integrate the schemes they have learned in the previous stages to form a more cohesive system of symbolization. The child learns the principle of conservation at this stage. Piaget used the term conservation to refer to a child's understanding of physical quantities. This concept is better explained through an example. Suppose a 4–year–old child is faced with two glasses of equal size filled with the same amount of water. When the contents of one of the glasses is then poured into a tall, thinner glass, this child may conclude that there is more water in the taller glass. If this child were in the concrete operational stage, however, she would understand that the liquids in the short and tall glasses are equal.

When a child masters the principle of conservation, she begins to understand time, space, and causality (cause and effect). In the context of entrepreneurship, understanding the concept of time is extremely important. Understanding time means that a child can think beyond immediate gratification. For example, she is more likely to save her money for a long time to buy a pair of shoes for school than to blow the money right away on candy. As you will discover later on, saving money is one of the first lessons a child should learn about money management. It is an important stage in the entrepreneurial process.

Mastery of conservation also allows a child to relate today to tomorrow and to plan for the future. The ability to delay gratification and to make plans for the future is an extremely important factor in the entrepreneurial process because without it children can never map out strategies for starting and running their businesses.

Until your child approaches the late preoperational stage or the early concrete operational stage, it is probably too early to teach her one of the earliest skills related to entrepreneurship—money management and planning for business ventures. Indeed, experts agree that from age six and up, kids should be taught how to handle money.

The formal operational stage (12–15 years)

The final stage in cognitive development as outlined by Piaget is the formal operational stage. The child no longer learns by trial and error. He can now form and test his own hypotheses. He can understand how things relate to each other and think imaginatively about his environment. At the formal operational stage, a child begins to sharpen his self–identity. He can now see himself as part of society, consider his responsibilities in society and his eventual occupation in life. With his heightened reasoning power, he can discuss such things as religion, sex, and other topics of relevance to society. In addition, he increasingly questions authority.

The formal operational stage is the right time for the child to go through an entrepreneurial experience. At this stage, he can understand the basic concepts necessary for running a business.

CAVEAT TO THE STAGES IN COGNITIVE DEVELOPMENT

The stages in cognitive development I have just described are not meant to be hard rules on how and when a child should acquire cognitive or problem–solving skills or guidelines as to when to begin teaching children about business. Since children develop at different rates, no hard–and–fast rule can apply to everyone. The stages of development that Piaget proposed are merely guidelines derived from observations of children. Obviously, environmental factors are very important in determining the pace of your child's cognitive development.

4

SELF–ESTEEM: THE KEY INGREDIENT FOR ENTREPRENEURSHIP

One of the most important characteristics of entrepreneurs is that they have a strong belief in themselves. They have the courage to reach for greater achievements and they believe that they can control their lives and their destinies. This same principle holds true even for child entrepreneurs. All of the young entrepreneurs I have met through my organization, the Center for Teen Entrepreneurs, have one thing in common: high self–esteem. If you are to encourage the entrepreneur in your children, you must make sure they have a healthy self–concept. With a healthy self–concept, your kids will reach for excellence, and ultimately will be good creative problem solvers—key ingredients in entrepreneurship. In this chapter, I will explain the dynamics of self–esteem and how parents can affect their child's self–concept.

DEFINING SELF–ESTEEM

Self–esteem is a measure of how your child feels about himself. When your child is born, he has no self–identity and no self–concept. As he grows, there are two ways he can acquire his self–esteem through:

1. You and other people in his environment.

2. His accomplishments.

The parent–child relationship is an extremely important variable in the acquisition of a high or positive self–esteem. Think for a moment about the life of a newborn child. From birth, he depends on his parents for everything: food, shelter, comfort, and love. The manner in which his parents fulfill these needs determines how this child sees himself. If they meet his basic needs, he will feel that his parents value his very existence and this belief creates a stronger sense of self–esteem.

In addition to the influence of his parents, this child's self–esteem may also be affected by the caretakers outside of the home. The caretakers can affect this child's sense of self–worth through the manner in which they satisfy the child's basic needs. Teachers and other relatives can also have similar influences. In short, other humans in his environment have the potential to affect his self–esteem positively or negatively.

Self–esteem is a dynamic quality. It can change daily and can fluctuate from moment to moment. For example, telling a good joke to your friends can make you feel witty, but stumbling in front of a large crowd can embarrass you. In both cases, the duration of the elevation or depression of your self–esteem may vary. You may feel good about the joke for a short while and then quickly forget about your comedic talents. On the other hand, you may forever remember stumbling in front of the crowd and, thus, always feel clumsy.

Self–esteem may also vary according to the activity in which a person is involved. For example, a person who considers himself to be a great tennis player may experience low self–esteem if he gets beaten badly by his tennis partner. Yet this same person's self–esteem is not threatened if he is beaten in a long–distance race.

Building your child's self–esteem started from birth. Even though your infant could not communicate verbally, you knew when to fulfill his needs for food, shelter, comfort, and love. You learned to watch for the signals that indicated his desire for these needs. Conversely, he learned to receive signals from you that indicated sadness, joy, contentment, and other emotions.

As your child grows, there are many more ways to build or destroy his self–esteem besides meeting his physical needs. His emotional needs become more important because many of the things he needed you to do for him when he was younger, he can do for himself as he gets older and stronger. As a parent, you should know that the things you do and say have a great impact on how your children see themselves and on their motivation to achieve. This motivation to achieve is one of the driving forces behind entrepreneurial behavior.

The following sections outline some of the factors that can hurt or help your children's self–esteem and how your children's self–esteem influences their desire to achieve and to reach their maximum potential. Once you are aware of these factors, you can begin to take positive steps to constantly build your child's self–esteem. Remember that self–esteem is something you have to work on every single day. The total sum of how you treat your kids will determine what they think of themselves. You have to maintain a sustained effort to bolster their self–esteem on a daily basis.

SELF–ESTEEM DEFLATORS

Ridicule

Many parents are not aware of how mere words can affect their children. Quite often, a parent may throw out a careless phrase or statement that children remember for a long, long time. I am willing to bet that there are some painful things that your parents said to you when you were growing up that you can still remember to this day.

Constant parental ridicule can shape the way children see themselves. One athletically built father often poked fun at his 13–year–old son for being fat. A week never went by without this father making a snide comment about his son's weight. What made things worse was that this boy also got picked on by other kids in the neighborhood. Ordinarily, you would expect this child's father to give his child emotional support when others are tearing away at his self–esteem. Unfortunately, this young, impressionable boy faced abuse both inside and outside of his home. The poor boy's self–esteem was battered from both ends.

When parents make fun of their children's inadequacies, the hurt cuts deeper because very young kids generally respect their parents' opinions more than those of their peers or friends. This should not be so surprising since young kids think of their parents as all–powerful and all–knowing.

Labels and name calling

You have probably heard the children's chant: "Sticks and stones will break my bones, but words will never hurt me." Kids usually use it to reassure themselves that they are fine as long as they are not being physically attacked. But of course, words can sometimes hurt more than sticks and stones. I am sure that there were times in your childhood when you wished you had been spanked instead of getting a tongue–lashing. The simple fact is that a spanking is short–lived pain. It is over and done with in a hurry. Hurtful names, however, can stay in an individual's memory for a long time.

Parents sometimes lash out at their kids in fits of anger. Many times what comes out is a string of caustic labels. Often, these labels are aimed directly at the children themselves—not at what they did. One day, as I was browsing at a department store, I saw a little girl pull down a stack of books. Her mother flung her around, slapped her and said, "You idiot. What the hell do you think you are doing?" I knew that this woman was justified in her anger. However, I felt that she did not have to use insulting labels on her little girl. Labels like "stupid," "moron," or other words that attack the whole essence of a child's existence may not be harmful if such outbursts are infrequent. But I find that parents who curse and label their children do it all the time. It is a bad habit that constantly nibbles at their children's self–esteem. Any child who faces a barrage of derogatory names will eventually wonder if the labels actually fit. This is dangerous, overt brainwashing. Parents should take care to criticize only their children's behavior—not the essence of the children themselves. Attacking the children and not their behavior tends to make them fearful and timid, and hence, less likely to exercise their decision–making skills.

A vote of no confidence

Your child's self–esteem can be influenced also by his perception of how much confidence you have in him. Simply put, if you constantly tell your child that he cannot perform a specific task, your words will become a self–fulfilling prophecy. Your child may in fact begin to meet your expectation of his incompetence. Some of you may be saying that if someone told you that you are not capable of doing something, you will try even harder to prove him wrong. Perhaps you feel this way because you have enough self–esteem to withstand such a vote of no confidence. However, your child may not yet have this strong sense of self. In addition, a repeated onslaught of negative messages will have a strong impact on a child's sense of self–worth. Such negative messages begin to brainwash the recipient into thinking that he is incompetent at the task at hand, as well as other unrelated tasks. John, now 37, recalls his childhood and how inadequate and incompetent his father made him feel back then. "My father never had much confidence that I could do things right. Even when I was 17 years old, he would not let me mow the lawn because he thought I would screw it up. I really internalized those feelings of my father's lack of faith in my ability to accomplish simple tasks. It has taken me a while to realize that, yes, I am a competent human being." This father's feeling toward his son's ability to perform simple tasks was blatantly clear. In the father's eyes his son could not do anything right.

Even innocent and subtle statements about your child's competence can hurt his self–esteem. One friend told me that when she was younger, her mother once tried to encourage her to work hard by telling her that she should study harder because she was not as smart as the other kids in school. While her mother thought she was encouraging her daughter to apply herself in school, her daughter's interpretation of the advice was that she (the daughter) was simply dumb. To this day, this friend still remembers the incident and admits that for many years she felt intellectually inferior.

Of course, one careless comment from a parent is not going to drive a child into a permanent state of a low self–esteem. Rather, a succession of statements that show that the parent has no confidence in his child will eventually erode the child's sense of self–worth.

Comparisons

Comparing your child with another child or even comparing your child's behavior with your behavior when you were his age is bound to lower your child's self–esteem. You certainly should point to other kids as role models for your child. However, it is very easy to go from merely showing your child role models to berating him for failing to possess the qualities you admire in these role models.

One fundamental principle you must understand as a parent is that all kids do not have the same set of skills or abilities. In any family, one child may be outgoing, while another may be shy. One child may show signs of brilliance that no other kid in the family can match. One child may be extraordinarily creative while the other may just be ordinary. There are too many factors that separate human beings as individuals. Using one child's characteristics as a benchmark for another child's qualities is a useless exercise. I honestly believe that every child has some good skills or characteristics that set him apart from the rest.

Concerned parents should not misunderstand my point on comparisons. Comparisons, if made in a sensitive way, can be a good technique for motivating children. For example, I once heard a friend of mine say to her 12–year–old son, "Your hair will look nicer if you combed it like John does. Ask him to show you how he does his." The mother could have easily said, "Why don't you ever comb your hair neatly like your brother." The mother encouraged her son to seek grooming help from his brother by making a subtle comparison between the two boys' grooming techniques.

Some parents look back to their childhood and reminisce about their angelic behavior. They then use this revisionist view about their past as a benchmark for their children's behavior. Such comparisons are useless because, for one thing, times have changed. Young people today face more problems than you did when you were their age. For example, 20 or 30 years ago a high school student considered himself a radical if he defied authority by walking in the school hallways without a pass or if he smoked in the bathroom. Today some high school kids in large cities in this country are defying authority by packing guns! Depending on where you live, kids are also confronted with drugs and violence in high school. The pressures you faced years ago cannot compare with those your kids are facing today.

Expectations

A child's self–esteem can also be affected by her parent's expectations. Having excessively high expectations for your child that are impossible for her to meet, lowers self–esteem. One of your most important tasks is to learn your child's capabilities. Their physical limitations are pretty obvious. For example, common sense tells us that a 10–year–old child will not be able to lift a 100–pound box. What is not apparent is this child's emotional and mental limitations. For example, I know a brilliant father who expected his 14–year–old son to get all A's on his report card. I knew that his son was a hard worker so his failure to get straight A's was not due to a lack of effort. The boy started to lose confidence in his intellectual abilities because he was not meeting his father's expectations. He went from getting B's and a sprinkling of A's to getting quite a few C's. The father later confessed that he felt directly responsible for his son's underachievement because he pushed him a bit too hard.

Before parents can encourage their children to accomplish certain tasks or goals, they have to ask themselves two questions:

1. How are my kids going to benefit from meeting my expectations?

2. Do I want my kids to do this for my own selfish reasons?

You must determine how your kids are going to benefit if they accomplish certain tasks or goals. Obviously, if the accomplishment is not very important, why bother? You must justify that the tasks or goals are worthwhile. Parents waste time trying to get their children to do things that don't really matter. For example, I once witnessed one parent insist that her daughter make a bigger bow when tying her shoelaces. The girl's shoelace looked fine to me, but I guess the mother wanted a more flamboyant knot. Another parent insisted that his son physically strike back at any kid who teased him about his dental braces. These demands are not tied to any universal laws of how things should be. Oftentimes they are tied to incidents that the parents themselves faced in childhood. For example, the parent who wanted his son to strike kids who provoked him may himself have been picked on by the local bully when he was a child. Encouraging his son to fight back could be his way of settling the score with his childhood bully.

Sometimes, parents want their kids to accomplish specific objectives for purely selfish reasons. When my younger brother was 12 years old, he played on a Little League team. I remember attending one championship game that was attended mostly by family members. In my opinion, the stands were filled with fathers who had dreamed of being major league stars in their youth but never quite got there. I say this because I have never seen such obsession for winning in my life. The parents questioned every call made by the umpire and they even cursed at some of the kids on the field. It is obvious that these parents had their self–esteem tied to their children's performance on the field. Such parents have self–esteem problems themselves. They see their children as extensions of themselves. They use their children's activities as a vehicle for boosting their own sense of self–worth. When their children fail, these parents oftentimes see themselves as failures. This situation leaves the child in a bind. He not only has to please himself, but he also has to make his parents happy with his performance.

The unfulfilled dreams of a stage career are still another reason some parents set unrealistic goals for their children. One mother who wanted her 8–year–old daughter to be a child actress, auditioned for parts herself when she was a child. This mother was the typical overbearing stage mother—tirelessly preparing her daughter for her big break under the lights. Unfortunately, her daughter was neither talented nor interested in acting. It was the mother who was interested in acting. This mother was merely fulfilling her own childhood dreams through her daughter.

Other parents set excessively high achievement standards for their kids for status reasons. These are the parents who brag about their children's straight–A averages or about their children's admission to an Ivy League college. On the surface, you may think these parents are just showing how proud they are of their kids. But if you look deeper, you will see that these parents are simply proud of their kids because of the status their children bring them.

Just as excessively high expectations can hurt a child's self-esteem, low expectations can do the same thing. If you don't expect much of your children, they will not expect much of themselves. They will also think that you have no confidence in them. In addition, if your expectations of your kids are low, they will have problems when they go out in the real world and deal with teachers and peers, who will undoubtedly expect more from them than you do.

SELF–ESTEEM INFLATORS

Trust

Respected psychologist Eric Erickson believed that the most fundamental ingredient in building your child's self–esteem is his faith and trust in you, and trust that his needs will be consistently met.

When your kids were infants, they began to trust you as you gave them the nourishment and comfort they needed when they needed it. As you fed them when they were hungry and as you comforted them when they cried, they began to depend on you to satisfy their needs. When your children grew older, they no longer had the immediate needs they had as infants. For example, they learned how to prepare their own food and to put themselves to bed. However, their self–esteem was still influenced by the degree of trust they had in you.

There are several ways for you to increase the amount of trust between you and your kids. One way is to be honest with your kids. As parents, we sometimes make promises to our kids simply because we want them off our backs or because we don't want to see the disappointment in their faces. By making promises we can't keep we increasingly make them suspicious of everything we say. I am sure you have at least one person in your life whom you have learned not to depend on over the years. When this person makes promises, you probably just think to yourself, "I'll believe it when I see it." As an adult, you take the promises this person makes with a grain of salt. Now imagine children who look up to what they consider omniscient and omnipotent parents. If you repeatedly fail to follow through on promises, your children will trust you less and less. The lack of trust leaves your children uncertain as to whether to depend on you.

Parents should also be honest about their feelings. Some parents believe that as authority figures they should always be the model of stability and serenity. These parents typically hide their true feelings from their kids and put up a front. Unfortunately, even though the lips of these parents are saying one thing, their actions are saying another. Take, for example, a father who comes home from work one day after arguing with his boss. As he walks into the house his young daughter greets him at the door and asks him, "Did you have a good day at the office?" He replies in the affirmative without an expression of joy in seeing his daughter. For the rest of the evening, he gives the whole family the silent treatment and goes to bed very early. His daughter of course has been tipped off by observing her father's body language. While her father says that everything was fine, she knows from his behavior that something must be bothering him. When your kids discover that your body language conflicts with your spoken messages, they learn to give less credence to your verbal communication and to look to your behavior for clues as to how you feel. Unfortunately, they also come to the conclusion that they cannot trust some of the things you say.

When your kids have to hunt for clues as to how you feel, they can also incorrectly attribute your behavior to something they themselves did. In the example above, the daughter could have easily concluded that the father was angry at her. She had no way of knowing that the father wasn't very happy because he had a bad day at the office.

Honesty with your kids does not require that you tell them all of your problems, thoughts, and feelings. When something is bothering you and you don't really want to discuss it with them, tell them so. The man who had a bad day at the office could have said to his daughter, "I had a hard day at the office but it is something that I'll have to resolve on my own." You should never tell them that nothing is wrong because your emotions will eventually expose your inner feelings.

Loving your child

Love means many things to different people. Some parents feel that because they give their kids lots of hugs and kisses their children feel really loved. Others feel that they can demonstrate love to their children by simply providing them with food, shelter, and clothing. Having been exposed to many different cultures, I can say that physical demonstrations of love through hugs and kisses are not the only means of proving love. There are many societies that are not openly affectionate whose children still grow up with the love they need for a strong self–concept. Providing kids with the necessary food and clothing is obviously not enough because the rich and famous have the same problems as the rest of the population.

No one can really tell you what love is. Before I take a stab at it, I'll tell you what love is not. Love is not tirelessly doing things for your children such as making their beds, doing their laundry or any other chores that they can do on their own if they are old enough. Love is also not avoiding chastising your kids when they have done something wrong, and it is not avoiding discipline or establishing moral and ethical guidelines.

True love exists only when you cherish your child simply because she exists and not because she has some skills or qualities that you admire. A parent who is proud of her child's accomplishments may be demonstrating conditional love to the child—a love that depends on the child's performance. Such love is temporal. Because it comes and goes depending on her performance, she cannot really depend on it. She will start believing that the only time the parent demonstrates love is when she is doing well.

The only definition of love that I know how to give is from a parental perspective. To me, love is simply a feeling of contentment when you are with your child or someone you care about. It's as simple as that.

Giving them attention

Spending quality time with your child is necessary for boosting his self–esteem. The very fact that you take time out of your busy schedule tells him that he matters to you. Though the number of hours you spend with him is important, the quality of the time you spend with him is even more important. These days, quality time has become a cliché, but it is still a useful factor to keep in mind. A parent who spends three hours a day around his children just to constantly criticize them probably helps lower their self–esteem. A parent who makes his children feel that they are stopping him from doing more important things also helps lower their self–esteem. In these two examples, the parents are certainly not spending quality time with their kids. Quality time refers to the amount of focused attention you give your children as you constructively interact with them.

The first stage in giving your kids quality time is to learn to listen to them. How many of you hear your spouse say something to you and two seconds later, you realize that you were not really listening. Everyone does it from time to time but some people are chronic nonlisteners. I am sure that if someone did a scientific study of what people actually hear and retain in a conversation, it would be less than 60%. Some parents tend to retain even less in conversations with kids.

Listening is a skill that can be improved if you work at it. It is a discipline just like any other discipline (such as reading or adding). As a parent, you have to practice this craft daily. Some parents find they can increase their listening skills with their kids by spending time with them without distractions such as television or radio. We are living in an age where the average family has the television on for about six hours per day. If you have conversations with your children in front of the television set, it is easy to be distracted by the latest fashions, videos, or news items that come blaring out of the television. I used to be a television junkie. I am now in recovery, but what started me thinking about my addiction was that when my son was 1 year old, I noticed that also his eyes were glued to the television set. He increasingly watched television instead of climbing all over me and trying to bite my nose off, like he used to do. At first, I thought he was just growing up. But when I kept the television turned off after coming home from work, I noticed that he once again began to frolic with me. Although he could not make any intelligible sounds at the time, it was obvious that the TV was, in a way, forcing us to drift apart. The nonverbal communication between us was diminished because when the television was on, my attention was fixed on it and so was his.

When you eliminate distractions like television, you will discover that you will be a better listener to both the verbal and nonverbal messages your child sends.

Listening to your children is not meant to be a solemn activity. You should not just quietly sit there and let them talk. If you do, they will get the impression that you are not really paying attention. If they are recounting a story about an encounter they had, ask them questions about it so they know that you are involved in what they have to say.

Another way parents can improve their listening skills is to empathize with their children's feelings. An 8 –year–old boy who is scared of the dark complains to his parents about being scared in his room at night. The parents tell him he should not be afraid because the darkness cannot hurt him. Right away, the child wonders whether he has a right to feel the way he does. The proper response would have been to recognize that child's right to his feelings. The parent could have said to him, "When I was your age, I was afraid of the dark, too. I understand how you feel." Then continue with the logic of not being afraid of the dark. To respond empathetically is to temporarily throw logic out the window and respond to your kids from the heart. Kids cannot always articulate how they feel. But when they make attempts to express their views or feelings, you cannot begin with logical reasoning to either change their mind or talk them out of negative thoughts. Children raised by empathetic parents generally feel that their opinions are respected and taken into consideration.

Another way to give your children attention is to participate in some of their activities. One mother whose high school daughter loved to paint set aside Saturday mornings to try her hand at painting. She had her daughter instruct her on different painting techniques. This mother essentially developed an interest in her child's hobby. If your kids don't have a hobby, maybe you can turn them on to hobbies such as kite flying or crossword puzzles. You might be saying to yourself, "I don't have that kind of time." My answer is that you do not necessarily have to do these things with your kids on a daily or weekly basis. I think most kids understand that their parents have very little leisure time. They do not expect constant attention—it is not necessary to be around them all the time. However, you have to periodically do some activities with them to show them that you care and that you want to be with them.

Treating them like individuals

Treating kids like individuals is a hard concept for some parents to embrace. For one thing, parents think back to the days when they were kids and how their parents made all their decisions for them. Their parents, as with many parents in those days, expected their kids to do as they were told without questioning their authority. This parenting style was possible because parents spent more time at home and, more than likely, the mother was a homemaker. With a mother at home full time, all of the responsibilities related to feeding the family and doing the household chores fell on her shoulders. These days, kids are growing up with both parents working. They are likely to come home from school to an empty house, to make buying decisions for the family, and to watch over their siblings. In short, kids today have to grow up faster than their counterparts a generation or two ago.

In addition, kids growing up today also have to be aware of other realities of life at an earlier age. Take, for example, the AIDS epidemic that is spreading across the globe. This disease has made it necessary to educate young people about sex and its consequences. A generation ago, people just had to worry about simple venereal diseases, which are curable. AIDS is deadly. It is just one more thing that forces young people to mature faster and become more aware of their environment.

All of these modern realities amount to extra pressure on young people to cope in an ever–changing world. It also means that kids are growing up faster and learning more about life than you did when you were their age.

With such forced maturity, it is important that you recognize your children's need for individuality. They need to feel that you see them as human beings with their own feelings and attitudes.

Whenever I speak of individuality, there are always those who think that I am saying that kids should do whatever they want to do as an expression of their individuality. A parent can allow individuality in his child and still maintain behavioral guidelines. As parents become comfortable with their children's individuality and independence, their children will acquire a stronger feeling of their self–worth.

PARENTING STYLE AND SELF–ESTEEM

Psychologist Diana Baumrind grouped parenting styles into three categories: authoritarian, permissive, and authoritative. Each one of these styles can heavily influence your child's self–esteem. You should be aware of them so that you can catch yourself when you are behaving in a way that will result in lowering your child's self–esteem and reduce his achievement motivation.

Authoritarian parenting

Eight–year–old John and his mother are in a shopping center. As they are walking through one of the department stores, he asks his mom for money to buy a piece of candy, but she refuses. He asks why he cannot buy the candy, and she replies angrily, "I don't have to give you a reason. The answer is no."

You have probably heard this kind of exchange between a parent and child before. The mother's statement implies that the child should do what he has been told without question. On the surface this seems like a harmless idea. But, while we want our children to be obedient, we also do not want them to be robots. This mother's answer cut off all possibilities of discussing the issue. If this is her general attitude toward her child, I would say she is a dictator. Such dictatorial behavior in family life squelches children's self–esteem and diminishes their problem–solving capabilities, their creativity, and their achievement motivation.

Authoritarian parents exercise complete control over their children. They rule with an iron fist, and they expect their children to accept their ideas about authority, obedience, work, and other values without questioning the rationale behind them. These parents also have the tendency to reject their children by dwelling on their shortcomings and by ignoring their opinions. Children raised in this manner are generally neither independent nor creative. In addition, because decisions about things that are important to them are being made by their parents, they are unlikely to develop any sense of control over their lives and hence, their self–concept is usually quite low. Steven, now 34 years old, recounts his experience with his authoritarian father. "My father believed that children should be seen and not heard. He was also such a strict disciplinarian. My younger brother was so terrified of him. I think my father's attitude was the direct cause of my brother's lack of confidence in himself. To some extent, my father's attitude towards us affected me the same way."

Permissive parenting

The permissive parent tends to indulge all of his child's wishes. If the child is disobedient, the permissive parent does not confront or punish the child. The most glaring aspect of this parenting style is that the parent does not enforce rules of acceptable behavior. Quite often, the child has no sense of social responsibility. He is also likely to be disorderly, overly aggressive, selfish and, most importantly, not particularly independent.

In some cases, children brought up by permissive parents tend to be hard on themselves. Phyllis Fonseca, a licensed social worker in the Boston area, says, "Kids generally need some behavioral boundaries in their lives and if these boundaries are missing, some will impose stricter behavioral standards on themselves or set formidable goals that they can never meet." A result is that these kids usually have low self–esteem because they can never measure up to their own standards.

Quite often, permissive parents are so because they are too busy to instill some discipline in their kids. This is the case with some so–called high–powered corporate executives. They work seventy hours per week at the office and when they finally see their kids, they allow them to do anything they want out of guilt. They feel so guilty about their absences from the family that they try to make up for lost time by indulging their children with material things. This strategy often backfires for one very good reason: the kids conclude that the parents don't care enough to spend time with them and are trying to buy them off. This leads to low self–esteem because the children feel unloved and sometimes unwanted.

Authoritative parenting

Authoritative parents make up rules for acceptable behavior for their children and are consistent in enforcing these rules. However, these parents encourage the exchange of ideas and opinions with their children. They explain their rules and regulations to their children, and they offer them alternatives, thereby encouraging them to exercise their decision–making skills. Authoritative parents also set high achievement standards for their children and are aware of what they should expect at various stages in the cognitive, social, and physical development of their children. These parents are also supportive of their children, but when they misbehave, they are told why their behavior was wrong and are then promptly disciplined. The punishment, whatever the form, is directed at their children's behavior, and not the children themselves. This parenting style is conducive to the development of high self–esteem.

The ideal parenting style

Obviously no parent is always authoritarian, permissive, or authoritative. These styles are often blended. What is clear, however, is that the best child–rearing practice lies somewhere between exercising complete control over a child and letting him do whatever he pleases.

Total control lowers the child's self–esteem, which consequently discourages the child's motivation to succeed. Parental permissiveness does not challenge the child enough for him to learn to pull resources together, compromise, improvise, and become a creative problem–solver because he has no restrictions on his behavior. This is why the authoritative parenting style is the best choice for bringing up well–adjusted, self–reliant, creative children with a high self–concept.

It is important for parents to realize that they can positively or negatively influence their child's adult life with their child–rearing practices. These practices have a profound effect on their child's self–esteem, which in turn affects their child's desire to succeed. Positive influences can be accomplished only by knowing your child's capabilities and then setting standards of behavior accordingly. Neglecting your child's feelings and capabilities is a negative influence that will affect your child's adult life.

NEED FOR ACHIEVEMENT AND SELF–ESTEEM

In his book, *The Achieving Society*, David McClelland presented a psychological model of entrepreneurs that still represents one of the most significant works ever written on the character of entrepreneurs and the factors that motivate them. He coined the term "need for achievement" to describe a person's desire to excel. With strong self–esteem, your kids can acquire a desire to achieve. By the same token, when your kids accomplish some important goals, their self–esteem is also increased. Self–esteem feeds on achievement and achievement feeds on self–esteem. To understand the achievement motivation, you need to understand the theoretical framework behind McClelland's need for achievement and how it relates to entrepreneurship.

McClelland researched the relationship between the need for achievement and entrepreneurship. McClelland's model showed that the need for achievement encouraged economic achievement, which in turn motivated people to become entrepreneurs. Societal achievement philosophies on such virtues as persistence, diligence, hard work, and responsibility have a direct impact on education and parental child–rearing practices. McClelland believed that when young people have been raised with such values, they are more likely to become economically prosperous because of their strong achievement motivation. He supported this model by gathering information from several diverse societies. Having devised a system for measuring the achievement motivation, he gauged it at various instances for each society. He found a correlation between a high need for achievement and economic growth. Through his research,

McClelland identified four characteristics of entrepreneurs that have withstood the test of time:

1. High–achievement individuals (entrepreneurs) set objectives for themselves that are neither too difficult nor too easy to accomplish. They are more likely to work harder when they are faced with assignments of moderate difficulty. In other words, they are moderate risk takers.

2. High–achievement individuals prefer situations in which they can take direct responsibility for solving problems. They thrive in situations where their efforts, and not luck, yield positive results. Taking credit for the resolution of the problem also boosts their achievement motivation. The higher the need for achievement, the higher their confidence in further successes. This confidence leads them to believe that they will succeed where others have failed.

3. Individuals with a high need for achievement like to receive objective measures of how they are doing. For the entrepreneur, this gauge of his competence can be profits, market share, or a feeling of having made a contribution to society.

4. Individuals with a high need for achievement are innovative and creative. They are more likely to try different ideas in their search for a way to exercise their skills. Innovators see problems as solvable. Creativity comes into play because the entrepreneur may see possibilities that others overlook. The opportunities do not necessarily occur because of new inventions, but also by new applications to old problems.

As I mentioned earlier, before an individual can acquire a high need for achievement, he must have a healthy self–concept. By the same token, realized achievement goals increase self–esteem. Obviously, parents can increase their children's need for achievement by increasing their self–esteem.

The family environment has the biggest influence on children's development of a high need for achievement. The need for achievement is promoted when parents set high realistic standards for their children. Encouragement of a high need for achievement starts at a young age. In fact, McClelland found that by the age of five, there are already differences in the need for achievement among kids. Have the children been given adequate responsibilities? Have the parents given children the opportunity to do simple tasks on their own? These questions are questions to be asked of every parent who wishes to encourage his child's need for achievement.

As far back as 1958, Marian R. Winterbottom showed that differences in children's need for achievement can be traced to the attitudes of their mothers. Winterbottom tried to measure the attitudes of the mothers of children (ages 8–10) she had already classified on the need–for–achievement scale. She elicited from these mothers, the age at which they expected their children to perform certain tasks and the age at which they expected the children to refrain from certain acts.

Table 1 shows a sample of the questions she asked the mothers.

TABLE 1

GENERAL QUESTION TO THE MOTHER: At what age would you expect a son of yours to have learned...

ACHIEVEMENT

1. To try new things without asking for help?

2. To be able to lead other children and assert himself in children's groups?

3. To make his own friends among children his own age?

4. To do well in school on his own?

5. To make decisions for himself, such as how he spends his pocket money, what books he reads, what movies he sees?

6. To know his way around the neighborhood so that he can play where he wants to without getting lost?

7. To be active and energetic in climbing, jumping, and sports?

8. To try hard things for himself without asking for help?

9. To have interests and hobbies of his own? To be able to entertain himself?

10. To do well in competition with other children? To try hard to come out on top in games and sports?

CARETAKING

1. To be able to undress and go to bed by himself?

2. To do some regular tasks around the house?

3. To be able to eat alone without help in cutting and handling food?

4. To hang up his own clothes and look after his own possessions?

By asking questions like these, Winterbottom found that children who scored high on the need–for–achievement scale had mothers who expected them to be self–reliant at an earlier age. The children were expected to be competent at certain tasks, and as soon as they displayed this competence, they were expected to uphold the same standards when performing the same tasks again and again. By contrast, children who scored low on the need–for–achievement scale, were found to have mothers who restricted them, thereby forcing them to be very dependent on adults. In other words, these parents employed the authoritarian parenting style. Expecting children to perform some tasks before they are ready can also lead to a low need for achievement.

The authoritative parenting style, which sets limits for children but allows them to make decisions and maneuver within those limits, is the best way to promote a high need for achievement. As children learn to make decisions when confronted with choices, they take credit for their successes and blame for their failures. They know that their actions matter.

LOCUS OF CONTROL AND SELF–ESTEEM

There are a multitude of researchers who have tried to identify the major characteristics of entrepreneurs. The works of the most respected researchers usually relate back to the need for achievement. One factor that these researchers have isolated as an important characteristic of the entrepreneur is the concept of the locus of control. Locus of control describes the attitude a person has about her ability to control her environment. A person with an internal locus of control believes that she can influence the outcome of events that affect her. A person with an external locus of control believes that the outcome of events is beyond her control. This person feels that she is destined to remain in her particular situation. In other words, she cannot change the course of events in her life.

Studies have shown that people with an internal locus of control also score highly on the need–for–achievement scale. These people are more likely to desire independence and are more self–reliant when trying to accomplish goals they have set for themselves. To put this in the context of entrepreneurship, a person with an internal locus of control finds the restrictive atmosphere of corporations stifling. Being very independent and self–reliant persons, they decide to take action to change their situations. Some just change jobs, but others decide to start their own businesses.

It should be clear that people with an internal locus of control also have high self–esteem. They feel that they can change their circumstances without depending on luck.

5

CREATIVE PROBLEM SOLVING AND ENTREPRENEURSHIP

Part of the definition of an entrepreneur is one who applies resources in unique ways to solve a problem. If you think about it, all this says is that entrepreneurs solve problems creatively. They do not always invent products, but they use available resources in new and different ways.

The experts say that problem solving is one of the single most important factors in encouraging entrepreneurship in children. Since entrepreneurs are basically creative problem solvers, anything that enhances your children's problem–solving capabilities will also encourage their entrepreneurial behavior.

One good example of a creative problem solver is third grader Maurice Scales of Suitland, Maryland. Maurice was a first–grade regional winner of the annual Invent America contest. Maurice came up with a device he called Baby No–Mash. This was a plastic device that went on top of doors to keep the doors from slamming on unsuspecting little fingers. When I first heard about this I thought to myself, "What a simple and elegant solution." Upon further investigation I found out that Maurice came up with his idea because he wanted to keep his baby sister from getting her fingers caught in a door. Maurice was truly a creative problem solver.

One of the most fundamental steps in cultivating entrepreneurship in children is to teach them problem–solving skills. Problem solving is basic to learning. Learning to solve problems allows children to overcome hurdles they might face in life. It also gives children the confidence they need to make decisions and allows them to inject creativity into their thinking process.

In the American and Canadian educational systems, emphasis is placed on teaching basic skills such as reading and mathematics. Very little time is spent teaching children how to use information and basic skills to think, solve problems, and come up with new ideas. The challenge for the nineties is to teach children how to think and, in particular, how to think creatively to solve problems.

To be a good problem solver, an entrepreneur must be able to think creatively. Creative thinking is the ability to think of many solutions to a problem. It is also being able to think of unique or original solutions, and to develop or elaborate on solutions. At times it is asking good questions to clarify a problem. Also, it is being able to translate ideas into forms of communication or expression that make it possible for other people to grasp the ideas or solutions. Problem solving and creativity are inseparable concepts. Many identifiably creative abilities such as fluency, flexibility, and originality, while measurable and trainable, are really just components of complex problem–solving behavior. Real–life problem solving is really creative problem solving in that it requires a wide range of creative, conceptual, and logical thinking ability. From this point on when I refer to problem solving, I am also referring to the creative thinking process.

There are several steps in this problem–solving process:

1. Defining the problem.

2. Thinking about possible solutions.

3. Gathering the information needed.

4. Choosing and trying a solution.

Not all of these steps are followed in solving every problem, and they are not necessarily followed in the same order. Here is a typical problem–solving opportunity that might arise in a household:

> *Joe had been playing with his toy cars on the floor. One of them rolled under the couch. "Oh, no," said Joe, as he heard it bang against the wall. "Mom," he shouted. "My car is under the couch." His mother came into the room. "Well, how can you get it out?" she asked. He stretched his arm under the couch, as far as it could go, but he couldn't find the car. "You try, mom," he said. His mother got down and felt around the couch. "That was a good idea you had, but I guess my arm isn't long enough either. Now what?" Joe had another idea. He would try with his foot. When his leg wouldn't fit in the space under the couch he tried the other leg, then gave the couch an angry kick. "Don't kick the couch," his mom said. "Think about why it didn't work." Joe's mother smiled, "What could we use that would fit?" Joe thought for a minute and said, "Hey, a stick." "Good idea Joe," she said. She then left the room and came back with a broom, which she put down beside him. It didn't take Joe long to figure out that he could use the broom. He poked the broom handle under the couch and out rolled the car. Joe smiled and crawled after it.*

Together Joe and his mother had solved a problem. Joe knew what the problem was and tried several ways to solve it. His mother just as easily could have moved the couch out of the way to retrieve the toy car, but she realized that Joe could learn something from this experience, even though the solutions that he was trying were not working. Had she retrieved the car for him, he probably would expect her to bail him out the next time the car went behind the couch and this would just start a cycle of dependency that is not healthy for him or his mother.

Joe's mother knew that she could help him by turning what could have been a frustrating experience into a good lesson in problem solving. She did this by:

1. Giving him attention when he asked for it.

2. Encouraging him to find a solution by himself.

3. Praising his efforts even when they weren't successful.

4. Giving him a start with a new idea so that he could finally solve the problem.

The next time Joe runs into a problem, he will most likely work at it more patiently. He may end up having to ask for help again, but at least he will have learned that he is able to solve problems. Children can learn to solve problems, and parents can help them learn.

Steps in problem solving

One of the first steps in problem solving is the recognition of the problem. A child must first figure out what is wrong. For adults, this is the most natural thing in the world to do. For example, if your lamp won't go on, you ask yourself, "Is it plugged in? Is the bulb any good? Is there something else wrong that has to be repaired?" Children, however, especially very young ones, may not even think to look for the problem. A 2 year old may only know that, as hard as he tugs, his wagon won't roll. In such a situation, you may have to point out where the trouble spot is, by saying something like, "Look! The wheel is stuck on that rock."

Older children with problems may have trouble recognizing them, too. Encouraging them to talk to you about the situation can help them get to the bottom of the trouble: "Tell me what's wrong. Maybe together we can think of an idea." It helps if you can stay calm while helping them solve the problem.

Children have to recognize the importance of a problem before they will be interested in solving it. It has to matter to them. It's also essential that you recognize its importance, too: "I know that you want to learn to whistle. I'll show you again."

Once children realize what the problem is, they should sit back and think about how to attack it. More often than not, however, young children try to solve a problem using the first idea that comes to them, without considering that there might be a better solution. As a parent, you may have to help them think things through by talking with them. Sometimes the way to go about this is to ask, "What do you think we should do?" or to suggest, "Let's try to find another way for both of you to play with the ball."

Finding another way to accomplish a goal is where creativity comes into play in problem solving. Creativity can be viewed as a process of change in thinking and action. Combining ideas into a novel idea or concept requires change. Increasing creativity in the home requires that parents create an atmosphere that is receptive to new ideas. A positive, reinforcing, accepting climate is the basic ingredient necessary for encouraging creative behavior. Many obstacles to creative thinking are emotional reactions to insecure feelings, which are caused by fear of new or different ideas or situations. By suggesting novel ideas, people open themselves to criticism. It is often easier to conform to the norm than to risk making a fool of yourself by expressing a new idea or thought. New or different ideas can flourish in a flexible environment.

In the home, a flexible environment is one in which parents should encourage and reinforce unusual ideas. Parental support and positive attitudes are the fuel necessary to power the positive motivational climate that will set the stage for the creative atmosphere.

As children grow older and gain more experience in problem solving, they learn to be more patient. Often they take the time to stand back from a problem, to think about possible ways to solve it. They actually like the idea of trying to figure things out for themselves and they feel a strong sense of accomplishment when they do.

Children should be praised for trying again and for finding new and different ways to solve a problem, even if the new ways do not work. Being able to think through several possibilities is a good problem–solving skill. Praise and support for problem solving may help a child learn to seek new ideas and different, more successful ways of thinking. Some problems require more information. Books may offer useful information, but discussion is often what's needed: "Let's find out why Patrick is angry and won't let you play with his toy." Other problems require asking for help. Children need to learn to ask for help too: "I see that you want to move the chair. It's too heavy for you to move by yourself. You can ask me to help you."

Children also need to learn that there are some problems no one can solve, not even parents. For example, a child may think that a dead pet can be brought back to life. Parents can help their children see that no matter how much they want to find a solution, some problems have none.

Once children have gotten all the necessary information or help and have chosen the best solution, they can try it out. If the solution works well, fine. If not, they may need to try out another solution.

Sometimes your child will decide on a solution that really is not a good way of handling a problem. It is your job as a parent to guide him to what you feel is a better answer. For example, suppose your son decides that the best way to wash the dog is to put him in the bathtub. If you do not feel that this is the way to clean the dog, you could go over the other possibilities and encourage him to try other approaches.

How problem solving develops

A newborn baby's problems must all be taken care of by someone else. Very soon, he tries to do things on his own and finds out about people and objects around him. He may try to do things like pulling the keys from a key ring or trying to fit all his fingers in his mouth at once. He wants to solve problems.

Three year olds can solve problems as long as the problems have to do with things that they can actually feel or see. They will try to get their zipper unstuck or put puzzle pieces together. Other problems may simply be beyond them. For example, young children may not even think of a solution for getting a ball back when it gets caught in the branches of a bush. They may even soon forget that it is lost and start to play with something else, or they may begin to cry but not really be able to tell you what happened. As their language skills improve, they become better able to explain their difficulties and ask for help when it is needed.

Soon they also begin to understand that there may be more than one way of going about things. They can remember several possibilities long enough to try them out, and if one solution doesn't work, they are able to go down their mental list of ideas and try another. At first, they might try to shake the branches of the bush to get their ball, and if that does not work, they might try to push it out with something else. They will keep trying to get their ball back.

By the time they reach school age, children can think through several possibilities in their heads and then pick out the most sensible one to try. They may still find it difficult to put their thoughts into words, however. Even when they are well into elementary school, they may have trouble explaining their problems in a way that makes sense to adults. For example, your child may not be able to explain why he feels unhappy or what it is that is bothering him.

As children get more practice in problem solving, they become more skilled at it and more eager to handle the day–to–day problems they face. Developing a positive attitude toward problem solving helps children become successful learners.

When children learn to solve problems, they pick up other skills as well. They learn to be patient with themselves and with others, to be alert to many possibilities, and to be careful observers. Learning to recognize that there may be more than one solution to a problem helps children become more open–minded. In addition, it increases their confidence, which in turn increases creativity, self–esteem, decision–making skills, and the feeling of being able to control their environment (or locus of control). As we discussed earlier, all these characteristics are important factors in the development of entrepreneurs.

HELPING YOUR CHILDREN LEARN CREATIVE PROBLEM SOLVING

Since your children spend so much time at home, many of their problems occur there. As a parent, you can help them learn to figure out solutions if you take their problems seriously, no matter how trivial they may seem.

Talking with your children

To help children become good problem solvers and creative thinkers, parents need to give them something to think about. The most common way of getting children to think is to ask questions. However, asking questions that require children to think takes much more thought by the parent than asking questions that can be answered by a yes or a no. Open–ended questions geared toward something that is of interest to the child can help him develop skills in information gathering, hypothesis formulation, and hypothesis testing. Here are examples of questions that will encourage a child to think:

> *How many different ways can you use a shoe box? A brown bag? A pine cone? A shovelful of sand?*
>
> *What would we do if the door blew shut and we were locked out?*
>
> *How many different ways can you think of to help a friend who is new at school?*

Here are some guidelines to follow in developing your own questioning technique:

1. The question must pertain to something in which the child is interested. For example, if the child is painting a picture with watercolors, a question that might encourage him to think in a creative way might be: "What colors can you mix together to get green?" The question must flow from the activities of the child. Any other questioning technique may be unnatural, and the child may lose interest in the problem–solving process.

2. Ask questions simply and directly and avoid excessive wording. Vary the way you word the questions.

3. Allow sufficient time after a question is asked so that your child can think and formulate possible answers or responses. Do not be impatient or rush your child into answering you.

4. Reinforce and encourage your child's effort to respond even though his answers may not be exactly what you expect to hear. Never ridicule or put him down. Let him know you admire his good ideas. Praise him for being able to think of more than one way to do things.

5. Remember that the process should be fun. Asking children their opinions and ideas gives them a sense of importance. "What things make you feel happy?" It encourages them to think and to put their thoughts into words. If you accept their opinions and respect their ideas, they will feel good about themselves. Read and tell your children stories about other people who had problems to solve: "Once when your grandfather was a little boy on the farm, his goat fell into a deep hole..." "When I was about your age, I lost a quarter in the sidewalk grating."

Provide practice in problem solving

Give your children things to do that have built–in problems. All kinds of puzzles are problem–solving games. Riddles, jokes, mysteries, brainteasers, and magic tricks are all activities that make children stop and think. Young children like to solve matching games and puzzles that fit together in only one way because they can see firsthand how successful they are at problem solving. Children may need encouragement to stay with an activity until it is finished, but when it is done, they know it is done well. This develops a good attitude towards problem solving.

Make a game of thinking of a problem situation in which there is more than one answer. Make problem solving fun. Children enjoy games that challenge them to think of many possibilities. Older children may want to keep score of how many different solutions they can list.

Sharing your own problem solving with your children

As you go about solving your own problems, your children watch and learn from you. Parents solve problems every day— some big ones and a lot of small ones. You figure out the quickest way to get chores done. You check the tires on the car, decide how to repair the fence, and determine whether the milk is spoiled. These are all good opportunities for teaching your children about problem solving. Take time to explain to a young child what you are doing and why. Learning that adults have reasons for what they do helps children to think reasonably. Share your thinking. Think aloud so that your children will understand what is going through your mind as you fix that leaky faucet. Show your children the resources you use. Let them see that you are reading the instructions and following them as you put together the new toy. Sometimes a solution doesn't work. Even parents make mistakes. When this happens show your children what good problem solvers do:

1. They try a different way.

2. They seek new information.

3. They do not give up until they have tried many solutions.

4. They ask for help when they need it.

Brainstorming

So far, we have discussed ways you can encourage your young kids to become creative problem solvers. However, if you have teenagers and you would like to help them develop these skills, you can employ the brainstorming technique to enhance their creative problem–solving skills.

Brainstorming is a technique used to produce an idea related to a particular problem, topic, or theme. It is an excellent technique for strengthening imagination. The brainstorming technique can be applied to any situation, such as a family crisis or even a recent world event. However, to get your kids interested, you should apply it to a problem they themselves are having or a decision that the entire family has to make. For example, if you are thinking of what to do for the next summer vacation, you can turn this into a topic for brainstorming. Brainstorming can also be used to invent products.

The ground rules in a brainstorming session are as follows:

1. Do not criticize or evaluate any ideas produced. Ideas should be free–flowing and unhampered.

2. The crazier the ideas, the better. Unusual or bizarre ideas may actually be usable when slightly modified.

3. The more the merrier. The quantity of ideas are important in the idea–finding stage. If enough ideas are generated, there are bound to be some usable ones.

4. As your kids produce their own ideas on how to solve problems that face them, you should also contribute your own ideas. It is permissible for you or your kids to modify an idea already suggested to come up with a new idea.

5. If you are in a position to do so, record all the ideas.

The secret to brainstorming is deferred judgment. This means that criticism is ruled out. Simply concentrate on getting as many ideas as possible.

After you and your kids have listed all the ideas you can think of to solve the problem at hand, you can all go through the list as many times as necessary to find the best or most promising ideas.

If you practice this brainstorming technique with your kids, you will find that they will automatically think of various solutions to solve problems or make decisions. Thinking creatively will become second nature to them because they will be used to starting out their problem–solving or decision–making process without constraints.

6

TEACHING YOUR KIDS
HOW TO MANAGE MONEY

Learning the fundamentals of money management is the first step in your children's financial education. Early financial literacy will arm your kids with the knowledge they need to understand the dynamics of starting and running their own businesses. While not all entrepreneurial ventures result in personal financial gains, most entrepreneurs have to know how to collect money, budget it, invest it, and even borrow it to run their businesses successfully.

One of the biggest causes of small–business failures in this country is that entrepreneurs lack budgeting and planning skills. At The National Conference on Entrepreneurship Education held recently in Toronto, Canada, Senior Vice President Dennice Leahy of The Royal Bank of Canada said in her address:

> *Preventive medicine is so important—we need to make sure entrepreneurs don't miss out on this basic financial education in the first place. As things now stand in our school system, they do. That's because we don't start this kind of training early enough.*

Coming up with good business ideas will not suffice. The business world is strewn with bankrupt entrepreneurs who have missed opportunities to capitalize on their creative business ideas because they mismanaged their start–up funds or underestimated their working capital (the money needed to sustain their businesses on a day–to–day basis).

There are three ways entrepreneurs can acquire sound financial management skills for their businesses:

1. Hiring financial experts.

2. Learning from their failures.

3. Learning money–management skills during preteen and teen years.

Hiring financial experts has its advantages. Financial experts make up for an entrepreneur's deficiencies in financial matters and leave the entrepreneur with more time to worry about the creative side of the business. Unfortunately, there is a significant downside. An entrepreneur who hires a financial expert can easily lose sight of her financial constraints when creating new products or when expanding her business. The reason for this is that once she leaves the financial decisions to someone else, she can become detached from profit–loss considerations. For example, she may try to create a product or offer a service that she cannot possibly make available to customers at a reasonable price or profit. In addition, relinquishing financial control also leaves her vulnerable to dishonest accountants or money managers.

A business starter who has sufficient money to make up for her ineptitude in handling her finances can afford to learn from her business failures. But many entrepreneurs start their businesses either on a shoestring budget or with borrowed funds. For these people, learning money–management skills by trial and error is likely to send their new ventures into bankruptcy in a flash.

The best time for would–be entrepreneurs to acquire money–management skills is long before they even start their own businesses. Parents must shoulder the responsibility for ensuring that their kids learn the basics of handling money in these early years. By their teen years, kids should already demonstrate the financial savvy necessary to run their own full–fledged businesses.

At first glance the task of teaching kids the basics of money management may seem formidable, but it is actually made easier by the fact that children have acquired a tremendous amount of economic power in the past few decades. This new–found financial power can be attributed in part to the changing dynamics of the American family.

These days, mothers are joining the workforce in unprecedented numbers, and consequently their kids are increasingly shouldering more purchasing decisions related to food, clothing, and other consumer items. In a 1994 survey, Rand Youth Poll—a research organization that has been surveying teenagers for forty–two years—found that teenagers shelled out $64 billion on daily expenditures for that year. In addition, Rand Youth Poll found that teenagers influenced or were directly involved in additional purchases of goods and services totaling $177 billion.

That's a total of $241 billion of economic clout! However, the fact that kids have control or influence over $241 billion does not necessarily mean that they know how to spend money wisely or that they have other good money–management skills.

Parents can view their children's economic clout as an opportunity for teaching them two of the most fundamental lessons in money management: how to save and how to plan for expenditures.

THE ROOTS OF FINANCIAL ILLITERACY

Parents go to great lengths to make sure that their children receive the best education that money can buy. They send their children to music lessons, ballet lessons, tennis lessons, computer summer camps, and other skill–intensive activities. Unfortunately, they neglect one of the most inexpensive and valuable skills their children can acquire: how to handle money.

The ability to manage money is a skill that must be acquired early in life. Saving, budgeting, and investing money are disciplines that should be incorporated into children's total education, particularly if parents want to encourage entrepreneurial behavior in their children.

According to the Rand Youth Poll, only 35% of parents talk to their kids about money. This means that the other 65% miss their best opportunity to teach their kids how to budget and spend money wisely.

Sometimes parents neglect to teach their children about money because they were brought up in families that kept financial matters secret and discouraged their participation in decisions involving money. "When I was growing up, my parents felt that we should be protected from the harsh realities of our family's financial condition," one mother says. "I suspect that since we never really had a lot of money, they didn't want me or my other siblings to focus on anything having to do with money. Maybe they thought that the more we knew about handling money, the more we would realize that we were not that well off." Another parent provides some insight as to why his parents were never interested in teaching him how to handle money when he was growing up: "My parents were very religious people. To them, the love of money was the root of all evil, so they avoided the subject at all costs unless it was absolutely necessary." Parents who were brought up in such environments are in turn applying the same flawed principles to the raising of their children.

WHEN TO START TEACHING YOUR KIDS ABOUT MONEY

You should consider the ages and maturity of your children before deciding when to start teaching them how to manage money. You must know what your kids are capable of learning at different stages of their development.

Child–care experts agree that parents should provide their children with opportunities to become financially literate as early as at the age of 4 or 5. Your first two goals should be to familiarize your kids with the currency and to help them understand the value of money as a medium of exchange. Let them learn the difference between pennies, nickels, dimes, and quarters. You can explore these currencies with your children through play or by introducing them to hobbies that involve keeping track of money. "I started teaching Janet about money when she was only 4 years old," a young mother told me. "I helped her set up a collection of coins. Each week, she added coins minted in a different year to her coin book. In a short while, she was familiar with all the coins and she knew their relative values."

Parents can involve kids as young as four in making choices about buying one item over another. For example, in supermarkets, you can give your young children money to pay for items themselves or you can even give them change so they can buy you newspapers and other small items.

Between the ages of six and nine, your children go through a transformation that makes it possible for them to begin to understand the basics of money management. Applying the Piagetian model (see Chapter 3), children in this age group begin to learn that they cannot have certain items without bargaining for them. That is, they begin to understand the value of merchandise. In addition, their sense of time begins to expand. They can see beyond the short horizon of one or two days, and thus they are able to plan for the future use of their money. All of these factors, combined with children's desire for independence, have convinced child–development experts that children can be taught the fundamentals of money management by the time they enter first grade. At this age, they should already know the difference between coins. They should also be able to count, even though they may not be able to understand numbers in the hundreds or thousands.

Parents can build on this basic foundation by involving their kids in small financial decisions. For example, if they accompany you to the supermarket, they can help you comparison shop. "When I take my 8–year–old son to the grocery store," one mother said, "he makes a game of comparing prices of particular items on the shelves such as two–liter bottles of different brands of cola or quarts of various milk brands."

Between the ages of ten and twelve, children's sense of time is further developed and they have the ability to save for anticipated purchases. They are better able to delay immediate gratification for the longer–term pleasure of buying something they really want. At this age, children should be included in the family's budgeting processes and decisions.

By age thirteen, your kids should be able to understand such economic concepts as supply and demand, profit, and other business–related ideas, although they may not know the proper business terms. In addition, they should be capable of understanding credit–related issues such as borrowing money, lending money, using credit cards, and making interest payments.

APPROACHES TO TEACHING MONEY–MANAGEMENT PRINCIPLES

Once parents recognize the importance of teaching their children about money, they have to find a suitable method to achieve this goal. There are three common approaches parents take to help their kids become financially literate: giving their children money on an as–needed basis, paying their children for doing chores, and giving their children regular allowances.

Giving children money as the need arises is one approach that all parents have taken at one time or another. For example, if your daughter wants to go to the movies with her friends and she asks you for the cash, you give her the exact sum she needs—no more, no less. It's fine to dispense money to your children in this manner on rare occasions. But if this practice becomes habitual, your children will never learn to budget their money or make decisions about future purchases.

One parent laments:

Unfortunately, even as my daughter approached her late teens, I still gave her money to buy small items like magazines or even snacks. I never gave her a regular allowance. Maybe I just wanted to maintain control over all her purchases. Now that she is in her mid–twenties, I can see the result of the way I taught her about money. She finds it hard to make independent decisions about what to buy and she still seeks my advice even for the smallest items.

Doling out money to kids on an as–needed basis is probably one of the worst techniques you can use to teach your children how to manage money because they never learn how to allocate their money.

Another approach some parents take in introducing their children to money management is to tie allowances to specific chores. A survey taken by Penny Power, a Consumer Reports publication for young people, revealed that 90% of the children who get allowances say that they are supposed to do some work around the house for it. For example, parents might assign a dollar value to taking out the garbage, mowing the lawn, vacuuming the house, and other chores. Using this approach, parents frequently also dock their children money for neglecting to do chores.

Unfortunately, with this approach, children learn neither responsibility nor money–management skills. Instead, they learn to expect payment for things that they should be doing for free, such as cleaning their rooms, setting the dinner table, or refraining from beating on their brothers and sisters. If parents tie allowances to chores, they run the risk that their kids will decide that for the amount of money they are "fined" for not doing their chores, it is worth not doing them.

One youngster confides, "My parents paid me a dollar for every day I made my bed. But some days, I just didn't feel like doing it so it cost me a dollar each time. I didn't really mind losing a dollar from time to time." Obviously, this youngster felt that the cost of neglecting to make her bed was an amount she could afford to lose. By tying chores to money, parents confuse teaching children how to be responsible family members with teaching them how to handle their finances. The message gets so muddled that neither lesson is absorbed by the children.

The third approach parents employ to teach their kids about money management is to dole out regular allowances with few or no strings attached. Children who get allowances can make up their own budgets and decide when and where to spend their money. For example, if your son wants to use his allowance to play video games with his friends, he shouldn't have to approach you for approval. As long as you have set guidelines for expenditures you will not tolerate, he should be able to spend his money on anything he wants.

The allowance method is consistent with the authoritative style of parenting (see Chapter 4) because children are given the freedom to spend money for items of their choice. This discretionary power enables children to develop their decision–making skills and to gain more self–confidence: two characteristics of entrepreneurs.

HOW TO DETERMINE THE PROPER ALLOWANCES FOR YOUR KIDS

There are two common mistakes parents make when it comes to deciding how much allowance to give their children. The first mistake is that they try to match the allowances given by other parents in the neighborhood. One parent told me that he doubled his 13–year–old son's weekly allowance because other kids were getting twice as much allowance as his son was. Such a blunder is the worst way to set allowance limits.

Parents who set allowances according to the amounts given by other parents relinquish their right to determine the money that is appropriate for their children. In addition, these parents may find that they cannot afford to dispense the same amount of money to their kids as the neighbors to theirs. One mother notes:

I tried to give my daughter enough so that she could buy all the things that her friends in the neighborhood were buying. But I knew that things were getting out of hand when she came home one day and asked me to raise her weekly allowance so that she could save enough money to buy a $200 designer pocketbook that all her friends were buying. That's when I realized that keeping up with the Joneses was going to drive me to the poor–house.

The second mistake that parents make in setting allowances for their children is to take into consideration the allowances they themselves received when they were growing up. As you attempt to figure out the appropriate amount for your kids, keep this in mind: inflation has probably distorted prices so much that using the allowances you received twenty years ago as a benchmark for the allowance to give your kids is a useless exercise. In 1996, even a movie can cost your children $7.50 in some areas of the country. This is probably at least three times the price of a movie ticket when you were their age.

One parent confesses:

My 16–year–old son and some of his friends go dancing at a nonalcoholic club about once a month. When he told me that the cover charge was $10, I was shocked because I remember paying $1.50 to get into dance halls when I was a teenager. I guess times have really changed.

Let's suppose that you are trying to figure out an appropriate allowance for your daughter. In figuring out an appropriate amount, you should monitor all expenditures you make for her over a period of about six weeks.

Put these expenditures in three categories:

1. Purchases such as shoes, clothes, and other big–ticket items that you make for her on an infrequent basis.

2. Small–ticket items that you anticipate on a weekly basis. Items like school lunches, snacks, or bus money.

3. Small amounts requested by your child for leisure or hobbies such as going to the movies, to the arcade to play video games, to a skating rink, and other recreational activities.

You must consider the leisure–time activities available in your area for kids. If you are new to the neighborhood, talking to other parents with children the same age as yours should help. However, do not accept suggestions that will leave you penniless.

Your daughter's maturity will determine whether you should dispense the money for all three categories of expenditures at the same time. Obviously, if she is 6 years old, she will not be able to handle money intended for infrequent purchases like shoes and clothes. She is still at the developmental stage where she craves immediate gratification and therefore cannot plan for future expenditures.

To determine an appropriate allowance for your daughter, discuss her weekly expenditures with her and ask her to help you list items that she would like included in an allowance figure. Her age should determine whether you should go through the list in great detail. By talking it over with her, you are telling her that her opinion counts even though you can overrule her. This gives her a sense of confidence in handling her affairs and assures her that you value her opinion. This technique is consistent with the authoritative parenting discussed in Chapter 4.

Compare your daughter's list with your own. You may be surprised at her ability to recall expenses that you missed. Her list may also contain some frivolous expenses. For example, she may try to convince you that she absolutely has to buy a piece of candy every day on her way back from school. It is up to you to set guidelines for the things she can count as legitimate expenditures. Merge the two lists.

If your daughter is between the ages of six and nine, you may want to give her enough money to cover only fun activities with her friends (category 3). Between the ages of ten and twelve, you can also include in her allowance, money for expenditures that can be anticipated on a weekly basis (category 2). If she is 13 years old or older, you can include money for the big–ticket items such as shoes and clothes (category 1).

Put some boundaries on her spending but give her as much leeway as possible. You wouldn't want her to use all of her weekly allowance on treats if you have determined for health reasons that she should not purchase these items. However, having indicated the items you forbid, let her spend the money any way she sees fit.

Keep in mind that the decision on how much money to give your child and what should be included in the allowance must be monitored from time to time to make sure that she is not misusing her allowance. Suppose you decide to give your child the responsibility to manage her money for essential items such as shoes and clothes but you subsequently discover that she is using the money for other purposes. In this case, you should make adjustments in the way you disburse her funds. For example, you may want to give her the cash for these items at the time she is to make these purchases. "When I discovered that my daughter was going without lunch in school because she spent her weekly allotment as soon as she got it," one father recounts, "I decided to give her lunch money on a daily basis. This way, I eliminated the temptation to spend a week's worth of lunch money." I am not advocating that you dispense money for all of her purchases as the need arises, but that you monitor her big purchases to make sure that she is using the money you give her for the purposes you intended. As she begins to show you that she is mature enough to handle money for bigger purchases, you can stop monitoring her expenditures.

It is a fact of capitalism that you can get laid off, demoted, fired, or lose your business. In such situations, your daughter's allowance should be reduced accordingly, unless you can truly afford to give her the same amount of money as before.

Do not try to shield her from the fact that your financial status has deteriorated. It is not necessary to tell her all of the financial details, but it is important that she understand the association between her financial well–being and your job. This is a particularly good lesson for young kids who have a hard time understanding the relationship between work and money. One father of four explained:

> *After the company I work for was bought out, 20% of its work force was laid off. I was lucky because I got to keep my job. Unfortunately, I had to take a 15% pay cut. I also cut my children's allowances by 15% after explaining to them what had happened at my job. My kids understood our predicament and they offered to take an even bigger allowance cut.*

HOW TO SET THE ALLOWANCE PERIOD

The period between each allowance can vary according to how your children handle their money. Some 12 year olds who are given an allowance on a monthly basis can make their allowance last until the end of the month, but others may spend it all in a week or a day. For children less than 13 years old it is probably advisable to give them weekly allowances. For older children, it depends on their maturity. If your kids cannot properly manage their money, you can try and shorten the period between allowances.

According to child–care experts, parents should dispense allowances at designated dates and times. This gives children the opportunity to plan the activities for which they will use the discretionary portions of their allowances. Since you want your children to plan their expenditures, you should not change the period between allowances without telling them in advance. In addition, you should never withhold allowance because your kids have been mischievous or have neglected to perform certain tasks. "Every Saturday morning," says one parent, "I give Susan her weekly allowance even if all her chores were not completed to my satisfaction. The way I see it, I get paid on my job every two weeks no matter what. It is only fair that I give my daughter her allowance at regular intervals."

DOLING OUT EXTRA MONEY

You may find that from time to time, you will have to give your kids extra spending money. There is nothing wrong with this practice provided they need the money for unanticipated expenditures. For example, if your kids have to go on a school field trip, they will probably have to approach you for extra money. If, however, you have already included money for specific activities or purchases in their weekly allowances, supplying them with more money for such activities defeats the whole purpose of giving allowances.

If your kids come in contact with relatives, they probably receive cash gifts from them on their birthday, holidays, or other occasions. Grandparents in particular do not care about the allowance limits you have set for your kids. One father told me that his mother–in–law once said, "It is my job to spoil my grandchildren, and your responsibility to discipline them." Birthdays, holidays, and other occasions can provide the opportunity your parents and other relatives need to carry out their master plan of spoiling your children. Most of the time, they will do it by giving your kids cash gifts.

If you are not watchful, these relatives can undo everything you have taught your kids about managing money. Your kids may take their cash gifts without letting you know, but it is up to you to sensitize their grandparents and other relatives about your money policy. You should request that when they give your children money, they tell you about it. You should also ask your children to let you know when they get money from anyone else besides you. Depending on their ages and maturity, if they receive money that is substantially higher than their periodic allowances, consider putting the money in savings accounts. If they are less than 10 years old, put the money away for them, but make sure that they realize the money is part of their savings. You can dole out the money at your discretion and talk to them about their intended expenditures when they want to draw from these savings. For older children, let them handle the cash gifts, but make sure that you monitor how they use the extra money.

HELPING YOUR KIDS SET LONG–TERM AND SHORT–TERM GOALS

Kids are traditionally instant pleasure seekers. From the time they are born to the time they go off to college, most children want immediate gratification. When they are old enough to understand the concept of money, they can easily settle into a buy–buy cycle unless their parents teach them good money–management techniques.

One of the biggest challenges you face is getting your kids to plan for expenditures. The easiest way to do this is to help your youngsters come up with their own money–management plan. An important step in helping your children develop a money–management plan is to have them set their own goals.

Goals are wants, needs, and future objectives your kids can set for themselves. Goals may be long–term or short–term. While you may consider long–term goals to be objectives you hope to reach in five or ten years, children have much shorter time frames. For a 7 year old, one month is an eternity. However, for a 16 year old, it is not that far in the future. Set the time horizon for your children according to their age and maturity. Only you know what they consider to be a long or short time.

Categorizing goals as either long–term or short–term will help your kids understand that financial goals can and should be prioritized. Help your kids evaluate whether their financial goals are realistic. For example, if your 14–year–old son wants to buy a $5,000 computer within a year and he doesn't have a penny in his savings account nor does he have a plan to supplement his weekly allowance, then he cannot possibly meet his goal. Questioning your children about how they intend to meet their goals should help stop them from coming up with unrealistic objectives.

HELPING YOUR KIDS COME UP WITH A BUDGET

After your kids have set their long–term and short–term objectives, the next step in helping them learn about proper money management is to have them come up with their own budgets. Budgets are simply plans for spending and saving. They will help your kids prevent impulse spending, decide what they can or cannot afford, know where their money goes, and increase savings. By learning how to set their budgets, your kids will be better prepared to run their own businesses. As you will see in the following chapters, the skills gained in making up a budget are the same skills needed for coming up with a business plan.

A budget may cover any convenient period of time—one week, two weeks, or a month. The period depends on how often your children get their allowances. If you give them weekly allowances, you should help them draw up a weekly budget. If your kids are old enough to work, they are probably mature enough to create a monthly budget. Once again, young kids have very short time horizons so tailor the budget to their ages and temperaments.

The first step in helping your kids come up with their budgets is to have them tally their income—all the money they will receive in the budget period. They should include in their income the allowance you give them on a regular basis, cash gifts from relatives, and money from part–time jobs, if any.

After your kids have determined their income for the budget period, they should estimate their expenses—all their expenditures in the budget period. Their expense list should include only items that they will pay for in an allowance period. The big items that you pay for, such as winter coats, shoes, sneakers, and other expensive goods, should be kept off the list.

One important item your kids should consider when coming up with a budget is how much they should save each budget period to meet their short–term and long–term goals. They should consider savings as a reduction in the income they will receive in this period. For example, suppose your child decides to save $8 each week, and he receives $20 of income each week. After he sets aside the $8 as his savings, he is forced to meet all of his other expenses with the remaining $12.

Once they have calculated their income and expenses for an allowance period, your children should simply subtract their expenses from their income to come up with a surplus or a deficit. If their income is bigger than their expenses, the remaining amount should be added to their savings so they can meet their short–term or long–term purchasing goals. If their expenses are bigger than their income in the allowance period, then they have to either increase their income or decrease their expenses to eliminate the deficit.

They should not touch the savings to close the deficit unless they absolutely have to balance their budget. They should try to reduce their other expenditures first to close the budget gap. Said one New York mother, "The first time Andrea figured out her weekly budget, she ended up with her expenses exceeding her income. At first she was upset that she did not have enough money to close the gap. But it didn't take her long to realize that cutting out some expenditures such as buying teen magazines or going to the movies, helped her meet her budget."

Working out a budget will help your kids understand the importance of planning for the future. In addition, it will help them see the consequences of their spending decisions even before they make any purchases. Your kids can use the worksheet below as a guide for coming up with their own budget. They can use it to itemize their income and expenses. Note that item C is for your children's savings. As you give them a copy of the worksheet, emphasize that to meet their long–term goals, they will have to put some money away as savings on a regular basis.

<u>WEEKLY BUDGET WORKSHEET</u>

SOURCES OF CASH

Money from parents and other cash gifts _____

Money from jobs _____

A. Total Sources of Cash $_____

EXPENSES (ITEMS YOU BUY)

<u>School–related expenses</u>

Lunch _____

Notebooks _____

Pens/pencils _____

Other school expenses _____

Snacks/food _____

Fun money _____

Clothing _____

Subscriptions _____

Transportation _____

Gas _____

Oil _____

Savings _____

<u>Other Expenses</u>

_____ _____

_____ _____

_____ _____

B. Total Expenses (Sum up all expenses) $ _____

C. Savings (A less B) $ _____

TEACHING YOUR KIDS HOW TO SAVE

Americans are known for having one of the lowest savings rates in the industrialized world. For example, the typical American worker saves five cents of every dollar he takes home while the average Japanese worker saves sixteen cents. Most economists will tell you that such a low savings rate deprives the United States of the capital needed for investments. However, I see another problem with a low savings rate—this low rate underscores the spend culture in this country, which can undermine your efforts in trying to teach your kids how to manage money.

The idea of saving for anticipated purchases is one of the most important lessons you can teach your children. By teaching them to save, you are teaching the idea of delayed gratification— that is, the postponement of immediate pleasure for greater pleasure in the future. With kids, this could mean accumulating daily bubble gum money to buy record albums or passing up a trip to the movies with their friends for several weeks so that they can use their money to buy a rare comic book.

A child who is able to postpone gratification can work toward specific objectives. This characteristic is absolutely essential to raising entrepreneurs. The concept of delayed gratification can be communicated through the money lessons you are teaching your children. It can be taught effectively to your children by guiding them and urging them to save some of their money for future purchases.

As your children's allowances grow and as they get more cash from other sources, such as relatives or part–time jobs, you should consider helping them open up bank accounts so that they can put away their savings. Increasingly, banks are trying to attract young savers and many have eliminated age restrictions for kids who want to open up passbook savings or time deposit accounts. As soon as children can sign their name, these banks will generally give them the same privileges as adults. The banks that *do* have age restrictions allow young people to open up accounts as soon as they reach high school.

When you help your kids open up their own savings or checking accounts, explain the banking processes to them. This discussion should include the mechanics of having the bank safeguard savings, the availability of their funds on demand, the interest they will receive on the deposited amount, and other services provided by banks. Without your patient explanation, your children may not understand that although the money is out of their sight, it still belongs to them. If your kids are very young, this discussion should make them a lot more comfortable with the decision to give up wads of bills in exchange for passbooks from a bank.

You should get your kids used to the idea of keeping proper records of their bank funds. If they have passbook savings accounts, the record–keeping is already done for them. But for other accounts, they should mark down the amount they withdraw or deposit and their remaining balances.

TEACHING YOUR KIDS ABOUT CREDIT

Credit card charges increased from $100 billion in 1982 to $474 billion in 1993 and are expected to reach $1.2 trillion by the year 2000 according to the *Wall Street Journal*. With hundreds of millions of credit cards in their pockets, consumers are increasingly using plastic instead of money. Unfortunately, this phenomenon makes it more difficult for kids to learn the basics of managing money. Children who are constantly exposed to credit–card transactions never quite learn the importance of saving before spending.

You may already know that credit cards are easy to come by for college students. According to *The Orange County Register*, "some campuses have evolved into marketing battlegrounds, where independent agencies that sign people up for Visa, MasterCard and other cards wage war for undergrad customer." Credit cards issued to college students have even attracted the attention of politicians. In 1994, Rep. Joseph P. Kennedy, D–Mass., began hearings on the availability of credit to students—a clear warning sign to the consumer credit industry.

The next battleground for consumer credit marketers may be for even younger consumers. In 1989, a savings bank in Denver, The Young American Bank, began issuing its "kiddie" MasterCard with a small credit limit of $200. What's more, Visa and American Express have been test–marketing their credit cards at fast–food restaurants.

The danger of "kiddie" credit cards is that children may learn to spend money before they have learned to save. You and I know that kids already have the apparent need to buy things on impulse. For kids, the name of the game is instant gratification. The only thing that usually stops them from making purchases is lack of money. If they are given credit cards, virtually nothing will stop them from buying things that they cannot afford.

Some argue that "kiddie" credit cards teach kids simply to be responsible borrowers when they become adult consumers. They say that since kids are going to grow up and use credit cards anyway, they should learn how to use them without getting themselves into financial difficulties.

Regardless of whether or not you agree that children should use credit cards, the simple fact is that your kids live in a society that thrives on credit. It is up to you to teach them good money–management skills so that they know that using plastic requires even more discipline than using cash.

In my opinion, the potential for the abuse of traditional credit cards pales in comparison to the potential for the abuse of future modes of transactions with:

1. Electronic cash—digital money that can be transferred to your computer's hard drive to be used for purchases.

2. "Smart" cards—electronically encoded cards that can be used for a wide variety of purchases from pay phones to taxis.

It should be apparent that the more removed a young person is from handling cash, the more difficult it is to teach him or her how to manage money. However, since this society is going cash-less, we have to do our best to equip our kids with good judgment about the use of money—electronic or otherwise. For now, I will concentrate on how you can teach your kids about the use of credit as it relates to traditional credit cards.

Teaching your kids about credit involves three basic steps: letting them know how credit works, making sure that they pay the credit card bills or at least watch you pay them, and showing them how to calculate the interest due on the cards. These three steps will ensure that your youngsters know that credit is not free.

If your kids are at least 8 years old, you can start teaching them the basics of credit. The easiest way to teach them is to have them accompany you when you make purchases for them with your credit card. For example, if your daughter needs clothes for the new school year, take her to the department store and charge the items instead of paying with cash. Don't just whip out the card and use it without telling her what you are doing. Explain to her that you have money set aside in the bank (or at home) to pay for the items but that it was more convenient to use the card on that particular day. Show her the receipt and tell her that the company will probably bill you within one month.

As you make credit card purchases for your kids, keep all your receipts so that when the bills come due, you can sit down with your youngsters and show them the charges you made for them. By matching the items on your bill to the receipts, your children can see the connection between the use of the credit cards in the stores and the bills. Your kids will start to realize that the charges have to be paid for sooner or later.

The next step is to actually pay the credit–card bills. You probably pay most of your bills with checks. Unless your kids are familiar with checks, however, this process could be quite mysterious to them. At this point, all you need to tell them is that you will pay the bill and that it will make your bank account go down by the same amount. Keep in mind that you should not phrase the depletion of your bank account in such a way as to make your kids feel guilty about using your money. Your only goal should be to clearly establish the relationship between using credit and actually spending money.

Depending on the ages of your children, you can teach them about the big interest payments for outstanding credit card debts. If your kids are 14 years old or older, they may be able to understand that paying up to 20% yearly interest on an outstanding credit card bill can substantially raise the cost of the items purchased on credit. For example, if you have a MasterCard outstanding balance of $1,000, your monthly interest charge will be about 1.67% per month (20% divided by 12). Applying this number to your outstanding balance, your interest charge for that month will be $16.70 (.0167 x $1,000). If you have the same outstanding balance for the whole year, your interest bill for that year would be $200. As long as your kids understand the concept of interest payments, they can appreciate the fact that buying items on credit can be quite expensive.

WORKING CHILDREN

If your children are between the ages of six and thirteen, you can probably keep them satisfied with a small weekly allowance, coupled with occasional handouts. But as they get older, you may find that they will want to make and keep their own money. The need to fit in with peer groups and the arrival of puberty dictate that your children spend more money. When you can no longer meet their financial needs and they are old enough to work, then it is time for you to consider allowing them to find extra sources of income.

When considering whether to allow your kids to work, make sure that you lay out the ground rules for the type of jobs or number of hours they can work. Consider the effect of after–school jobs on their extra–curricular activities and on their study time. After students attend six or seven hours of school and go to work, even for three hours, their leisure time is completely gone. If your child wants to earn extra income by working, you should insist that the job does not eat up all of her leisure time. I recommend work that can be done on weekends and, if need be, once or twice weeknights.

Children can learn responsibility while earning money with a part–time job. However, not all jobs can accomplish these objectives and encourage entrepreneurship at the same time. Your kids should seek unstructured jobs that allow them to take initiative, be creative, or solve problems. For example, some kids get jobs at fast–food restaurants such as McDonald's or Burger King. In these jobs, the fries, pies, hamburgers, and onion rings are cooked with precision by automatic fryers. The cashiers do not even have to know how to add. The computerized cash registers provide the right change for customers with little prodding from the cashiers. This kind of service is great for customers, but it turns employees into mindless drones who just follow instructions. For these reasons, I do not recommend such regimented jobs. If you want your kids to develop the skills they need to become successful entrepreneurs, encourage them to look for the following types of jobs:

1. *Jobs that the kids create themselves.* For example, working for themselves as painters, lawn–mowers, baby–sitters, computer consultants, and typists.

2. *Jobs that bring them closer to their hobbies or interests.* For example, a teenager that aspires to become a photographer should try to work in a store that sells photography equipment.

3. *Sales jobs that pay on commission* . For example, working at a clothing store.

The jobs that kids create for themselves are the jobs in which they can best learn good money–management skills. As kids lay out strategies for their own businesses, they have to consider all the financial factors that can make these businesses successes or failures. Moreover, when kids try to make money by working for themselves, not only are they forced to exercise their money–management skills, but they also begin to learn what it takes to become economically self–sufficient. Good money–management skills and economic self–sufficiency are the cornerstones of successful entrepreneurship.

7

MOTIVATING YOUR KIDS TO START THEIR OWN BUSINESSES

Most parents who want to motivate their kids to start their own businesses do it for one reason: they feel that in the long run, their children will lead a more satisfying life by being self–employed. While this may be an honorable reason, your kids will not be swayed to start a business by this logic. Take it from some-one who has been advising young people for years on how to start their own businesses—kids are not interested in the lofty goal of becoming entrepreneurs today so their lives will be easier five or ten years from now. Kids have a short–term view of the world. They are always interested in the here and now. They will want to know how entrepreneurship is going to benefit them in the short run. Fortunately, there are steps you can take to show your young-sters the significance of the long–term and short–term implications of starting and running businesses now. These approaches abandon the intellectual arguments parents try to use to motivate their kids to start their own businesses. Rather, they are tangible approaches that have proven effective in encouraging kids to at least try entrepre-neurship before succumbing to the lure of being ordinary employ-ees.

Over the years I have found the following approaches to be quite effective in encouraging kids to start businesses: providing them with role models with whom they can identify, encouraging them to use their creative talents or hobbies in a business, presenting entrepreneurship as an avenue for making extra money, and presenting entrepreneurship as a way to help others lead a better life.

ROLE MODELS

Your kids are bombarded daily, through the media and in school, with images of professionals who collect a paycheck. Television in particular glorifies the corporate life. It constantly parades corporate role models in front of your kids, and consciously or subconsciously, they absorb the message that being an employee is better than being an employer. Providing your children with entrepreneurial role models can go a long way to countering the effect of this massive media brainwashing.

The importance of having a role model was driven home to me when I was still in high school. I joined the Lawrence High School track team in the eighth grade. Within two years, each one of my three younger siblings also joined the track team in succession. I am convinced that if I had not been a successful runner, they would not have followed in my footsteps. Such examples are quite common. In fact, you often see kids getting involved in sports, music, acting, or other activities because they aspire to be like their heroes.

You can apply this role model concept when trying to encourage your kids to become entrepreneurs. The sources of adult role models can be found in business magazines on your local neighborhood newsstand. In the next chapter, I will give you several examples of such business magazines.

While adult business role models have always been abundant in business publications, examples of teen and preteen entrepreneurs have been somewhat harder to find until the past five years. More newspapers and magazines such as *Wall Street Journal, USA Today*, and *Forbes*, are printing stories about self–employed kids. If you run into these stories, clip them out or photocopy them for your children. These articles can be interesting sources for dinnertime conversations.

I have found that young people are fascinated by examples of other kids their age who are running their own businesses. One father collects articles on child entrepreneurs and frequently discusses them with his kids: "My three teenagers love to hear stories of young kids running their own businesses. In fact two of them were so fascinated by a story I clipped about how a 14 year old ran his own lawn–care service that they went into the same business the next summer."

One parent of a 12–year–old girl once told me that her daughter was delighted to learn about child entrepreneurs: "Janet was really interested to hear about how young kids her age were running real businesses," said the father. "One particular article I clipped from *Entrepreneur* magazine was about how a girl her age created her own card game. I couldn't really quite figure out why that particular article fascinated her. Then it finally dawned on me. In all previous cases, I talked to her about young boys who were running their own businesses. It never occurred to me that I needed to give her examples of young girls doing the same thing." This to me is a perfect example of how the proper role models can really pique a child's interest. You too can present your daughters with entrepreneurial role models they can relate to. If your daughter is in her teens, buy copies of some of the women's magazines that deal with business start–ups. One monthly magazine, *Working Woman* magazine, often features female entrepreneurs. In addition, I urge you to contact An Income of Her Own—an organization which gives girls and young women the tools, knowledge, and experience to help them become economically independent (see Chapter 18). "Take Our Daughters to Work Day" sponsored by The Ms. Foundation for Women is another way to get girls one step closer to economic independence.

African–Americans should also try to provide their children with Black role models they can relate to along with examples of entrepreneurs from other groups. If you are an African–American and your kids are in their teens, *Black Enterprise*, *Essence*, and *YSB* (Young Sisters and Brothers) magazines may provide your kids with good entrepreneurial role models.

Another effective way to motivate your kids to consider starting their own businesses, is to expose them to books that specifically focus on the child entrepreneur. These publications often have inspirational examples of kids running full–fledged businesses. You will find a list of books for aspiring young entrepreneurs in Chapter 18.

There are other ways to present your kids with role models to help motivate them to start their own businesses. You can seek out entrepreneurs in your neighborhood or in your family who can tell your kids all about the joys and problems of running their own businesses. Arrange to have these entrepreneurs talk to your kids about starting their own businesses. A mother of a 15–year–old boy describes her experience when she took her son to talk to her brother who was a software consultant. This mother said of her son:

John has loved computers since he was 10 years old. This year, for our vacation, I decided that we should visit my brother Donald, who owns a computer consulting company. From the moment we got there until the moment we left, John and Donald talked about computers. By the time we got home, John had already decided that he would follow in Donald's footsteps and start his own company. He now gets paid for advising kids in his school on what type of system to buy and how to use their computers.

Of course, not all children are going to be immediately inspired to start their own businesses when they talk to entrepreneurs. But I can guarantee you that when your kids come in contact with real, live entrepreneurs, they will at least realize that starting and running a business is an attainable goal.

When you find entrepreneurs that can inspire your children, make sure that they tell your kids about the difficulties encountered in starting a business along with all the good points about starting a business. Here are four topics that you should ask the role model to discuss with your kids:

1. *Their motivation for starting their businesses.* If you ask most entrepreneurs what they like most about their businesses they will tell you that they enjoy their freedom. Freedom from having to answer to anyone but themselves. Freedom from the time clock, and most of all,

freedom to be as creative as they want, doing what they like. Your children's entrepreneurial role model should convey this benefit to your kids.

2. *The hard work involved.* Having worked with young entrepreneurs, I know that they sometimes look too far ahead to the good things that come with entrepreneurship such as creative freedom and money. Some don't consider the enormous amount of work it takes to start and run their own businesses. The role model you find for your kids should emphasize the hard work involved in becoming a business owner. Have this role model tell your children how many hours he worked in his business when he first started.

3. *Their failures.* All entrepreneurs have failed at one point or another. It is part of the learning process. Have your children's entrepreneurial role model talk to your kids about their failures and how they picked themselves up and started all over again.

4. *The importance of education.* In this technologically advanced society, it has become critical that everyone get a good education. The need for a good education is obvious when you look at the manufacturing jobs that used to be taken by people who didn't even graduate from high school. Today in the automobile industry, for example, some of the manufacturing processes are run by robots controlled by computers monitored by a factory worker. I don't need to tell you that this factory worker has to be a bit more educated than his predecessors. He simply won't do a good job if he cannot even read and understand the complicated procedures manuals for the machines he operates. The role model you find for your kids should stress the importance of attending a post–high–school institution such as a four–year college or a junior college. While many older entrepreneurs do not have college degrees, younger business owners are finding out that the lack of a college education is increasingly becoming a hindrance. Lack of a college education, for example, can

hurt entrepreneurs when they are trying to acquire loans for their businesses. Venture capitalists consider the educational level of a prospective borrower when evaluating a loan application. All things being equal, a college–educated borrower will get money faster than a high school dropout. In addition, advanced education can help entrepreneurs hone skills they need to run their businesses. Accounting, for example, is an essential part of running a business. Good math skills, marketing skills, and finance skills can also help make an entrepreneur successful.

The role model you find for your kids should stress the importance of getting a good education. Even if he is not college educated, he should tell your youngsters how education will help them in running any business. In addition, the entrepreneur should tell your kids which skills they can acquire in school that can best help them in running their own businesses.

SHOWCASING CREATIVE TALENTS OR HOBBIES

Quite often, child entrepreneurs start their businesses because they have talents or hobbies they want to explore or share with the world. Sure, they consider the financial viability of their businesses, but money is generally an afterthought. Their main concern is to do what they love to do.

16–year–old Mark Andelbrandt of Hinsdale, Illinois, began his catering service for school events because he loved to prepare delicious pastries. Mark's dishes are so delectable that he won Hinsdale Central High School's Culinary Arts festival competition. His high–school cooking teacher praises him for his culinary skills as well as for his food management talents. Mark plans to open his own restaurant after attending the Culinary Institute.

Mark was lucky enough to get a lot of encouragement from his high school food teacher. However, many other youngsters who have highly developed skills are not so lucky. If you have kids who have hobbies or talents, perhaps they too can turn them into businesses. The problem I have found with some young entrepreneurs is that their parents did not recognize or value their talents. One 30–

year–old potter, who now runs a $90,000–a–year business, laments the lack of support she received from her parents when she was in high school:

> *My parents meant well, but they never showed much interest in my pottery when I was in high school. My designs then were about the same as they are now. In fact, I think I did my best work when I was about 16 years old. I dropped pottery completely until I was 28 years old.*

You should start paying closer attention to your children's creative activities. You also have to recognize that you may not be the best judge of which creative work is of good or poor quality. You may know exactly what you like, but you cannot tell what everyone else is going to appreciate. I am not saying that anything your children create should be considered artistic or salable. I am saying that your standards may not be the benchmark for the world. If you have ever been to a modern art exhibit, you know what I mean. Someone appreciates these drawings, even if it isn't me. The same thing goes for your children's designs or ideas.

A talent or skill that is ignored withers away in the same way a leg in a cast atrophies. You have got to pay attention to your children's creations or hobbies. It is not necessary to latch onto everything your children do as a testament to their creativity. However, when your kids consistently and diligently follow their hobbies or talents, it is time to pay closer attention. Do some research on his skills or hobbies so that in your conversations with him, he knows that you have taken a special interest in helping him further develop his talents. Seek out people who may be able to tell you if your kids are talented. For example, if your child makes pottery, you should take some of his work to a potter to get his opinion as to whether his work is good. I am not suggesting that you latch onto your children's interest to see if it can be exploited for commercial purposes. But if your kids have good ideas or talents, you can encourage them to develop them.

MAKING EXTRA POCKET MONEY

Your kids don't have much of a choice when it comes to putting extra money in their pockets. They can either get the money from you or work for it. As I discussed in Chapter 6 on money management, it's generally not a good idea to give your children money whenever they need it. For one thing, you may go broke. More importantly, a periodic allowance is the best way to teach your kids how to save and plan for purchases.

If your kids need extra money, they could consider getting a job. However, child labor laws can prohibit young people less than 16 years old from working in many establishments. In addition, even if they are lucky enough to get a job, their hours will be severely restricted. If they are old enough to work more hours, you can bet the pay will be lousy—a little over $4.00 per hour. Let's face it, most of the jobs out there pay peanuts, their hours conflict with after–school activities, and they are really boring. One look at the empty faces of the kids working in fast–food restaurants tells the whole story.

If your kids are faced with these obstacles to getting more money for reasonable purchases, you can suggest that they start their own businesses to make extra money. One parent of a 14–year–old girl made such a suggestion to his daughter. The girl started an unusual baby–sitting business. Instead of baby–sitting for the neighborhood parents, she became a baby–sitting broker. She matched up baby–sitters with parents and got a fee for the arrangement. The father said:

> *I didn't really expect my daughter to take me seriously when I told her to start her own business if she wanted extra pocket money. I just wanted her off my back. To my surprise she actually started working on it within one week. I wish I had told her earlier that starting a business is a rewarding way to earn money.*

The mere suggestion that your kids start a business will not necessarily motivate them unless they see examples of how other kids have supplemented their allowances by working for themselves.

HELPING–HAND ENTREPRENEURS

The desire to help other people out is also a big motivator for young would–be entrepreneurs. A helping–hand entrepreneur is a person who is motivated by the desire to help others live a better life. Their initial desire isn't making money, even though they may eventually turn a profit. Seventh–grader Aamir Raza of San Jose, California, invented an Anti–Sunburn Band Meter. This special headband tells kids when the sun is too harsh on their skin. Aamir said he came up with his idea because he wanted to help reduce the incidence of skin cancer. He received first prize for his invention in the annual Invent America competition held in Washington, D.C.

No matter what motivates your kids to start their own businesses, the end result is that once the entrepreneurial bug bites them, they will find that self–employment is infinitely more satisfying than working for others. Once again, the goal is to show your children that there are alternatives. The sooner your kids realize this, the better off they will be in the long run.

8

HELPING YOUR KIDS DEVELOP BUSINESS IDEAS

SOURCES OF BUSINESS IDEAS

Starting with hobbies

I have found that kids who start businesses related to their hobbies or interests, enjoy the entrepreneurial process a lot more than others who just choose businesses for which they have no real passion.

Consider how 16–year–old David Hall of Denver, Colorado, turned his love of cars into a business. David started his own car detailing business as a way of staying in touch with fine automobiles. He specializes in thoroughly cleaning the exteriors and interiors (including underneath the hood) of foreign luxury cars such as Mercedes Benzes, BMWs, and Jaguars. For each car he makes immaculate, Dave pockets $50. Dave says of his business:

> *Ever since I can remember, I have always liked cars. Two years ago, I decided to start my own car detailing business. I work hard at my business, but I also enjoy it because I work with some high–powered cars and sometimes even antiques. Getting paid for doing what I like makes it easier for me to do my job. The money is great, too.*

Like David, most teenagers who start and run businesses related to their hobbies, don't mind the hard work necessary to make their businesses financially rewarding

Inventions are not required

Lots of kids start businesses by simply applying resources around them in new and different ways. It is a rare young entrepreneur who actually invents a new product. Many kids must think of new ways to make existing products or services better. Their imagination is their only limitation.

Sometimes, young people can offer customers cheaper and better quality products or services than local stores. Ten–year–old Brandon Bozek of Miami, Florida, started his own weekly flower delivery business called Bloomin' Express. Once a week, Brandon buys his flowers from wholesalers and then delivers them to his customers. Brian started his business because he noticed the poor quality of the flowers that were sold in the local supermarket. He felt he could deliver fresher and less expensive flowers to his customers. Brian now has eight customers, and he is shooting for seven more subscribers. He collects $20 monthly from each customer, or $160 in revenues each month, half of which is pure profit that he puts away as savings.

Brian simply took advantage of the opportunity presented to him. He did not have to invent anything. He was perceptive enough to know how to lure some customers away from the local supermarket.

Inventions are welcomed

Some kids are creative enough to invent products that even grown–ups have not thought about. Take fourth–grader Theresa Gentes for example. She noticed that her mother often lost her needle while quilting, so she came up with the idea of spraying the needles with neon–colored paint, which makes the needles fully visible in the dark.

If your youngsters are as creative as Theresa and other young inventors, they may be able to profitably market their inventions. For information on how your children may be able to profit from their inventions, contact reputable invention organizations. Inventors Workshop International, as described in Chapter 18, is one such organization. The Invention Bookshop, also described in Chapter 18, can provide your kids with books that get help them market their inventions.

Considering service business

Your kids should consider offering services instead of selling products. To sell products, your kids either have to make it themselves, or buy and then resell them with a price mark–up. In service businesses, your kids provide services to their customers by doing physical or mental work for them. This work can range from computer programming to car washing or painting.

Many young people choose service businesses because these businesses are less costly to start than businesses in which they have to sell manufactured products and tie up funds by storing inventory. Your kids can start service businesses with little or no money. Seventeen–year–old entrepreneur Brad Dole of Brooklyn, New York, said of his business:

> *I didn't have much money to start a business so I decided to use my muscle. My company, Quick Movers, just loads customers trucks when they are moving. They provide the transportation, and we load and unload their property. When I first started the business, I didn't have to invest a penny buying equipment. I got two other guys who worked out with me at the gym to help me move customers. I don't know any other business where I could make $40 to $60 an hour with no investment.*

Of course not all kids have the muscle power to do rough physical work such as moving furniture. In fact, I don't recommend such work for your children unless they are healthy, strong, and are covered by insurance. Nevertheless, there are other service businesses that require very little capital investment or muscle. For example, some kids who have keen interests in computers are starting their own computer consulting businesses.

Considering businesses to help others

There is no universal law that says that entrepreneurs must only engage in money–making businesses. In fact, some of the most enterprising people I have ever met, run nonprofit organizations or participate in activities designed to help other people. Indeed, there are innovative young people who have started organizations just to help their communities. In the Introduction, I mentioned Melissa Poe who started an environmental awareness group, Kids For A Clean Environment, which now has 200,000 members. This is just one example of the young people across this country that are taking the initiative to better the world.

Your kids can probably dream up businesses and organizations that will help others in your community. The activity can be as simple as starting a mentoring group for kids in the community, or as sophisticated as teaching other kids how to use a computer. The possibilities for doing good are endless.

There are organizations that encourage entrepreneurial activities among young people who want to find solutions to problems in their communities and indeed, the country. For example, Do Something (described fully in Chapter 18), offers $500 grants to young people who come up with innovative ideas to make life better for people in their communities. Inventors Workshop International (also described fully in Chapter 18) runs an Eco–Inventors Contest for kids ages 6–18 years old who have ideas on how to help the environment.

Considering the Internet

The personal computer may turn out to be one of the biggest money–making tools of all time with the advent of the Internet, or as it is commonly known, the "information superhighway". With your computer, you can now access over 30 million other users through electronic mail, or through newsgroups—the "bulletin board" of the Internet.

The products that can be marketed on the Internet are endless. One easily identifiable group of products that can be offered on the Internet by just about anyone, is information. Anything that can be printed on paper such as recipes and books can be readily sold (or at least marketed) on the Internet. To see what else can be easily marketed on the Internet, I suggest that you subscribe to a service and just have your kids navigate through the various newsgroups and the electronic malls on the Internet called the World Wide Web (which can display pictures of consumer goods and other information).

The Internet can also be used for market research in order to test ideas or just gather information. For example, I sent an electronic mail message to people on the Internet for kids who are running their own businesses for use in the book you are now reading. This is only a taste of the reasearch power that the Internet can bring to your children's fingertip.

There are rules and regulations regarding what is considered blatant advertising on the Internet so your kids should find out about the proper etiquette for each newsgroup they access on the Internet.

The equipment you need to hook up to the Internet are as follows:

1. a personal computer.

2. a modem.

3. a telephone line.

4. a communications program.

5. a printer (this is optional but good to have for research purposes).

You will then need an Internet link through an Internet access provider. As an example of the cost of access, Netcom charges $19.95 per month and gives 40 free hours per month to its users. Here are a few access providers you can contact for more information:

- America Online   800–827–6364
- Compuserve   800–848–8199

- Delphi Internet Services 800–695–4005
- Netcom with NetCruiser Interface 800–501–8649
- Pipeline (in New York only) 212–267–3636

Don't be confined to this list of access providers because there are many more that may have better prices and terms. When you contact access providers, tell them what type of computer system you have and ask them whether their software will be compatible with your hardware. For example, some access providers may only offer windows based communications software for IBM compatibles, while others may offer Mac–based communications software. More detailed information on connecting to the Internet is available at your local bookstores and libraries.

If you can afford it, get your kids online as soon as possible so they can start browsing through the Internet to see what other people are offering to other subscribers. They may get some good business ideas on the system.

If you hook up to the Internet, my electronic mail address is as follows:

modu@ix.netcom.com

Considering other businesses by other kids

In your neighborhood, there are probably kids who are running their own small businesses. If not, there may be young entrepreneurs in your children's schools. If your kids are interested in the same kind of businesses other kids are running, they have to answer one question: Is there room enough for me to get my own customers? It is possible that the other youngsters have taken all the customers in the neighborhood and your kids may not be able to muscle their way into the business.

If your kids want to start the same businesses as other children in the neighborhood, they may do well if they add a new twist to the venture. That is, they can create their own market specialty within the same type of business. For example, if there are lots of kids in your neighborhood who mow lawns, perhaps your children could start a business tending to shrubs and flowers. This way, your kids can be considered the experts in one particular aspect of lawn care.

Your children can also compete with other young entrepreneurs by offering better or less expensive products or services. The more savvy your kids are about analyzing the features of their competitors' products or services, the easier it will be for them to offer a better version of these same products or services. I advise kids to make a list of all the features and benefits associated with the businesses they want to enter. They should also note how the features of their businesses compare to those of their potential competitors.

They should consider new fads

New fads can also be a source of ideas for your kids. For example, if the cool thing to do is for kids to wear painted high–top sneakers, maybe your kids can paint sneakers for a price. Or if fancy T–shirts are in, maybe they can take advantage of this trend to make some extra money. One young girl capitalized on the popularity of dinosaurs in her school and sold wooden models of them to her classmates.

Twelve–year–olds Josh Bashow and Brian Clegg of Winterburn, Alberta, Canada, design and sew their own sportswear. They decided to make their own wild and colorful sweat pants and shorts because they felt that the prices at the local mall were too high. With some help from Josh's mother, the two seventh graders learned how to modify an existing pattern for sweats to make them as baggy as the latest fashions kids were wearing. They even cut their own fabric and learned how to sew straight seams. When the two enterprising youngsters wore their newly created fashions to school other kids wanted to get their hands on this wild and colorful sportswear that Josh and Brian called BJs. Josh and Brian's sweat pants sold for $12.50 compared to an average price in stores of $20. The boys made $2,000 last year. By their estimation, this translates to about $6 per hour. This sure beats minimum wage.

A fad can be very profitable. Its biggest drawback, however, is that it is sometimes difficult to determine when the popularity of the fad will wane. When the Berlin Wall was finally dismantled, some entrepreneurs sold pieces of it to consumers through popular department stores. Now that the euphoria behind German reunification is over, pieces of the wall are no longer in demand. I am certain that somewhere in this country, someone has a big inventory of unsold pieces of the Berlin Wall. There are many more examples of the quick death of fads. If your kids try to capitalize on them, they should be aware that by nature they can be short–lived.

Grown–ups can be customers, too

Your children should not limit themselves to businesses geared towards other kids. Other kids may have little money to spend on the products or services your kids can provide. Because adults have more money, your young entrepreneurs should consider starting businesses that are aimed at them. Even if your children want to sell their products or services to other kids, they should make it appealing to parents because parents have deeper pockets than children.

If you live near colleges or universities, perhaps your kids can sell their products or services to the students in these institutions. Sixteen–year–old Sandy Bennet of Cambridge, Massachusetts, capitalized on her 60–words–per–minute typing speed by starting her own word processing company called Type Power. Sandy started her company by soliciting business from other students in her high school. Sandy finally sought customers from the local colleges around Cambridge because she wanted to get more typing jobs.

Sandy says of her business:

> *I made very little money when I was typing term papers for other kids in my high school. When I decided to get my customers from the universities around me, I started charging $2.00 per page instead of the $1.00 per page I charged high school kids. I actually had to turn down business because I couldn't keep up with the demand—I only had 10 hours a week for my business and in that time I could type about 60 pages. That's over $120 per week. I hope to hire other kids in my high school who type over 50 words per minute to help me in my business.*

Magazines and books can help

There are many magazines out there that can help your kids with ideas about businesses they can start. Some of these magazines are geared toward small–time entrepreneurs. Magazines for small businesses can help keep your kids abreast of what is going on out there in the entrepreneurial world. Have you ever thought about subscribing to business magazines for your children's benefit? Your kids can get some pretty good business ideas from magazines that small–business owners read.

Here is a partial list of magazines that may help unearth the entrepreneurial talents in your kids:

1. *Entrepreneur*, 714–261–2325

2. *Inc.*, 212–326–2600

3. *Success*, 212–551–9500

4. *Black Enterprise*, 212–242–8000

5. *Essence*, 212–642–0600

6. *Opportunity Magazine*, 312–346–4790

7. *Income Opportunities*, 212–557–9100

8. *In Business* (for ecology entrepreneurs), 215–967–4135

9. *Business Start–Ups*, 800–274–8333

10. *Working Woman*, 800–234–9675

11. *Gift and Stationery Business Magazine* (GSB Magazine) 212–626–2272

Other publications that frequently feature entrepreneurs and highlight business trends include:

1. *Wall Street Journal*, 212–416–2000

2. *Forbes*, 212–620–2200

3. *Fortune*, 212–552–1212

4. *Business Week*, 212–512–2511

5. *Nation's Business*, 202–463–5650

You may be able to read these publications at your local library. If they are not in your neighborhood library, you can get samples from the publishers. The numbers next to the magazines are the phone numbers of the publishers or the agencies that handle the advertising. Call them for free samples. Some may require that you pay a nominal fee for the samples.

After you receive the magazines, look them over to see whether they are appropriate for your young entrepreneurs. If so, let your kids browse through these publications to see if they have any interest in subscribing to them.

Teaming up with other kids

Your kids might be better off teaming up with other kids who have complementary skills. They say that two heads are better than one and this is especially true when kids start businesses. Great ideas can come out of a team of kids trying to come up with salable products or services.

When your children team up with other kids to start businesses, they not only benefit from business ideas their partners provide, but they can also take advantage of their partners' special skills and talents.

One of the biggest myths about entrepreneurs is that they don't depend on anyone else to run their businesses. This myth portrays entrepreneurs as so individualistic that they do everything themselves. I have found that entrepreneurs who feel that they can do it all don't last very long. Their downfall is usually that they fail to delegate and fail to recognize their own shortcomings.

Jane Pyle and Jody Knoll of Houston, Texas, teamed up to start their own directory that listed all the important social events in their county and surrounding counties. Jane and Jody got their idea by brainstorming about the types of businesses needed in their area and about the types of skills they each had. They finally decided on the directory. They parceled out the work based on each person's skills and expertise. Jane's job was to call the local newspapers and organizations to find out about upcoming events. She was also responsible for calling local advertisers to sell them ad space in the directory. Jody, on the other hand, wrote the short pieces about the events and compiled them in their bimonthly directory.

As you can see, Jane and Jody came up with their idea by discussing several business ideas and then finally choosing one. Had they not put their heads together, it is possible that they would not have thought about the possibility of starting their own directory.

Organization and programs for young entrepreneurs

There are several organizations and programs that can help your kids become entrepreneurs. I discuss them fully in Chapter 18, but here are a few:

Center for Teen Entrepreneurs
Junior Achievement
National Foundation For Teaching Entrepreneurship
Young Americans Bank
Future Business Leaders of America
Business Kids
DECA

A FEW SIMPLE BUSINESS IDEAS

Some kids have no hobbies to translate into businesses. Even though they have no business ideas, they would still like to explore entrepreneurship. For those kids, I am presenting a few business ideas that most young people from 12 to 18 can start on their own. Keep in mind, however, that it is up to you as a parent to decide whether your children are old enough and mature enough to handle the businesses they would like to start.

The businesses discussed here are actually being implemented by young entrepreneurs across the country. Some are harder to start than others. However, if your kids need help with any of the business ideas or if they would like other ideas, they can contact the

Center for Teen Entrepreneurs at Box 3967, New York, New York 10163–6027L.

Buying goods from auctions and reselling them

When I first started writing this book, I wanted a laser printer so that I could send a legible manuscript to my publisher. After shopping around in computer stores, I could not find any decent laser printers for less than $1,000. My wife, whose hobby of late has been going to auctions, suggested that I look for a printer at one of these auctions. I finally attended an FDIC government auction of a failed savings and loan. At the auction, I purchased a Unisys laser printer for $275. Still glowing from the euphoria of buying a laser printer for such a low price, I quickly called Unisys to find out the value of my new purchase. I was shocked when they told me that I had just acquired a $3,780 printer. I purchased the printer for less than one–tenth the original price!

While I was at the auction, I couldn't help thinking that a young entrepreneur, who had time in the summer, could purchase goods at government or bankruptcy auctions and then resell them to individuals on his own. At the auction I attended, there were IBM typewriters going for $20 and very nice lamps going for $5. At such low prices, your kids can easily buy the goods, resell them, and pocket some nice change.

You are probably wondering how kids can participate in the madhouse world of auction purchasing. Believe me, the process is so simple, it's ridiculous. Because your kids are probably less than 18 years old, they probably cannot bid on the items being auctioned because they are not old enough to enter into contracts. This is only a small barrier because an adult can bid on the items for them. If you or an older relative or friend have the time, perhaps you can accompany your children to these auctions. On the other hand, if your kids have a registered business and they have a tax identification number, they can participate in these auctions on their own.

Several days or weeks before the auction, your youngsters can usually get a list of the items being auctioned. Using this list, they can determine whether it is worth their time to attend.

Typically in these auctions, each item is numbered and the attendees are given several hours to inspect all of them to decide what to bid on. Once the bidding starts, the auctioneer may open with a number and then wait for bidders to compete with each other until there are no further challenges to the highest bid.

My advice to your children when they attend these auctions is to set a limit on how much money they are willing to spend on each item. For example, if your kids are interested in buying lamps, they can set a $10 maximum. In setting the limit they should consider how much cash they have on hand and how much they can get from selling the lamp.

If your kids bid on an item and win, they will have to put down about 20% of the value of the bid and then bring the rest of the money when they actually pick up the item. In some auctions there is a 10% buyer's premium added to the final bid price. Of course, tax is levied on all final bids (unless the buyer has a tax ID number).

One difficulty with these auctions is that the auctioneers expect you to clear out the items you purchased within two days.

To find out about the auctions in your area, look in the Sunday edition of the largest–circulation newspaper in your area. In my case, I looked in the Sunday *New York Times*. If you live near a large city, get the newspaper that services that metropolitan area.

T–shirts

A T–shirt business is one venture that can help your kids make extra money year after year. There seems to be no end in sight to the demand for them. As long as your kids can come up with new and innovative designs, logos, and slogans, they can start and run a profitable business selling T–shirts to fellow students and adults.

Your kids can produce T–shirts with slogans that capitalize on current events. One teenage entrepreneur had T–shirts printed with George Bush and Mikhail Gorbachev shaking hands.

There are lots of manufacturers who make blank T–shirts of varying quality. Your kids can buy blank T–shirts wholesale, and then decide on what logos or slogans to print on them. The design on the T–shirt need not be produced by your kids. They can get other kids who may be artistic to create designs. If there aren't artistic kids around, your kids can try a graphic arts designer. One young entrepreneur went to a local arts college to hire a graphic arts student for his T–shirt design.

With camera–ready copy of the design, your children can go to a printer and have the new T–shirts printed with the design. Of course, the printing costs might be high, so your kids have to make sure that they can get enough customers to cover the expense and make a profit at the same time.

If your kids can draw, they can also choose to paint designs on the T–shirts with special paints for clothing instead of getting the T–shirts printed.

Helping the elderly

This is one nonprofit business that is needed in many of our neighborhoods. As people get older, they find that they cannot do with ease and flair all the things they did in their younger days. Quite a few senior citizens live by themselves and they have no one around to run errands or move furniture or install a window–unit air conditioner.

Your youngsters can help by providing a service to help them. The only requirement is that your kids should be good organizers and leaders.

The idea behind this service is for your kids to be a clearing house for older people who need help doing things. This should be a nonprofit organization. However, there should be a minimum charge to the users of the service to take care of all the expenses associated with providing the service.

Your children should solicit senior citizens to join the service. The customers should pay a small membership fee to be registered. As these senior citizens call, they should tell your kids the type of help they need on a regular basis. However, the subscribers to the service should be allowed in the course of their membership to make other requests as well.

Your children should set up a card for each member in their filing cabinet, which should include the following information:

1. Name and age of member.

2. Address and phone number.

3. The type of help needed on a regular basis.

4. The type of requests made in the past.

5. Comments by the kids who help.

Here is how I envision the service working. Senior citizens will call your youngsters if they need something done, such as mowing their lawns, moving heavy items, or going shopping. Your kids should have some guidelines as to the sort of services they will perform. They should be able to come up with permissible requests as they get more experience with the service.

At the same time your children are soliciting members for the club, they should also try to recruit kids who will actually perform the services. My suggestion is that your kids recruit other kids from religious organizations, the Boy or Girl Scouts, or other organizations that encourage community service.

Once they have volunteers to help the senior citizens, they should get these other children to commit to a certain time of the day or week when they will be available. Chances are that most kids will have time only during the weekends unless school is not in session. These young people should be told what kind of work they may be called upon to do, and then they should sign up according to their skills and abilities. For example, some youngsters may not be able to move furniture around, but they can run errands to the local grocery store. Your kids should set up a card in a filing system for each young volunteer. The information on each card should contain the following information:

1. Name and age of volunteer.

2. Address and phone number.

3. Days and time available.

4. The assignments he or she is willing to take.

5. A list of each assignment he or she has completed.

6. Comments from the customers he or she has helped.

Remember that the membership fee your kids charge will help them to take care of incidental expenses associated with running the organization. Items such as advertising and telephone calls cost money and will have to be paid for somehow. In addition, if your children find that the members need other services that cost money, they can use the membership fees for these services.

If more money is needed, your kids should try to solicit money from businesses in your area. If local businesses sponsor such things as Little League baseball teams, why can't they donate money to your children's services?

If still more money is needed, perhaps your kids can charge the senior citizens each time they use the service. They should keep in mind, however, that senior citizens quite often live on a fixed income, so they don't have a lot of money to throw around.

Car cleaning

People are proud of their cars, whether they are old jalopies or souped up sports cars. Car owners are forever washing and buffing their cars to make them look sparkling new. Your kids can provide this service to car owners. They can start a business to do a complete cleaning of the interior and exterior of cars.

To start the business, your children can come up with a catchy flyer to be passed out to all the car owners in the neighborhood. They should advertise that their service is a package deal in which both the inside and outside of the cars are thoroughly cleaned for $20. For extra services such as carpet cleaning, they can charge an extra $10. They should make sure that they use the proper solvents and equipment to clean car carpets.

Lawn service

This is one business that has stood the test of time for young people. It is relatively easy to start and a young entrepreneur can add more services to the typical mowing jobs to make good pocket money.

Of course, two of the most important requirements for a lawn service are that your kids have access to a mower and that they are old enough to safely handle it. Even if there is no mower in the house, your kids may be able to use the client's mower or they may be able to rent one at U–Haul or other rental centers. Of course, if they rent a mower, they will have to make sure that they have enough mowing jobs to make it worth their while. In addition to having access to a mower, your kids should have some safety gear, such as steel–toed shoes and leather work gloves.

To most kids, lawn service just means cutting grass. But savvy young entrepreneurs know that they can also offer other lawn–related services such as shrub maintenance, weeding, and sidewalk grass trimming.

A lucrative lawn service business depends on the demand for it in your neighborhood. If you live in an area with lots of apartments, chances are that your children won't get many jobs because apartment complexes usually have their own maintenance crews. However, if you live in a residential area with houses, your kids should get plenty of jobs because lawn care is a drudgery for many home owners.

Your children's customers will fall into the following five categories:

1. People who are too lazy to take care of their lawns.

2. People who don't have the time to take care of their lawns.

3. People who are on vacation.

4. People who are moving and want to sell their home.

5. People who are disabled or elderly and unable to do lawn maintenance themselves.

The best way for your kids to reach these customers is to go around the neighborhood, ring doorbells, hand out advertising flyers, and talk to people about the possibility of becoming their regular lawn mower.

Your children should ask potential customers the following questions:

1. Is there someone besides a family member mowing their lawns? If so, is the job they are doing satisfactory?

2. Would they be interested in having their lawns mowed on a regular basis? Once a week? Once every two weeks? Or just on demand.

3. Would their lawn mower be available for mowing the lawn?

4. Would they pay $10 an hour for the job?

Your kids could also advertise in the neighborhood newsletter or newspaper to reach more customers.

House and apartment–cleaning services

House and apartment cleaning is becoming more popular these days. Years ago, people were assumed to be wealthy if they had their apartment or house cleaned periodically. These days, however, both parents in the house may have full–time jobs so there is less time to do the cleaning. More and more families are choosing to hire a house or apartment cleaner to keep the house clean.

An apartment–cleaning or house–cleaning service is perfect for your kids if they have little or no start–up funds and no experience. If they can dust, vacuum, make beds, and empty trash cans, they can be successful at this business. This business also requires that your youngsters have a lot of energy because it is hard work.

To get customers, your kids should go around the neighborhood to families with working couples. They can also advertise in the neighborhood bulletins or the local newspapers.

When they get a customer, they should tell them what type of cleaning they are willing to do. Here is a short list of the types of chores that customers will frequently ask for:

- Changing the sheets
- Vacuuming
- Dusting and polishing
- Cleaning the bathroom
- Doing dishes
- Doing laundry
- Mopping floors
- Washing windows

Your children should decide which of these services they are willing to offer. Their decision should depend on their ages and strength.

Your kids should charge anywhere from $8 to $12 per hour. For an accurate price quote, have them take a look at the house or apartment. When they go to the appointment, the prospective client should tell them exactly what items need to be taken care of. Your kids and the prospective clients should walk through each room, and your children should record everything they are to do.

When your kids have gone through the entire house, they should sit down and calculate how much time each task will take. For example, they might estimate 20 minutes for the vacuuming, 5 minutes for polishing a table, etc. Then your children should give the prospective client an estimate of how much time it will take to clean the entire apartment or house.

With this type of business, your youngsters could hire other kids to help them out. Of course, the wages have to be negotiated, but I recommend that your kids pay other kids no more than one–third of their hourly wage.

One word of advice. Before your children accept a customer, you should visit these potential customers to get a feeling for the type of people your kids are dealing with. Although you probably know many of the people in your neighborhood, it is best to go to their home and speak to them about the type of things they want your kids to clean in their home or apartment.

Posters

Like that of T–shirts, the appeal of posters depends on the slogans or the designs on them. A young entrepreneur can also take advantage of current events to sell lots of posters. One sharp teen-age entrepreneur sold posters with a nice picture of Nelson Mandela in his traditional garb during the leader's visit to New York City after his release from prison. With a captive audience of several hundred thousand onlookers during the Mandela parade, this kid was selling posters for $8 a shot. In a span of less than 30 minutes, I saw him sell about 20 posters. I approached him to ask him how he got the posters printed in time for the Mandela visit. He told me that he had been planning his venture for weeks, looking for a good re-producible picture of Mr. Mandela for the posters.

If your kids have a good slogan or artwork that might capital-ize on current events, they, too, should consider coming up with their own posters. Posters will sell particularly well in parades and other festivities. The posters your kids sell at these functions should of course be related to the event. They should not attempt to sell Columbus Day posters at a Labor Day parade.

Your children should check with a number of printers to find out how much it costs to have posters made to order.

Other ideas

Typing service
Christmas wreath construction
Computer consulting
Tutoring
Selling sports collectibles (such as baseball cards)
Bicycle repair
House painting
House sitting
Window washing
Errand service
Gift basket sales
Newsletter publishing

9

HELPING YOUR KIDS DEVELOP BUSINESS PLANS

Seventeen–year–old Gerald Jordan of Philadelphia, Pennsylvania, lacked the money to start his sportswear business, Slam Dunk Fashions. He put together a business plan and went looking far someone to finance his idea. Luckily, he found an investor who was willing to give him $1,000 to develop Slam Dunk Fashions.

Without a clear plan that described the business and its profit potential, Gerald would not have gotten anyone to help him finance his venture. Business plans make investors more comfortable about handing over their hard–earned money. Good business plans tell them that entrepreneurs have thoroughly thought about all aspects of their proposed businesses. In addition, business plans help entrepreneurs focus on their goals and objectives. Doing without them is like getting lost in a forest without a compass or a map. Your kids should write up a plan, no matter how scanty.

Sooner or later, your kids are going to need some money to start their own businesses. Chances are that their savings will not be sufficient to cover the initial investment they need to start their businesses. Before you give them a dime, make sure they come up with business plans to show you how they intend to use your money. Even if they receive no money from you, you should still discuss how a good business plan can help them become successful in their businesses.

How elaborate the plan should be depends on how old your kids are. Obviously, a 10–year–old child may not be able to come up with a plan that is more than one or two pages long. Teenagers, on the other hand, should be able to fully describe their ideas and create a comprehensive marketing and financial plan.

This chapter describes the basic components of a basic business plan. I urge you and your kids to go to your local library or bookstore for books which gives more details on how to prepare and present business plans.

DEFINING THE BUSINESS

The first items your children's business plans should include are complete descriptions of their business ideas. What are they going to be selling? They should practice writing short, specific statements describing their products or services.

When 16–year–old Sue Hansen of Pittsburgh, Pennsylvania, decided to start a T–shirt business, she knew she had to sell a product that no one in her area had ever before offered. She came up with a great concept called ArtShirts. She described her business in very simple terms: "My business is to sell T–shirts with hand–drawn colorful works of art." Sue was an accomplished painter and she had won numerous art competitions in her area. To her, Art-Shirts was a labor of love.

Help your kids focus on the type of products or services they will offer by encouraging them to make a list of what their customers will get from them. I find that kids realize how much work will be involved in their businesses only when they jot down what they intend to do for their customers. Two teenagers who wanted to start a wallpapering business thought it was going to be easy. When they finally started making their list, it included the following arduous tasks: removing the old wallpaper, lining up the edges in the corners, making sure the paper was not buckled, and other difficult tasks. They decided that it was too much work and they tried their hand at something else.

THE MARKET

After your kids have described their basic business ideas, the work begins. Their next task is to find out if anyone will be interested in the products or services they intend to sell. This is the most fundamental task your kids have to do before they invest a penny in their proposed businesses. Unfortunately, for kids and adults alike, it is one of the most overlooked aspects of business start–ups. Every entrepreneur has made this mistake at one point or another. For some, it is a fatal mistake. For others, it is an expensive way to learn a lesson. Kids in particular always feel that there is great demand for their products or services before they do the simplest of investigations or research to confirm their feelings. Many of them don't understand that not everyone shares their opinions about the value of their products or services. Over the years, I have found that as long as young entrepreneurs focus on how their products or services can benefit their customers, they can more readily determine whether anyone will be interested in what they have to sell.

Your kids have to first decide to whom they would like to sell their products or services. Will the customers be parents? Homeowners? Other kids? They should at least consider the profile of their ideal customers. Initially, Sue Hansen of ArtShirts wanted to sell her T–shirts to the kids in her neighborhood. After talking it over, she and her father decided that introducing T–shirts with school–related themes and selling them to her fellow students would provide her with a broader market. She changed her focus to both kids in school and their parents. To the kids, she would sell T–shirts with popular slogans on them. To both parents and kids, she would sell ArtShirts at high school sporting events. In a swim meet, for example, she made up twenty Art–Shirts with two of the school's champion swimmers painted on them. By talking to your kids about their market, you too may be able to open their eyes to possibilities they had not previously considered.

Your children's business plans also have to include an up–to–date analysis of their competition. Why? Because they need to plan their market position. Will they be offering completely new products or services? Will their products or services be variations of businesses that already exist? What benefits can they build into their products or services that their competitors don't offer?

Once your kids have identified their target markets, they should figure out how to gauge the size of these markets and how to get in touch with potential customers.There are several techniques other kids have used in figuring out the number of potential customers for their products or services. The right technique for your children depends on what they are offering.

Young entrepreneurs who have neighborhood businesses, such as lawn mowing or house painting businesses, can poll residents in the area to gauge customer interest in patronizing their businesses. They can accomplish this by personally talking to their potential customers. They can interview these neighbors to see if they will be interested in patronizing your children's businesses. Before one high school student started his lawn–care business, he approached 60 of his neighbors. Here are some of the questions he asked these neighbors:

1. Is someone besides a family member mowing your lawns on a regular basis? If so, are you satisfied with the work?

2. Would you be interested in having your lawn mowed on a regular basis? Once a week? Once every two weeks? Or just on demand?

3. Would your lawn mower be available to use for cutting the grass?

4. Would you be willing to pay $10 per hour for the service? (Of course before he asked this question, he had already explained what services he intended to offer. In addition, he knew the going rate for lawn mowing. More on pricing later.)

This teenager was doing his market research by going directly to his potential customers: those who had lawns to be mowed.Your kids can also find a way to contact their potential customers to estimate customer interest in their products or services. However, if your kids are just sizing up the market, they should tell these potential customers so. It would be wrong for them to pretend that they are already running their own businesses when in fact they are just doing research.

Another approach that will help your kids determine the demand for their products or services in the neighborhood is distributing advertising flyers that include phone numbers where customers can reach them. The potential customers can then contact your kids if they are interested in the products or services. Once again, when these potential customers call, your kids should let the potential customers know whether they are in fact going to start the business or whether they are just gauging consumer interest in their product or services.

The flyer distribution technique for gauging demand is less work than actually talking to potential customers, but the information gathered from this impersonal approach to market research is not as reliable.

If your kids are starting school–based businesses, they have to take a different approach to gauging the size of their markets. They have to show samples of their products or services to the other kids in their school. Sue Hansen of ArtShirts wore her colorful hand–painted ArtShirts to school. For two straight weeks, she wore a different design and color. The ArtShirts proved to be so popular in Sue's high school that kids were approaching her in the hallways to ask where they could get them. In one day, twenty students asked her about the shirts. In addition, she captured the attention of the football coach when she wore an ArtShirt that featured her high–school football quarterback and the quarterback of the team's perennial rival. The painting on her T–shirts was so well done that the coach mentioned the T–shirts to the football team. One week later, the whole team decided to order a set of Sue's ArtShirts to get them pumped up for the game.

Sue's market research also included an estimate of what she could charge for her ArtShirts. Before she wore her painted T–shirts to her school she spent many hours in the local malls searching for painted T–shirts that looked like her own creations. The closest products she found were some crude artworks ironed on to poor quality T–shirts. And the cost of these T–shirts were $14. This piece of market research gave her an idea of the quality and prices of her competitors' products. In addition, it helped her give her fellow students an idea of what it would cost them to purchase Art-Shirts. She eventually quoted her customers a price of $10 for splendid designs on good quality T–shirts. For personalized Art-Shirts, she charged $15.

The response Sue got from her fellow students helped her determine the market size for her colorful ArtShirts. From the reactions of the students in her school, she decided that she could sell about 200 personalized ArtShirts to other kids. In addition, she became confident that she could sell as many to parents who attended her high school's athletic events.

If your kids have a product or service for other students in their high school, there are other ways to get the word out. They can make up flyers describing what they are selling. They can also use their school's bulletin board or even the school newspaper as advertising vehicles. In addition, if there are any entrepreneurship classes in your children's high school, perhaps they can get a student in those classes to sell their products. If there are fund–raisers in their school perhaps they can get kids to sell their products or services with part of the proceeds going toward the fund. Whatever marketing campaigns your kids intend to do in their school, they should first talk to their principal or other school officials for approval.

As your kids are working on their plan, they should also think about when their product or services can be offered. Are their businesses seasonal or do they sell their items all year round? Naturally, demand for their products or services can fluctuate during the year because of factors that they cannot control. One ninth–grade student makes more than $1,000 each year selling Christmas wreaths. Obviously, she sells her wreaths only from late November to late December because no one would want to buy a wreath after Christmas.

There are other businesses that are short–term or seasonal. A lawn–care business lasts about five or six months of the year in the New England area. Sue Hansen, the 16–year–old owner of Art-Shirts, runs her business during the school year because most of her sales are to students and parents who attend school athletic events.

FINANCE

Revenue

So far, I have discussed how your kids can define their products or services and figure out the number of customers they may be able to get. Now your kids have to use this information to determine the amount of money they can make. Once again, I will use Sue Hansen's ArtShirts to illustrate how your kids can handle the financial end of their business.

Judging by the response she got from other kids when she wore her painted ArtShirts to school, Sue Hansen figured that she could sell at least 200 ArtShirts during the school year. That is about 20 shirts per month to be sold to kids in school and spectators at athletic events.

Once your kids decide how much they can sell each month (or in any other period) they can then calculate their revenues. Sue calculated her monthly revenue for her ArtShirts by simply multiplying her monthly sales by the cost of each item. Her potential revenue was $10 x 20 = $200 every month. However, Sue had to consider the following factors:

1. The revenue is based on the assumption that all of the estimated 200 potential customers will actually become real paying customers. Unfortunately, sometimes people may show interest in a product or service but then, when push comes to shove, they don't pry their wallets open to make any purchases. Your kids have to be wary of overestimating their customer base.

2. Expenses have to be deducted from the revenue to calculate real profit.

3. It takes a lot of work to make this money. Customers will also want satisfaction and they may demand their money back if they don't like the shirts.

4. The time she had on her hands was limited. With school taking up most of her time during the week, she may not be able to take on all of the business by herself. It may just be physically impossible to meet the demands of her business.

Expenses

After your kids get the upper limit on their revenues, they have to figure out the expenses that they will incur while running their businesses. This process is critical to the success or failure of their ventures. Give your kids the opportunity to think about all the foreseeable expenses in their businesses. You can sit down with them and use the brainstorming technique (see Chapter 5) to think of all the possible expenses they will face in their businesses. There may be some expenses they have not considered and, likewise, there may be expenses that you have not considered that will drastically change the profit potential of the products or services. In helping Sue think of her expenses for her painted ArtShirts, her parents reminded her that she could not do all the painting in her room because it was too small and the fumes from the paint could be noxious. Her parents then suggested that she could rent the family garage for all of her equipment, and the family car would be parked out in the street.

You may be wondering why Sue's parents even charged her for using the garage. They charged her rent because they wanted her to know that in the real world, she would have to consider the expenses associated with the building where she would be conducting her business. In helping your kids figure out their expenses, do not give anything away free. Charge them something for the use of your assets even if the amount is minuscule. This will at least get them used to considering expenses they would not ordinarily have thought about. Remember that you are charging them to make a point, not to fully recover the overhead costs.

As you and your kids are coming up with expense figures, you should advise them to actually go out and price the materials they need for their businesses. They can do their research at the local supermarket, hardware store, art supply store, or other establishments that can supply the materials they need for their businesses. In addition, you should suggest that they look for used equipment or other substitutes for their businesses. For example, Sue purchased a couple of metal buckets from a garage sale for washing her paintbrushes. Here are some of the expenses your children must include:

1. *Direct material costs.* These are the costs of the raw materials.

2. *Direct labor costs.* These are the wages your kids will pay to employees. Depending on the kind of business your kids start, they may need some help from other kids. For example, a garage–cleaning service may require two people to help move heavy equipment out of the way. One person probably cannot do it alone. In some cases, it may be worth it for your kids to hire someone to help them accomplish specific tasks in their businesses.

3. *Overhead expenses.* These expenses include rent, gas, electricity, telephone, packing and shipping, delivery and freight charges, cleaning expenses for the office, insurance, office supplies, postage, repairs and maintenance, or other expenses that cannot be directly attributed to one unit of the product or service provided.

Here are the expenses Sue and her parents came up with for her business:

White T–shirts (wholesaler)	$30.00 a dozen
Fabric paints	$10.00 for 10 shirts
Brushes (3)	$15.00 for all shirts
Blotter	$8.00 every 20 shirts
2 Buckets	$4.00 for all shirts
Cleaner for brushes	$8.00 every 20 shirts
Overalls for painting	$20.00 for all shirts
Exhaust fan for fumes	$40.00 for all shirts
Garage rental	$20.00 for all shirts
Advertising	$20.00 for flyers for all shirts

Notice that there are some non–recurring expenses on Sue's list, such as the buckets, the overalls, and the exhaust fan. For our purposes, we will assume that she has to purchase these items only once for the entire life of her business.

The next step is to break the expenses down on a per–job basis. This requires knowing how long each item is going to last. For example, Sue has to replace the paint cleaner after painting about twenty shirts. Likewise, your kids have to know what each item on their expense lists will cost them for the products they produce or the services they render. Sue broke down her expense per T–shirt in the following way:

1. *White T–shirts (from wholesaler)*. $30.00 a dozen, or $2.50 each.

2. *Fabric paints*. $10.00 for 10 shirts, or $1 per shirt.

3. *Brushes (3)*. $15.00 for all 200 shirts, or 7.5 cents per shirt.

4. *Blotter*. $8.00 every 20 shirts, or 40 cents per shirt.

5. *Two buckets*. $4.00 for all 200 shirts. Since the buckets will last for the projected 200 ArtShirts, the cost per shirt will be 2 cents.

6. *Cleaner for brushes*. $8.00 for 20 shirts, or 40 cents per shirt.

7. *Overalls for painting*. $20.00 for all 200 shirts. Since the overalls will last for the projected 200 ArtShirts, the cost per order will be 10 cents per shirt.

8. *Exhaust fan for fumes*. $40.00 for all 200 shirts. Once again, this item will last for as long as Sue produces her painted T–shirts and probably beyond. On a per–job basis, the cost for the fan is 20 cents per shirt for the 200 shirts.

9. *Garage rental*. $20.00 for all 200 shirts. Since the garage rental will be for the time it takes to make the projected 200 ArtShirts, the cost per order will be 10 cents per shirt.

10. *Advertising*. Sue's advertising consists of flyers she created on her parent's computer and copied at the local
print shop. On a per–job basis, advertising costs was 10
cents per shirt.

Sue's total cost per shirt was as follows:

White T–shirts (wholesaler)	$2.50
Fabric paints	$1.00
Brushes (3)	$. 08
Blotter	$ .40
2 Buckets	$ .02
Cleaner for brushes	$ .40
Overalls for painting	$ .10
Exhaust fan for fumes	$ .20
Garage rental	$ .10
Advertising	$ .10
	$ 4.90 per shirt

According to Sue's calculations, she will make about $5.10
per shirt ($10 – $4.90 = $5.10). If she sells 20 ArtShirts per month,
her profit will be about $102 per month (20 ArtShirts x $5.10 =
$102).

It takes Sue about half an hour to paint her shirt, so her hourly
wage is about $10.20 per hour (2 T–shirts painted per hour at a
profit of $5.10 per shirt). This definitely beats minimum wage.

You can help your kids figure out how much it will cost to offer their products or services in the same way Sue Hansen has done
for her ArtShirts. Your kids should make comprehensive lists of all
of the items they need for their products or services and then break
these expenses down on a cost per product or service basis.

Pricing

Sue Hansen's approach to pricing her product was to look for
T–shirts at the local mall similar to the ones she was selling. As I
said earlier, she found inferior products for $14 apiece and then de-
cided to price her own T–shirts at $10. Sue priced them so low be-
cause she felt that people, especially students, would not be willing

to pay more than $10 for T–shirts—no matter the quality of the artwork. I disagreed with her on this point because of the excitement her products, particularly her customized shirts, generated in her school. Be that as it may, your kids should never lowball the prices of their products or services.

There are basically three approaches entrepreneurs take to setting their prices: using competitors' prices as a benchmark, tacking on the desired profit per item, or considering both the competitors' prices and the expenses per item.

Using the competitors' prices as a benchmark is a respectable way your kids can price their products or services. Your kids can use this method by first checking the competitors' prices and then adding or subtracting money from these prices, depending on how their product or service compares to the competitors' products or services. The only problem with this method is that your kids may not be able to find products or services that are comparable to what they are selling. If your children's businesses are innovative, there certainly will be no competitors they can use as benchmarks for determining what they should charge. Even if your kids offer products or services that are slightly better than their competitors, they are faced with the task of pricing the added value. For example, if your kids start a house–cleaning business in which they clean windows and their competitors do not, they will have to figure out what to charge the customers for the extra service. This is not an impossible task, but it complicates matters a bit.

Adding on a profit figure to the cost per item is also used by many entrepreneurs to figure out the prices they should charge. If, for example, Sue Hansen of ArtShirts wanted to make $10 profit for every T–shirt she painted, she would have to add $10 to her expense per shirt figure of $4.90 for a total of $14.90. The problem with this method of pricing is that the desire to make a specified level of profit does not necessarily mean that customers will pay the prices set for the products or services. If Sue had marked up her ArtShirts to $14.90, it is possible that the price would have been out of range for most of the students in her school.

The proper way for your kids to price their goods is a combination of the two methods just described. Here are instructions your kids should follow to price their products or services:

1. Calculate the costs per item produced or services rendered.

2. Find out the competitors' prices. In addition, have them compare the quality of their products or services with their competitors'.

3. If your children's products or services are exactly like those of the competitors, they will have little choice but to price like the competitors. If your kids subtract their expenses per item from this price and get a negative number, they should not go into the business. They should try something else.

4. If their products are slightly different from those of the competitors, they should probably use the competitors' prices as a benchmark and then make appropriate adjustments to reflect the differences in quality.

5. If your kids have a completely new product or service, they must set their prices above their costs. How far they can set their prices above cost is the million–dollar question. Your kids can start off by adding a modest amount to the cost depending on how much time it takes them to create the products or render the services. One way to determine this amount is for your kids to decide what they would like to earn on an hourly basis. Of course they will have to keep in mind that the minimum wage is $4.25 per hour. If they want to make $6 per hour, for example, and it takes them one hour to make their product or render their service, then they should add $6.00 to the cost per item. Of course, the possibility exists that customers will not be willing to pay such prices. In that case, your kids should probably lower their prices to attract more customers.

One more word about new products or services: because there are no price benchmarks, your kids have to experiment a little with prices. They should adjust their prices upward or downward to see if they can take in more profit. They may lose customers if they adjust their prices up, but they may get more total revenues none-theless. It's also possible that they could get more revenues by low-ering their prices. The opposite is also possible. Increasing prices may reduce the number of customers and total revenues at the same time. Reducing prices may increase the number of customers will-ing to purchase the product or service, but at the same time reduce total revenues.

Capital Investment Required

So far, we have discussed how your children should calculate their expenses, set their prices, and estimate their profit per product or service. But we have not talked about how much seed money they will need to start their businesses or how to get it.

Once again, I will use Sue Hansen's ArtShirts business to il-lustrate the process of calculating the required start–up funds. The start–up funds should include the money your kids will need to open their businesses and keep it open until they start getting paid for their product or service. Let's take a look at Sue's expenses again:

White T–shirts (wholesaler)	$30.00 a dozen
Fabric paints	$10.00 for 10 shirts
Brushes (3)	$15.00 for all shirts
Blotter	$ 8.00 every 20 shirts
2 Buckets	$ 4.00 for all shirts
Cleaner for brushes	$ 8.00 every 20 shirts
Overalls for painting	$20.00 for all shirts
Exhaust fan for fumes	$40.00 for all shirts
Garage rental	$20.00 for all shirts
Advertising	<u>$20.00 for flyers for all shirts</u>
	$175.00 for all items

Sue had to buy a lot of supplies and equipment to open up her business. Every single item on this list had to be paid for in ad-vance. Sue had to come up with $175 before she could open up for business. She was lucky enough to have put enough money away in her savings account to finance her business.

Unless your kids have money saved for their new businesses, they will have to approach you or an investor for start–up money. If they *do* borrow money from you, charge them interest. If Sue's parents had charged her interest of say 10% for borrowing $175, she would have had to pay them $17.50 per year. That would add about 9 cents per item ($17.50/200) to the expenses associated with producing her ArtShirts. In addition, she would have to pay back the principal based on a schedule. If her parents wanted her to pay back the loan at the end of one year, that money would have to come out of the revenue she would make during the year.

Break–Even Analysis

What I have described so far is a simplified version of how your kids can calculate revenue, expenses, price, and profit. If your kids have had basic arithmetic, they can muddle through the calculations with little or no help from you. Break–even analysis is another way your kids can figure out the potential for their businesses before investing time and money.

If your kids are 14 years old or older, and they are comfortable with math, they can use the break–even technique for measuring the profitability of their prospective businesses. The mathematics involved is just slightly more complicated than what we have just gone through in the previous sections, but the technique is much more powerful. Use your judgment to determine whether you can introduce this method to your children. Since kids don't have to know this technique to run their businesses, you don't have to explain it to them unless you feel they can understand it.

Break–even analysis implies a level of operations at which a business neither makes a profit nor loses money. At break even, revenue is exactly enough to cover expenses. Break–even analysis allows an entrepreneur to study the relationship between volume, expenses, and revenue.

The first step in applying break–even analysis is to separate expenses into fixed and variable components. Fixed expenses are expenses that do not depend on sales. In Sue Hansen's ArtShirts business, one obvious fixed expense is the $40 exhaust fan. No matter whether Sue planned to make 1 or 100 ArtShirts she had to spend $40 for the fan. In other businesses, big fixed expenses are usually the cost of building a factory, investing in machinery, and the cost of utilities such as gas and electricity.

Variable expenses are expenses that will increase or decrease with sales. In Sue's business, the cost of the unpainted T–shirts is an example of a variable expense. For each ArtShirt Sue sells, she must use a blank T–shirt that cost her $2.50.

Once again, I will use Sue's expenses to illustrate the break–even concept. Here are Sue's expenses broken down into their fixed and variable components:

Fixed Expenses

Overalls for painting	$20.00 for all shirts
Exhaust fan for fumes	$40.00 for all shirts
Brushes (3)	$15.00 for all shirts
Garage rental	$20.00 for all shirts
Advertising	$20.00 for flyers for all shirts
2 buckets	$ 4.00 for all shirts
	$119.00 for all shirts

Variable Expenses

White T–shirts (wholesaler)	$2.50 for each shirt
Fabric Paint	$1.00 for each shirt
Blotter	$ .40 for each shirt
Cleaner for brushes	$ .40 for each shirt
	$4.30 for each shirt

Earlier, Sue figured that she could get 200 people to buy her ArtShirts. But suppose she did not really know how many people would buy her T–shirts. If this were the case, then she may want to know the minimum number of customers she will need in order to break even. Once she finds out this threshold, she can work toward exceeding it. I will now go through the process of how your kids can use break–even analysis to find this threshold.

The formula for arriving at a profit is simply the following:

Equation A

$$PROFIT = [(P - V) \times Q] - F$$

Where P = price of each unit sold
V = variable expenses per unit sold
Q = number of units sold
F = total fixed expenses

If Sue wanted to find out how many ArtShirts she had to sell in order to break even, she had to solve equation A for Q and then set profit equal to 0.

Equation B

$$PROFIT = [(P - V) \times Q] - F$$

solving for Q,
$$Q = \frac{F + PROFIT}{(P - V)}$$

Plugging in the constants for Sue's ArtShirts, we obtain:

$PROFIT$ = $0
P = $10
V = $4.30
F = $119

$$Q = \frac{\$119}{(\$10 - \$4.30)}$$

Answer: Q = 21 ArtShirts

These calculations show that Sue had to sell 21 ArtShirts to break even. I can prove to you that this is correct. If Q equals 21, P equals $10, V equals $4.30, and F equals $119, then:

$$PROFIT = [(P - V) \times Q] - F$$

$$PROFIT = (\$10 - \$4.30) \times 21 - \$119$$

Answer: $PROFIT = 0$ (actually, the profit is 70 cents, but I am rounding it off to 0).

Even though Sue assumed she would get about 200 customers, the break–even equation tells her that if she gets more than 21 customers, she will still make some money. Equation B gives her an idea of how low her sales can be without losing money.

Your kids can follow the same process to figure out the minimum sales they need to break even. If they calculate they need a certain level of sales to break even and they don't feel they can make that many sales, then they should try other businesses.

Of course just breaking even should not be the goal of any business. It should not be your children's goal either. Equation B is typically used to figure out the sales needed to yield a certain level of profit. To break even, we set profit equal to 0. However, profit can be set to any level, and then sales level, Q, can be figured out accordingly.

Suppose that Sue would like to make $2,000 profit in the coming year. Although the desire to make that kind of money does not mean she will be able to rake in such profits, she could have figured out the level of sales she would need to meet her profit target for the year. Once again, we can use equation B, except this time we will plug in $2,000 for profit.

$$Q = \frac{\$119 + \$2000}{(\$10 - \$4.30)}$$

Answer: Q = 372 ArtShirts

Three hundred and seventy–two ArtShirts is an ambitious number of painted T–shirts for Sue to sell in her school. Of course, had Sue seen this figure, she probably would have decided either to settle for a profit less than $2,000 or to forget the business entirely. Herein lies the usefulness of the equation. It can help your kids set a profit level and back into the unit sales associated with that profit level. It may well turn out that after your kids see the sales numbers, they will realize that they cannot possibly get that many people to buy their product or service. If this is the case, they will have to either lower their minimum profit level or find another business venture.

The break–even equation has another important function. As long as your kids know four variables in the equation, they can always solve for the fifth. For example, given a particular level of profit, fixed expenses, variable expenses, number of customers, they can solve for the prices they will have to charge customers. Of course, as we discussed earlier, this is not a sensible way to set prices, but it does show the flexibility of the break–even formula. As long as your kids know everything to the right of the equals sign, they can solve for the variable to the left. Here are useful things your kids can do with the equation.

Figuring out units needed:

$$Q = \frac{F + PROFIT}{(P - V)}$$

Figuring out profit:

$$PROFIT = [(P - V) \times Q] - F$$

Figuring out price:

$$P = \frac{F + PROFIT}{Q} + V$$

where P = price of each unit sold
     V = variable expense per unit sold
     Q = number of units sold
     F = total fixed expenses

BUSINESS PLAN WORKSHEETS

DEFINING YOUR IDEAS

1. What is your business idea?

   _____
   _____
   _____

2. Who are your customers?

   _____
   _____
   _____

3. What special skills do you have that will help you with your business?

   _____
   _____
   _____

4. List exactly what you will do for the customers (step by step).

   _____
   _____
   _____

DEFINING YOUR MARKET

1. Is your product or service completely new?

   _____
   _____
   _____

2. If not, who are your competitors?

   _____
   _____
   _____

3. Where are your competitors located?

_____

_____

_____

4. What are your competitors' prices?

_____

_____

_____

5. How will you advertise your product or service?

_____

_____

_____

6. How may customers do you think you can get per week? per month? per year?

_____

_____

_____

FINANCIALS

1. Figure out your revenue (by week or month) by doing the following:

   Revenue = (number of units sold) x (price per unit)

2. List all of your expenses in making your product or offering your service.

_____

_____

_____

_____

_____

_____

3. Break the expenses into cost per unit.

_____
_____
_____
_____
_____
_____

4. Figure out how much money you need to start your business.

_____
_____
_____
_____
_____
_____

10

RECORD KEEPING

Keeping accurate and up–to–date business records is, for many kids, the most difficult and uninteresting aspect of operating their own businesses. Because this is an area of business management your kids may find tedious, it is never too early to start thinking of how to make it easier for them.

Proper record keeping is important for several reasons. For one thing, the U.S. government wants to get its share of your children's profit. A well–designed record–keeping system will simplify the process of complying with government regulations.

In addition, a simple, well–organized system of records, regularly kept up, can actually be a time–saver for your kids by bringing order out of disorder. Some of the young entrepreneurs I have counseled through the Center for Teen Entrepreneurs have found that with a good record–keeping system, they can service their customers better, and they can better keep track of the money they are owed or the money they have to pay.

Your children will need to know periodically what their profits are. Profit and loss information is an important aid in decision making. Information gathered by your young entrepreneurs from a review of their record–keeping system can indicate past trends in their company's operating effectiveness. This historical data can be used to answer specific questions about the change in profitability over time, the volume of sales at different times of the year, the most or least profitable lines of merchandise or services, and so on.

In this chapter, I provide your kids with forms that will help them develop good record–keeping habits. I will also point out simple ways you can encourage your kids to create their own record–keeping system.

EFFECTIVE RECORD KEEPING

Record keeping, as presented in this chapter, can be defined as the process of identifying what records need to be kept, how they are to be entered and maintained, and how they can be used effectively. A record is defined as basic information that documents financial, personnel, inventory, supply, or customer activities. This information is normally recorded as the result of a transaction or event in the course of conducting business.

Even though your children's businesses may be small, it is never too early to show them the basics of proper record keeping. In advising young entrepreneurs, I generally tell them to keep records of all of their sales activities regardless of whether their businesses are making money or not. If their businesses fail, I usually go over their records with them to see where they went wrong. Sometimes by going through their receipts, I often discover that the actual cost of offering their products or services was much higher than they predicted in their business plans.

There are three factors you have to keep in mind when helping your kids set up a good record–keeping system: simplicity, accuracy, and timeliness.

Simplicity

What your children are capable of learning about record keeping depends on their ages. If they are less than 14 years old, they may have a hard time grasping debits and credits of assets and liabilities. Indeed, it would be a waste of time to try to teach them double–entry accounting. Older kids can grasp these concepts, so I recommend that they take basic accounting classes in high school. My approach to record keeping is that kids can learn the basics without invoking sophisticated accounting principles. As long as your kids have the proper guidance, they can keep good records.

Accuracy

The necessity for maintaining accurate records seems obvious, but it can not be overemphasized. A common problem, for example, when kids record numbers is that they are sloppy. When they go back to read their handwriting, they find that they cannot understand what they have written. Consequently, they can easily interpret a customer's order incorrectly or even neglect to service their customers. Sometimes, inaccuracy in record keeping is a symptom of a disorganized business. One teenage entrepreneur who created database systems for his customers sometimes overcharged customers by mistake because he never kept records of the software features he gave his customers. Sure, he had a price list of what each feature will cost the customers, but he just did not write down what the customers chose. Of course, when he undercharged customers, these customers did not care that they were not billed properly. But when he overcharged them for software features he failed to include in the customized systems, he got an earful from irate customers. This young entrepreneur was not dishonest—he was just so disorganized that he was sending out inaccurate and incorrect bills to his customers.

Timeliness

Timeliness is an important element in a good record–keeping system. Consider the statement, "I made $200." Without the element of time, this statement has little meaning. Add "in one month" and the statement has more meaning. Or add "in one week" and the meaning changes dramatically. One consideration of record keeping, then, is time. Young entrepreneurs have the tendency to figure out their profits without considering how much time it took them to make that money.

The more obvious reason for timeliness is the need for the young entrepreneur to receive information as early as possible to make decisions affecting the business.

MINIMUM RECORDS REQUIRED

There are four basic records that you kids must maintain in their businesses:

1. Sales records.

2. Records of money received from customers.

3. Records of money owed by customers.

4. Money used for business purchases.

In this section, I present worksheets your kids can use to help them keep such records.

Sales records (see worksheet #1)

Your kids must keep a record of all sales as they occur. They should be aware that sales may result in cash or arrangements may be made to receive payments at a later time. In either case, the sales records should reflect that the sale has occurred.

Because your children's businesses will be small at first, they probably won't be using cash registers, which generate a combined sales and cash receipt. This means that they have to manually record their sales. For each sale, they can use the sales record worksheet to keep track of their sales and to generate a receipt for the customer. Your kids should fill out two sales records for each sale with each one containing the same information. One sales record should go to each customer and your kids should keep the duplicate for their records. The sales record should be used only for customers who pay your kids at the time they receive their products or services. If the customers are to pay them at a later date, then your children should use the accounts receivable form (Worksheet #2B).

WORKSHEET #1

SALES RECORD AND CUSTOMER RECEIPTS

Customer Receipt

Customer Name_____

Item or Service Purchased_____

_____

Date of Purchase_____

Payment_____

Method of Payment (cash, check, or credit card)_____

A Copy of the Customer Receipt (for your records)

Customer Name_____

Item or Service Purchased_____

_____

Date of Purchase_____

Payment_____

Method of Payment (cash, check, or credit card)_____

Money received from customers and money owed by customers (see worksheets #2A,#2B)

Your kids will receive cash at the time of the sale or as payment on account for credit sales. In any case, all cash should be recorded as it is received (column B on Worksheet #2A). Small businesses (like your children's) without cash registers, can enter all weekly or monthly transactions in the sales and cash receipts form showing the name of the customers, the date of their purchases, and the dollar amount of the sale.

If your kids provide products or services to customers and agree to accept payment at a later time, they create account receivables (or money owed by customers—column C on Worksheet #2A). An accounts receivable record normally contains information pertinent to billing and receiving payment from a customer after the product has been delivered or the service rendered.

I advise most young entrepreneurs to try to get paid right away when they provide products or services to avoid the confusion of who owes them what. The problem with this policy though is that they run the risk of losing customers. Some customers would rather be billed for the products or services they receive especially when kids are providing these products or services. Adults usually expect the worst from young entrepreneurs until they have proven to be reliable. If your kids can get more customers by selling items or services on credit, then collecting their money later may not be so bad. However, I strongly recommend that your kids do not sell anything on credit to other kids. I have seen many instances where kids refuse to pay their debts. Your young entrepreneurs will find that collecting money from other kids is like pulling teeth.

Your kids should keep good records as to who owes them money and when they are supposed to be paid. The accounts receivable form (Worksheet #2B) should help them keep track of their debtors. Notice that I have provided a lot of space for your kids to thoroughly describe the item or service purchased. It is extremely important that your kids write down precisely what the customer received from them. This is necessary because customers often forget what services or products they received on credit when it comes time to pay their bills. If your kids keep impeccable records about what they did for the customers, they will always have reliable documentation to prove that the customers owe them specific amounts.

WORKSHEET #2A

WEEKLY CUSTOMER RECORDS

(Date: From_____ To _____)

Customer Name	(A) Date of Sale	(B) Money Rcvd. from Cust.	(C) Money Owed by Cust.
_____	_____	_____	_____
_____	_____	_____	_____
_____	_____	_____	_____
_____	_____	_____	_____
_____	_____	_____	_____
_____	_____	_____	_____
_____	_____	_____	_____
_____	_____	_____	_____
_____	_____	_____	_____
_____	_____	_____	_____
TOTAL		══════	══════

WORKSHEET #2B

ACCOUNTS RECEIVABLE OR MONEY OWED ME BY CUSTOMERS

Customer Receipt

Customer Name_____

Item or Service Purchased_____

_____

_____

Date of Purchase_____

Date Payment Is to be Received _____

Payment to be Received _____

A Copy of the Customer Receipt (for your records)

Customer Name_____

Item or Service Purchased_____

_____

Date of Purchase_____

Date Payment Is to be Received _____

Payment to be Received _____

Money used for business purchases (see Worksheet #3)

Your kids should record every penny they use in their businesses. This is important because their net profit will depend on how much they spend each period for business expenses.

WORKSHEET #3:

WEEKLY PURCHASE RECORDS

(Date: From_____ To _____)

Item Bought	Date of Pchs (A)	Money Paid (B)	Money I Owe (C)
_____	_____	_____	_____
_____	_____	_____	_____
_____	_____	_____	_____
_____	_____	_____	_____
_____	_____	_____	_____
_____	_____	_____	_____
_____	_____	_____	_____
_____	_____	_____	_____
_____	_____	_____	_____
_____	_____	_____	_____
_____	_____	_____	_____

TOTAL ═══════ ═══════

PUTTING IT ALL TOGETHER

If your kids are diligent about keeping good sales records, cash receipts, accounts receivable, and cash disbursement records, then they should be able to periodically put together good summary of sales and cash receipt records. These records will help them track the money flowing in and out of their businesses.

WORKSHEET #4

SUMMARY OR SALES AND CASH RECEIPTS

(Date: From_____ To _____)

MONEY TAKEN IN THIS PERIOD

1. Cash sales $_____

2. Collections on account $_____

3. Miscellaneous receipts $_____

4. **Total receipts to be accounted for** $_____
   (Add 1 through 3)

CASH ON HAND

5. Coins, Bills, Checks $_____

6. Money deposited in bank account $_____

7. Money used to buy supplies $_____
   (Add up all Purchases)
            Purchase #1   _____
            Purchase #2   _____
            Purchase #3   _____
            Purchase #4   _____
            Purchase #5   _____

8. Refunds $_____

9. Payments on accounts $_____

10. **Total cash accounted for** $_____
   (Add 5 through 10)

RECONCILIATION

11. Cash short $\underline{\hspace{3cm}}$
   (Item 4 less Item 10 – if Item 4 is larger)

12. Cash over $\underline{\hspace{3cm}}$
   (Item 10 less Item 4 – if Item 10 is larger)

First note that the summary of sales and cash receipts (Worksheet #4) can be filled out on a daily, weekly, monthly, or yearly basis depending on how often an entrepreneur wants to evaluate his cash position. I recommend that your kids make a copy of this form and fill it out weekly. If they wait for one month or one year before filling it out, I can guarantee you that they will not remember what happened to the cash they took in or how much money they are owed.

From this point forward, I will assume that the forms will be filled out on a weekly basis. Here is the definition of each of the lines in the summary of sales and cash receipts:

1. *Cash sales*. This is the amount of money your young entrepreneurs collect from their customers when they make sales during the week.

2. *Collections on account*. This is the money that was owed to your kids, which they received from their customers during the week. If you know a bit about accounting, it is the amount of the accounts receivable that have been collected.

3. *Miscellaneous receipts*. This represents money that your kids receive during the week that is not related to sales of their products or services. For example, if your kids get a refund for purchases related to their businesses, the money should be recorded in this line.

4. *Total receipts to be accounted for*. This is essentially all the cash that was received during the week. It is the summation of items 1 to 3.

5. *Coins, bills, checks*. This represents the cash your kids received from running their businesses. This is money they have not yet deposited into a bank account.

6. *Money deposited in a bank account*. This is the money from your children's businesses that they have put away in their savings account. It is a good idea to encourage your kids to immediately put any substantial amount of

money ($30 or above) into their account. This takes away the temptation to use the money for frivolous purchases.

7. *Money used to buy supplies.* Chances are your kids will need to use some of the money they get from their businesses to buy supplies. For example, if they need stationery supplies, they will take the money out of their cash receipts for these purchases.

8. *Refunds.* Amount of money your kids refunded to their customers during the week.

9. *Payments on account.* This is the amount of money your kids owe to third parties that they paid off in the week. For example, if your young entrepreneurs buy items on credit, they will record the payment of that money in this line. This is analogous to a decrease of accounts payable in accounting jargon.

10. *Total cash accounted for.* This is basically all the cash your kids have on hand before paying for expenses and refunds.

11. *Cash short.* This represents the money that your kids cannot account for. They must have done something with the money they received; they should investigate what happened to the cash.

12. *Cash over.* This represents money your kids received from unidentified sources.

PROFIT AND LOSS STATEMENT

Perhaps the information your kids will want most about the performance of their businesses is their profitability. For a particular period of time, did their companies make or lose money? The profit and loss statement (sometimes called an income statement) describes the net results, over a period of time, of revenues less expenses.

The so called "bottom line" refers to the last line on a profit and loss statement—the line indicating the company's net profit (or loss). Stated simply, the profit and loss statement is represented by the equation:

Revenues–Expenses = Income

The profit and loss statement form (Worksheet #5) shows the type of categories commonly found on a profit and loss statement. The first thing to notice on the statement is the date on the top. A profit and loss statement always covers a particular period of time—a week, a month, a quarter, a year, and so on. This means that revenue was earned and expenses were incurred during the time indicated. The element of time should be kept in mind when examining the various accounts listed on the statement.

WORKSHEET #5

PROFIT AND LOSS STATEMENT

(For Current Month)

INCOME

1. Money received from customers
   or owed by customers $_____

2. Refunds to customers $_____

3. **Money left over** $_____
   (Line 1 less Line 2)

EXPENSES

4. The cost of items sold $_____

5. Wages to employees $_____

6. Interest on loans $_____

7. Purchases made on credit $_____

8. **Total expenses** $_____
   (Lines 4 through line 7)

9. **Total net income** $_____
   (Line 3 less Line 8)

The components of the profit and loss statement are self–explanatory. However, I would like to point out some important lines in this statement:

- *Money received from customers or owed by customers (line 1)*. This represents the total sales by your kids. It includes the amount of money collected by your kids in the relevant month as well as the amount of money for services or products sold on credit in the relevant month (i.e., accounts receivable for the month).

- *Refunds to customers (line 2)*. From time to time, your children's customers may want to get a refund for items they purchased. Because this results in a decrease in revenue for your kids, this refund must be subtracted from item 1 on the worksheet.

- *The cost of items sold (line 4)*. This is essentially the cost to make the product or offer the service. Earlier, I discussed how your kids are to come up with the per–unit cost of their products or services. Remember that they should include the overhead costs per unit in this number.

- *Wages to employees (line 5)*. If your kids hire other people to help them run their businesses, then they will have to recognize the labor expense for the period.

- *Purchases made on credit (line 7)*. If your kids make a small business purchase that they have not yet paid for, they should still recognize it as an expense for that month even if they will make the payment in a later month.

The profit and loss statement is for your children's information. Your kids should keep an eye on how much money they are making monthly to make sure that it meets the financial projections they made in their business plans. In addition, the profit and loss statement is important because it can be your children's working tools. Using the statement to compare performance with the previous month gives your kids some real guidelines to follow in managing the business. If they notice big changes in their net income, they will be prompted to go back to their records to look for factors that contributed to the change.

TIME SPENT ON RECORD KEEPING AND ORGANIZATION

If your kids do a little bit of record keeping every day, the task will not seem so formidable. When kids put off record keeping until a crisis occurs or until they have to show their monthly profit, it is too late to try to find old receipts.

Your young entrepreneur should get a folder to hold each of the forms shown in this chapter. Each time they fill out the forms, whether weekly or monthly, they ought to save them in the folders. There should be one folder to hold each of the following documents: sales receipts to customers, accounts receivable, profit and loss statements, sales records and sales receipts.

11

LEGAL AND TAX ISSUES

Starting a business takes more than coming up with a viable idea and a good business plan; it also takes an understanding of the legal requirements governing the establishment and operation of a business imposed by federal, state, county, and city governments. Once a child expresses serious interest in entrepreneurship, parents should ensure that the child becomes familiar with all necessary legal requirements (registration, licensing, taxation and, copyright, trademark and patent, if applicable) for starting and running a business. In addition, since this book focuses on youth entrepreneurship, an understanding of the laws and regulations that apply to the operation of a business in general, and by children in particular, is important.

A word of caution. This chapter is intended to serve as a basic guide to laws and regulations that a child should know before starting a business. It is not the definitive word on the laws that might apply to a child's business. Because state and local laws and regulations vary greatly, it is impossible to devise one set of guidelines that will apply to all the different types of businesses that young entrepreneurs can start.

While you may decide that it is your young entrepreneur's responsibility to fill out the forms required to operate a business, you should at least supervise her compliance with federal, state, and local regulations. In some instances, you may want to seek legal and financial counsel. In general, parents should review forms completed by their children in connection with starting or running their own businesses.

CHILD–SPECIFIC LAWS

Basically, children operating their own businesses are subject to the same federal, state, county, and city laws and regulations as adults. However, as minors, children must also be cognizant of state laws concerning their right to make contracts. In addition, parents must be aware of their rights to their children's income or services.

Children and the right to contract

In many states, children have a limited capacity to contract. Legally speaking, this means that when one of the parties to a contract is a minor, the contract is considered void *ab initio* or voidable. A contract which is void *ab initio* is invalid from its inception. In a voidable contract, the law permits one or both of the contracting parties to disaffirm or back out of the contract. In most states, a contract with a child is voidable.

For potential customers, voidable contracts at the election of minors conjure up fears of last–minute cancellations. Imagine someone contracting with a minor to cater a dinner and just as the guests walk through the door, the youngster calls and says, "I am a minor and I disaffirm our contract. Sorry, dinner's off." As a practical matter, if a child makes a habit of backing out of contracts, that child will find that no one will want to pay for his or her products or services. In addition, in most states, the child's right to back out of a contract is not without consequences. Aside from the obvious—the likelihood that the child will lose potential customers—many states, frown upon a child frivolously backing out of contracts. In some states the law does not allow a minor who voids a contract to enjoy the benefits of the contract. For example, if a youngster contracts with someone to make a dress and backs out of the contract after having received the fabric to make the dress, the fabric must be returned. In other states, if a minor makes a contract in the course of conducting her business, she cannot back out of the contract if it is a reasonable one.

If the law in your state is weighed in favor of children so heavily that it is unlikely that an adult would like to do business with them, you can be a party to the contract. However, although being a party to the contract will provide a great deal of comfort to hesitant customers, you will also be liable in the event that customers are dissatisfied with your child's service or product.

Realistically speaking, in most instances, children who run their own businesses are assisted by their parents so this fact alone should make their potential customers more comfortable.

Your right to their earnings

Most people know that parents are legally obligated to provide for their children's well–being. In other words, they must provide their children with basic necessities such as food, shelter, clothing, medical care, and education. What most people do not know is that parents have the right to the services and income of their children. This rule applies unless:

1. there is an express agreement between a parent and a child to the contrary; or

2. the circumstances show that there was an implied agreement between a parent and a child that the parent did not expect the right to the child's income; or

3. the child has reached his or her majority.

The right–to–income rule can be helpful in situations where parents want to ensure that their children are conducting their businesses ethically. For example, if you were to discover that your child is not conducting her business ethically and is short–changing customers, you can, in effect, garnish her income to reimburse her customers. Of course, if your young entrepreneur continuously engages in shady practices or produces shoddy products, much more drastic measures are required (see Chapter 14 on Business Ethics).

GETTING STARTED: LEGAL REQUIREMENTS

Obtaining a social security number

You cannot work for anyone else or have your own legitimate business without a social security number. Thus, if your son or daughter does not already have a social security number, it's time to get one. With an original or certified version of a birth certificate plus some other form of identification like a baptismal record, a social security number can be obtained from the Social Security Administration of the U.S. Department of Health and Human Services.

Registering the company

If your child does not intend to use her own name as the name of her business, she must register her company with the county clerk. If she does intend to use her own name as her company's name, it is recommended but not mandatory, that she register her business. This procedure is relatively painless because it takes very little time or money. The registration fee usually ranges from $5 to $30. The purpose of registration is to protect both customers and businesses by ensuring that the name of your child's business is not used by anyone else within the same county.

Business registrations *do* expire over a certain period of time (approximately 4 years or less). Therefore, they must be periodically renewed if the child is still operating the business past the original expiration period.

Obtaining a license

The procedure involved in obtaining a license, if indeed a license is even required, varies significantly from city to city and community to community. For example, according to the Licensing and Consumer Services Department in Minneapolis, Minnesota, children can obtain a license for those businesses that the city of Minneapolis has determined must be operated with a license. The exception to this rule: minors are prohibited from obtaining liquor licenses. In Newark, New Jersey, the procedure is very different. Before a minor can obtain a license to operate a business, she must obtain working papers or a working permit from the

Board of Education. Once she has obtained this permit and presented it to the appropriate authorities, she can obtain a license to operate those businesses that can be operated only with a license. In the District of Columbia, the requirements are stricter. There are approximately 128 different types of businesses that can be operated with a business license; a number of these cannot be operated by minors. Find out from your county official which businesses are off limits for minors and the requirements for business licenses.

Copyrights, trademarks and patents

It may be necessary for your young entrepreneur to apply for a patent, register a trademark or obtain copyright protection, depending on the type of business she runs.

A patent is a grant of a property right by the Government to the inventor "to exclude others from making, using or selling the invention." If a child invents a product and intends to sell the product, it is recommended that a patent application be filed so that the child, and not the purchaser of the invention, is recognized as the true inventor.

A trademark is either a word, phrase, symbol or design, (or combination of words, phrases, symbols or designs) which identifies and distinguishes the source of the goods or services of one party from those of others. A service mark is the same as a trademark except that it identifies and distinguishes the source of a service rather than a product. If a child wishes to identify her product or service, for example, with a logo or catchy phrase, it is recommended that the logo or phrase or other identifier gets registered as a trademark or service mark.

A copyright protects an original artistic or literary work. If a child writes a book and wishes to sell it to the public, it is recommended that the she apply for a copyright of the book.

Information with respect to patents, trademarks or service marks, including how to apply (or register) for them, can be obtained from the Patent and Trademark Office of the U.S. Department of Commerce at 703–557–4636. Information concerning copyrights, can be obtained from the Library of Congress at 202–707–3000.

Deciding the form of the company

One of the first things children should do when they want to start their own businesses is to decide the type of business structure they would like. Basically, they can choose from among three organizational structures: sole proprietorship, partnership, or corporation. Of the three, corporations are the most expensive and time consuming to operate. In addition, they are subject to numerous government regulations. For these reasons, I strongly recommend that children stay away from setting up corporations.

A sole proprietorship has only one owner–manager and has several advantages for the young entrepreneur who is eager to get her enterprise off the ground. It is typically the simplest and least expensive business structure to operate. In most instances, it requires only a social security number and possibly, a business registration and business license. Many children who start their own small businesses choose this form until it becomes practical to enter into partnerships or to be incorporated.

Since the sole proprietor is the only boss, she has absolute authority to manage her operations and can make quick decisions. In addition, a sole proprietorship offers tax advantages. Unlike corporations, which are taxed on their profits while the corporation's shareholders are taxed on dividends they receive, a sole proprietorship is not subject to double taxation.

The sole proprietorship does offer one major disadvantage, however. The sole proprietor is subject to unlimited personal liability. For example, if the product or service offered by a sole proprietor harms a customer, the customer can sue the sole proprietor and if he wins, can go after the sole proprietor's assets. This may mean that the sole proprietor can end up loosing her house, car, and other personal assets. However, with the exception of a child who has a significant amount of personal assets that creditors or dissatisfied customers may be able to go after, the disadvantages of a sole proprietorship are generally outweighed by its advantages.

Partnerships are another form of business organization available to the young entrepreneur. In a partnership two or more people agree to share ownership and, sometimes, management of a business. In a partnership, each partner can act on behalf of the firm to conduct the firm's business. Since there are more people responsible for running the business, all the work does not fall on any one person as is the case for a sole proprietorship.

A partnership is relatively easy to organize. Also, like a sole proprietorship, a partnership is not a taxable entity. The income is passed through to each of the partners who record individually their share of income, expenses, and losses.

Partnerships are the appropriate structure for children who do not possess the skills or resources to handle all the major aspects of their businesses on their own. In addition, some young entrepreneurs see partnerships as a good way to get equity capital for their businesses. For example, by taking on a partner, a young entrepreneur might require that the partner put up half the money for the venture.

Partnerships can also present certain problems. As in the case of the sole proprietorship, creditors of the partnership can go after the personal possessions of the general partners. In this situation, the partner with the most assets will lose the most. Also, the more partners in a partnership, the more bosses there are and, in turn, the longer it takes to get anything done and the greater the possibility of disputes.

In deciding whether to operate as a sole proprietorship or as a partnership, your children should think carefully about what potential partners could contribute to the businesses. They should consider the values, work ethic, and prior work experience of any potential partners. It is generally not a good idea for children to start businesses with friends unless the children are sure that their friends are really going contribute to the businesses.

If your children do decide to operate partnerships, make sure they draw up agreements that state the specific obligations of each partner. At a minimum, each partnership agreement should:

1. Stipulate the amount of start–up capital each partner will contribute.

2. Specify how the business will be managed.

3. Establish methods for handling differences and arbitrating disputes.

Employees

It is not recommended that young entrepreneurs hire employees when first starting their businesses. If their businesses grow and become modestly successful, however, it may be necessary to hire employees.

If a young entrepreneur *does* hire employees, depending upon the type of business involved, federal and state labor laws and regulations may be applicable to her business. In addition, if a young entrepreneur hires employees, even if it is only one person, they must obtain an employer identification number and a state unemployment tax number. Applications for employer identification numbers are obtained from the Internal Revenue Service (IRS). The appropriate form to request is form SS–4. Applications for state unemployment tax numbers can be obtained from the local office of your State Unemployment Commission.

Businesses that employ children must be conducted in accordance with federal and state child labor laws. Child labor laws do not apply to children who start their own businesses; they are exempt from such laws as self–employed entrepreneurs. However, if they employ children in their businesses, they must conform to the federal child labor laws—specifically, those provisions of the 1938 Fair Labor Standards Act and any legislation that their states have passed governing minors that work.

Most laws concerning working children were designed to prevent adults from exploiting children by having them work long hours, under horrendous conditions, and for little pay. If you can remember tales about children working in coal mines and meat packing operations years ago, you will understand the reason behind federal and state child labor laws.

In 1994, due to dramatic increases in child labor law violations, the Department of Labor stiffened the maximum fine for child labor law violations from a flat $10,000 to $10,000 for each violation leading to the serious injury or death of a child. Under the old standard, which had been previously increased in 1991 due to escalating child labor law violations, the fine could not exceed $10,000 regardless of the number of violations. In addition to increasing the penalty for child labor law violations, the

Department of Labor is considering revising the Department's existing child labor law regulations.

Here are some of the more important provisions of the federal child labor laws:

1. Children ages 16 and 17 can only work in non-hazardous occupations. They can work in these non–hazardous occupations for an unlimited number of hours. Roofing operations, work that entails exposure to radioactive substances, and logging and saw milling are considered hazardous occupations.

2. Teens 14 and 15 years of age may not work in hazardous jobs, nor may they work in other specified jobs such as manufacturing or mining. In addition, they may only work to three hours per day during a school week.

3. Children 11 and 12 years old are prohibited from working except in very limited instances, such as delivering newspapers or acting in television or commercials.

The easiest way to get information on child labor laws is by contacting the U.S. Department of Labor or your state Department of Labor.

Taxes

There are two misconceptions that parents have about taxes as they relate to their young entrepreneur's business. First, parents think that money a child makes from odd jobs is nontaxable. Second, parents worry that their budding entrepreneur can no longer be claimed as a dependent.

Many people believe that if a single dependent earns less than the standardized deduction ($3,800 for someone with a filing status of single on her 1994 tax return), they are automatically exempt from filing taxes. This is not always true because it depends on how the income is earned.

There are two situations which would require a child to file taxes with the IRS. First, the IRS will hastily inform you that any self–employed person who operates a small business must pay income taxes if her net income exceeds $400 per year. The IRS says "net" income because it allows expenses such as advertising, travel, and supplies to be subtracted from the total income received.

The IRS defines "self–employed" very loosely. In general, any type of income that is received by a person from someone other than that person's employer is considered self–employment income. The self–employment rule applies to children as well, except that the income they receive from taxable interest and dividends (unearned income) and income from their parents for doing chores is not subject to this rule. However, subject to these limited exceptions, any income a child receives from self–employment is subject to taxation if the net amount is greater than $400.

Not only is a child's income subject to tax if she satisfies the $400 net income threshold, but she must also file her own separate tax form. In other words, her parents cannot report her business earnings on their tax forms. Thus, if your child operates a small business and nets over $400 per year, the IRS requires payment of income taxes on that money. The proper forms to file are:

1. A 1040 tax return.

2. A Social Security Self–Employment Tax Form (Schedule SE).

3. A profit or loss from business form (Schedule C).

Schedule SE is for social security tax purposes and is one page long. For some reason, newspaper carriers under the age of 18 are exempt from filing this form.

There is a second condition under which a child will be required to file income tax returns. If a child's unearned income (taxable income and dividends) and earned income (self–employment income) exceeds $600, the child must file an income tax return. In this situation, income tax returns must be filed even if the child's net earned income is less than $400. Basically, this rule is important in situations where a child's total income (unearned and earned income) exceeds $600 and is received from interest or dividends over $200 with income from self–employment being less than $400.

As I mentioned earlier, parents also worry that they cannot claim their children as dependents if their children file their own tax returns. This is incorrect. Claiming a child as a dependent does not depend on whether that child files her own tax return.

To claim each of your children under age 19 as a dependent, you must satisfy the following requirements:

1. The dependent must be a member of the household or a child of the taxpayer.

2. The dependent must receive more than half of his or her support from the parent (this support test doesn't apply if the dependent is the child of divorced or separated parents or where there is a multiple support agreement).

3. The dependent must be a U.S. citizen, a U.S. national, or a resident of the U.S., Canada, or Mexico at some time during the calendar year.

It should be noted, however, that if parents claim their children as dependents on their tax forms, their children may not be able to take the standard deduction of $3,800 (1994 tax return) for single taxpayers when they file their own tax forms. As a dependent, a child can take only the standard deduction for dependents which is determined by completing the Standard Deduction Worksheet for Dependents included in the Instructions for Form 1040.

The IRS has a toll–free number you can call to get information (800–829–1040). If you have any questions about how your child entrepreneur's tax returns should be filled out, call the hot line. This is an excellent service to use to obtain up–to–date and accurate tax information.

Unfortunately, state, county, or city tax requirements are so varied, it is impossible to cover them in this book. However, it is important that the local authorities, such as the taxation division of the state treasury department are contacted to determine what tax obligations your child may be required to follow. Frequently, these departments have taxpayer information hot lines just like the IRS. Moreover, the Small Business Administration in your area is another useful place to start for information on local tax obligations.

In addition to inquiring about a child's tax obligations with the state and local authorities, it is important to ask about state and city sales taxes. Children that sell products or services directly to the public are subject to state or city sales tax and, in all likelihood, will be required to obtain sales tax permits. Once again, requirements vary from one area to another, but generally sales tax permits are required when selling products or services directly to consumers as opposed to selling products or services to stores. In many cases, when children sell to stores for resale, they are not required to obtain a tax permit, but they are required to apply for a wholesale exemption certificate in order to be excused from paying sales tax.

Zoning ordinances

Zoning ordinances determine the type of functions permitted in buildings and locations. Many people are surprised to learn that specific ordinances control how they utilize the space where they live and work. For example, many people rent out a spare bedroom in their house or convert their basement into an apartment without realizing that the zoning ordinance in their community may prohibit such activities.

A zoning ordinance may restrict your children's ability to advertise on your front lawn or to store supplies and equipment on your property. Some ordinances may even prohibit people from running businesses (or having employees) in the home. For this reason, it is important to check with the local zoning department to determine what businesses may be started in your home or at any other location.

As a practical matter, the subject of zoning will most likely be raised by your neighbors if they disapprove of, or are inconvenienced by, your children's activities. Neighbors are the ones who ordinarily contact the authorities when a zoning ordinance is violated. Therefore, it is important that your children consider, and try to minimize, any potential annoyances to your neighbors. For example, noxious odors emanating from your home or trucks barreling through the neighborhood at odd hours of the day will not be looked upon favorably by your neighbors and they will contact the authorities.

The thing to remember about zoning laws and indeed any of the legal obligations that apply to a child's businesses is that forewarned is forearmed. It is best for your young entrepreneur to know from the outset what can and cannot be done before investing a great deal of time and energy in establishing a particular business.

Insurance

When operating a business, children must guard against the following three types of potential liability problems:

1. Physical injury on the premises (someone slips on a banana peel that was dropped when your son was making banana bread for his bread business).

2. Product injury (your son's customer breaks his tooth on a walnut shell when biting into a piece of your son's banana bread).

3. Personal injury (your son is sued for false arrest after he mistakenly has a customer arrested for stealing his banana bread).

If you have homeowner's insurance (also called personal liability insurance, public liability insurance, or premises liability insurance), it is important to check with your insurance agent to see if your policy guards against physical, product, or personal injury arising from your child's business operations. The extent of coverage under homeowner's insurance depends entirely upon the specific provisions of your policy and the circumstances surrounding the accident or injury. Therefore, you want to ask your insurance agent questions about the extent of the coverage and any exclusions under your policy.

Insurance contracts frequently contain exception clauses that specify who is not covered by the policy and what types of injuries are not insured. Read these clauses carefully and discuss them with your insurance agent. For example, make sure that your policy protects all members or residents of your household or family. You would probably be surprised to learn that some policies contain specific exception clauses that exclude injury to children from coverage.

A number of homeowner's insurance policies contain an exception clause commonly known as a "business pursuit" clause. This clause generally states that the policy does not cover an injury that results from any business pursuits of the insured, other than activities that are ordinarily incident to non–business pursuits. This is a fancy way of saying that if someone is injured on your property as a result of a business being conducted on your property, your homeowner's policy will not cover the injury.

The business pursuit clause is intended to apply to those activities that you, or any other insured person under your policy, do on a continuous or customary basis for profit. A continuous business pursuit is an activity that is done five days a week. A customary business pursuit might be an annual bazaar that you hold every year to raise money.

There is one narrow exception to the business pursuits exclusion. If you can show that the person's injury is of the type which normally occurs on a homeowner's property outside of business, the policy may apply. The only problem is that courts do not consistently apply this exception. For example, in one case a grandmother was baby–sitting her granddaughter for free and another couple's child for pay. The other couple's child was injured. The insurance company claimed the grandmother's policy did not cover the injury because of a business pursuits clause. The court said that since grandma was also baby–sitting her granddaughter free of charge and the injury was the type of injury that could happen in a non–business setting, the insurance company had to cover the injury. Unfortunately, courts have made the opposite ruling in similar situations. Thus, as you can see, courts have a hard time figuring out what injuries are incidental to non–business operations.

If your policy contains a business pursuits clause, talk to your insurance agent about a new policy. If you are lucky enough not to have a business pursuits clause, talk to your insurance agent anyway and explain what type of business your child will be operating. Make sure that your policy will cover the possibility of injury that may result.

Insurance is a protective measure to guard against risk. It is one of those things that you hope you never have to use but if you do, you're glad that you have it. Make sure that in the event of a mishap in connection with the operation of your child's businesses, both you and your child are adequately insured.

12

COMMON MISTAKES MADE BY
YOUNG ENTREPRENEURS

Even though some child entrepreneurs show enormous amounts of creativity and sensibility in starting and running their own businesses, many others make fatal business mistakes that are easily avoidable. Here are some guidelines about the type of mistakes to watch out for when your kids start their own businesses.

NEGLECTING TO INCLUDE ALL COSTS

I was once advising a 16–year–old boy on how to run his baseball card business. Every two months, he would make a one–hour bus trip to Chicago to buy more cards for his business. When I asked him to calculate how much money it cost him to make this trip into the city, he came up with a figure of $10. When I asked him to include the cost of his meals and miscellaneous expenses during his trip, he increased his expense figure to $24. When I told him that he should include these expenses in pricing his cards, he protested. "I enjoy going into the city to buy new cards. I don't see why I should charge my customers for this trip." When I asked him whether he would go into Chicago as frequently if he didn't have a baseball card business, he said no. When I asked him whether he subtracted any of his travel expenses when calculating his net profit, he said no. I then said to him, "You are not making as much money in this business as you think you are."

This young entrepreneur's problem was simply that he did not consider all of his true expenses when figuring out the cost of each of his cards. Many kids with their own businesses make the same mistake. They forget that small expenses add up to big numbers and therefore should be included in the cost of their products of services.

Some kids are also not aware that they should include the cost of their equipment in making their products or offering their services. Take a typical teenage business such as lawn mowing, for example. Many kids who start lawn mowing businesses use their family's lawn mower. As with all other mechanical equipment, the more a lawn mower is used, the more likely it is to require servicing. If the youngsters mowing the lawns neglect to include the cost of periodic servicing of the mowers, then they are overestimating the profit figures in their businesses.

One way to guard against underestimation of expenses is to charge your kids for using your assets in their businesses. If they borrow your lawn mower for business purposes, charge them for it. If they use your paint or your paintbrushes to start their house painting business, charge them. Just keep in mind that these extra charges are designed to do one thing: to sensitize your kids to the fact that they should include all expenses (no matter how incidental) when setting their prices or when calculating their profits. The proper calculation of expenses can make the difference between whether your children decide to start their businesses or not.

Another effective way to make your kids aware of all of their expenses is to have them write down the process they will go through to make their products or offer their services. Every single activity that is taken as a result of the business should be included. For example, the young baseball card entrepreneur who traveled to Chicago every two months should include his bus fare, his transportation costs once he gets into Chicago, his meals while on the business trip, entrance fees to baseball card conventions, and other incidental costs.

CONSIDERING ALL MONEYS FROM CUSTOMERS AS PROFIT

Common sense tells adult entrepreneurs that revenue, the money collected from customers, is made up of two components: profit and expenses. They know that to calculate their profits they have to subtract all their expenses from their revenues. Some young entrepreneurs, however, spend or pocket all of the money they receive from their businesses. They forget some expenses for which they have not yet received payment. For example, one 13–year–old entrepreneur borrowed $200 from her parents to start a neighborhood T–shirt business. She made 50 T–shirts and charged $10 for each shirt. This young business owner collected $500 for her T–shirts over a period of two months from her customers. By the time her parents started asking for their $200 back, the girl had already spent $400 of the money she collected from her customers. Needless to say, the parents were able to collect only $100 of the $200 they were owed. This young entrepreneur was not trying to cheat her parents. What happened was that each time she sold some T–shirts, she used the money to buy clothes, magazines, and candy. Before she realized how much she had spent in the two–month period, it was too late. She had spent all but $100 of the money she had collected. Even if this young entrepreneur had used her own savings instead of borrowing $200 from her parents, she still should have replaced the money. In other words, the amount of money in her savings account should have been bigger by the time she finished her business.

One way to help your children understand that revenue is not equal to profit is to encourage them to set up a schedule of how they are to pay back all the debts they have incurred to start their businesses. By debt, I am not just talking about money they have borrowed, but also money they have taken from their own accounts. For each product they make or each service they render, they should put aside a portion of the money they get to repay the debt. If they have borrowed money from you, you should ask for partial payment of the loan periodically. If the money comes from their savings, you should advise them to periodically replace a specified amount of cash.

To avoid frivolous spending, your kids should open an account for their businesses. Even if they already have a savings account, they should open another one for all the money they get from their customers. As soon as they accumulate a specified amount of cash, they should immediately deposit it into their business account. This will help them separate business money from personal money.

MILKING THEIR BUSINESSES

During my business–school days, the term cash cow was used to designate a business that provided its owners with a steady stream of profit with little or no reinvestment. Young entrepreneurs sometimes consider their businesses to be cash cows. They think that their businesses will continue making money even if they do not reinvest some of their profits back into the businesses. This type of short–sighted thinking will doom any business.

One high school entrepreneur wanted to start a typing service. He wanted eventually to buy a word processor because it would make it much easier for him to edit his work. Because he didn't have enough money to buy a word processor, he decided to use his family's typewriter until he could save enough money from his profits to buy one. As his business grew, he was making $50 per week. Unfortunately, he never put any money away for the word processor. As it turned out, he got so much business that he began returning papers late to his customers with lots of errors. Eventually, he started losing his customers. Had he saved some of his profits for a word processor, he probably would have saved a lot of time with each document he typed, and he would have been better able to turn in error–free copies using the built–in spelling checker.

When your kids start their own businesses, you should encourage them to think ahead about how to improve their productivity in the future. In the beginning they may not be able to afford all the equipment they need to make their products faster or deliver their services more efficiently. But as their businesses grow, they should put some money away to improve their products or services. One entrepreneur who used to paint houses with ordinary brushes reinvested money in his business by buying a power paint sprayer. He cut the time for painting a house by 30%. Your kids can always find a way to improve the efficiency of their businesses. It may mean that they forfeit using their profits for now. But, in the long run, reinvesting their profits will make their businesses run more smoothly and help them look more professional.

TAKING ON BUSINESSES THEY CANNOT HANDLE

One of the qualities I admire in all young entrepreneurs is that they are optimists. They all feel they can make their businesses work. Unfortunately, optimism is not good enough when it comes time to realistically figure out the steps to take to actually operate their businesses. Coming up with a business idea is just a start. The efficiency of day–to–day operations is probably a more important determinant of the success or failure of a business. Efficiency is determined by the ability of the young entrepreneur to handle the business. Here are some of the things you have to think about when your kids decide to hang out their shingles.

FAILING TO CONSIDER THEIR PHYSICAL ABILITIES AND MATURITY

Some kids decide to start businesses that they cannot possibly handle because of their age and physical abilities. I know one 17–year–old boy who wanted to start a moving business because he had access to a big van. When I first heard about it, I thought that maybe he wanted to be the broker who found movers for families. On the contrary, this 98–pound weakling actually wanted to lug furniture around. I discouraged him because I felt that he would hurt his back, get a hernia, or worse.

Even if this kid had been strong, I would not have recommended that he start a business that needed a lot of strength. For one thing, he could have gotten hurt. Entrepreneurs who have businesses that last are usually the managers of people who do the physical work. If this young entrepreneur had decided to be the contractor to find movers for families, I would have supported him.

The age of your children should also determine the type of business you should allow them to start. I am sad to say that, yes, there are crazy people out there who will molest children. For this reason, your kids should be mature enough to understand when someone is trying to take advantage of them. Obviously, I expect you to investigate the customers your children may attract. I know of one case in which a high school student got so interested in Japanese massage that he opened up his own massage business. Even though this kid was genuinely interested in massage, he was not aware that sometimes this art form provides cover for prostitution rings. Although most of his customers really wanted a good Japanese massage, some wanted something more. This is just an extreme example of why it is important to know your children's potential customers. If your children are not mature enough to recognize morally questionable behavior by their customers, restrict their entrepreneurial ventures to businesses you think they can handle.

The maturity of your children is also important because it can determine how they deal with customers. An overwhelming number of your children's customers will be honest people. But your kids will inevitably run into people who will take advantage of them. One young entrepreneur I was advising told me that he had one customer who would never pay him on time for clearing his driveway of snow. This young kid was afraid to demand his money on time because he was intimidated by the customer. When I asked him why he continued to remove snow from the man's driveway, he told me that he was afraid not to do it. To you and me, this does not sound logical. But this made perfect sense to the boy. A more mature child would probably tell his parents and immediately stop servicing the customer.

TAKING ON TOO MUCH BUSINESS

Some kids take on too many customers. They first figure out how much money they want to make, and then calculate how many customers they will need to meet their goal. If they are lucky enough to get as many customers as they want, they may find that they created another problem: there aren't enough hours in the day to make the product or deliver the service. One high school entrepreneur started his own desktop publishing business. He bought some expensive computer equipment and started looking for writers who wanted to get published. He took on two writers and then the nightmare began. All of the administrative work he needed to do in order to publish the books was his undoing. First, he started skipping school to work on his business. Then he started staying up until 2 a.m. Finally, he closed his business. This young entrepreneur's problem was twofold. First, he did not thoroughly investigate all the steps he had to take to become a legitimate publisher. He found out the hard way that producing a book requires more than just good writers. It requires that the publishers edit the work and perform all other administrative services such as copyrighting the book and preparing to have it carried by national distributors. This young entrepreneur's second problem was that he took on more than one writer at a time. He should have gotten his feet wet in the business with one customer before acquiring more. When I asked this kid about his blunder he said, "I really didn't know how much work it took to publish a book. I figured that with a computer and a good printer I could easily start my own desktop publishing business."

One of the more serious problems kids face when they take on too much business is that they start pushing school down on their priority list. If your kids get so much business that it starts interfering with school or other important activities, you should pull the plug on their businesses unless they can reduce the amount of time they spend on it. Always keep in mind that a good education is still the best way to guarantee that your kids will lead a successful entrepreneurial life.

There are several ways your kids can reduce the amount of time it takes to run their businesses. For one thing, if they have too many customers, one obvious remedy is to increase their prices. This action typically lowers demand for a product or service. They should increase their prices enough so that they have the number of customers they can comfortably handle.

Another way your kids can decrease the amount of time it takes to run their businesses is to increase their productivity. As I discussed earlier, they can do this by buying equipment that can eliminate unnecessary work. For example, in a typing business, a word processor is infinitely better than an ordinary typewriter because it is easier to edit and information can be stored in memory.

Productivity can be increased also by better production scheduling and better time management. Production scheduling is simply the smooth scheduling of jobs in a sensible sequence. For example, one young entrepreneur who gives computer lessons in his city, schedules as many customers as possible in one area. "I try to set up the lessons so that when I am done visiting one customer, my next customer is a few streets away" he declared. "This way, I don't have to waste time zigzagging across town to get to my customers." Time management is simply the efficient use of time in accomplishing a goal. With the proper management of their time, your kids will be able to deliver on the goods and services they are offering. For example, one young entrepreneur with a cookie business wakes up at 6:00 a.m. on Saturdays to begin baking his cookies for his bakery business. During the week, he prepares dough for one hour when he comes back from school each day and refrigerates it. "I try not to waste time when I get back from school," he says. "Instead of watching music videos when I get home, I prepare my dough for baking my cookies on Saturday." Your kids, too, may find that they can squeeze small amounts of time from their day to prepare for their businesses.

Finally, if your children's businesses are eating up too much of their time, they should consider hiring other people. That's right—they should become employers. There may be other young people around who have the skills your kids need to help them in their businesses. Because your kids will have to pay these employees, they must consider adjusting their prices to reflect this increased expense level.

The employees your kids hire can do some of the more labor intensive work. Fourteen–year–old Susan Dunn of Atlanta, Georgia, had a business in which she folded letters and stuffed envelopes for local print shops. She charged about $100 for folding and stuffing 1,000 three–page documents into envelopes. Because it was taking her over seven hours to do this job, she decided to hire one of her friends for five dollars an hour. It now takes both her and her friend less than four hours to complete the job. She pays her friend $20 and pockets the rest.

When your kids look for other kids to help them in their businesses, they should first make a list of the qualities they require in an employee. Perhaps your kids require someone who is good in math, someone who is physically strong, or even someone who has a nice voice. Your kids have to decide on the skills and qualities that are important to them. A word of caution: hiring friends is fine but your kids should make sure that their friends can carry their own weight. Needless to say, no matter who they hire, their employees should be responsible. If your children's friends are not responsible, encourage your kids to find someone else that can help them run their businesses. Suggest that they look for other kids in their school with similar interests. One young entrepreneur who had a design business found someone in his school's art class to help him draw designs on clothing.

DEPENDING ON FAMILY AND FRIENDS ALONE TO BE THEIR CUSTOMERS

Kids considering starting their own businesses often think that their families and friends are the only customers they need to make their businesses viable. I jokingly tell these potential entrepreneurs that their family and friends can't possibly provide them with enough people to sell to unless everyone in their town is either related to them or is a friend.

It is easy to see how kids can operate under such illusions. Their reasoning goes like this :

1. My family will buy my product or service because they know me very well and they will want to help me out.

2. My friends will also buy my product or service to help me out.

True, friends and family may patronize your children's businesses once because they want to help out. But for sustained patronage, kids have to offer quality products or services that people truly need—particularly if the products or services are expensive. Even if family and friends need the products or services, they may not provide your kids with a big enough customer base to ensure the survival of the businesses.

As a parent, you may be tempted to buy your children's products or services. But as one parent discovered, resisting the temptation to rush to your children's assistance eventually pays off. This parent told me that when his daughter started selling candy around the neighborhood, he wanted to buy up a whole box to give her a boost.

When she first started selling the candy, business was so slow that I wanted to buy 20 bars from her. It's a good thing I didn't because she eventually developed a clever sales pitch and began selling 20 bars each weekend. Before that, she was selling less than 10 bars every weekend. If I had bought lots of candy from her, she wouldn't have used her creative energy to come up with a good sales pitch.

This example illustrates why being your children's best customer is not necessarily in their best interest. Part of the entrepreneurial process is to allow children to let the market dictate the survival of their businesses. Handouts from you may help in the short run. However, handouts just delay the inevitable. Eventually the business will fail if no other customers want the products or services.

Parents who become their children's best customers are also more tolerant than others of shoddy products or services. If you do decide to patronize your children's businesses, do it because you genuinely want the product or service. You should demand the same level of excellence you expect from other business people.

USING THE PRODUCTS OF THE BUSINESS

A few years ago, I was teaching a Junior Achievement class called Applied Economics in a New York City high school. In this class, I was supposed to help the kids understand the business principles behind running a business. The class collectively decided to start a business selling big vials of Tootsie Roll candy for $2 each. Each of the vials was to be filled with pieces of Tootsie Rolls. The class had 500 vials to fill but by the time the kids had finished filling the vials with the available candy, we ended up with only 450 vials. Some of these kids had been eating more candy than they were stuffing into the vials!

This example shows how kids can use up the assets that belong to their businesses. There is really only one way to help your kids avoid this problem. You should encourage them to keep good records. If they maintain good records, losses they incur by using their products or services will become more apparent. For example, in the case of the Tootsie Rolls, the 50 missing vials of candy represented a loss of $100 because we were to sell each of the vials for $2. This figure represents the cost to the class of consuming the candy instead of selling it. When kids start viewing their products in this way, they will be sensitized to the fact that they actually cheat themselves when they consume items that should go toward running their businesses.

LACK OF COMMITMENT TO THE BUSINESS

Some child entrepreneurs start their businesses expecting immediate profits. When the profits aren't forthcoming they quickly lose faith in their businesses. Young entrepreneurs have to be patient enough to try out their business ideas for a specified period. In that period, they should try their best to make their businesses work. Once impatience sets in, they start making irrational decisions.

LACK OF PUNCTUALITY, DEPENDABILITY, AND A PROFESSIONAL IMAGE

Kids who start their own businesses often don't know the importance of winning the trust of potential customers. Many adults are already skeptical about buying products or services from young entrepreneurs. When the entrepreneur compounds the problem by arriving late or not arriving at all, these customers rarely give them a second chance. Kids that are serious about their businesses make an extra effort to prove to their customers that they can be as punctual and as dependable as adult entrepreneurs.

Here are some things your kids can do to earn the trust of their customers:

1. If they can afford it, your kids should get business cards and stationery with the company name and a description of their businesses on them. This shows the customers that they are serious about their businesses.

2. Your kids should dress neatly when in contact with potential customers. A neatly dressed young entrepreneur sends the message that he cares about the way he looks and, hence, is likely to care about the quality of his work.

3. Your kids should be prompt when they show up to do the job or give customers an estimate of what it will cost to provide the service. Nothing irritates customers more than waiting for someone to arrive.

4. Your kids should go out of their way to be courteous to potential customers when soliciting their business.

5. Your kids should offer guarantees on every product they sell or every service they provide. A guarantee tells the potential customers that young entrepreneurs have enough confidence in their business to guarantee the quality of their product or services.

POOR TIME MANAGEMENT

Young people who want to start their own businesses have to become good time managers. They have to manage school and homework, recreation, the responsibilities of family life, and their businesses.

As a parent, you are responsible for making sure that your kids do not push school down on their priority list. One way you can do this is to help them establish a schedule for when they can work on their businesses.

I know parents who justifiably stopped their kids from running their businesses except on weekends because their kids were not spending enough time on their studies.

13

BUSINESS CONCEPTS YOUR
KIDS SHOULD KNOW

There are some basic business concepts that your kids should be familiar with. In some cases, your kids will pick up these concepts without even realizing it. For example, supply and demand will be abundantly clear to your young entrepreneurs if they are supplying products or services no one wants to buy at the prices they have set. Other concepts, however, are more subtle.

Some educators claim that some business concepts are too difficult to teach to kids. In fact, the educators seem to go out of their way to make these concepts so difficult that everyone is lost. But organizations that advocate economic and entrepreneurial literacy for kids have proved that young people can in fact pick up basic business concepts without much trouble.

In this chapter, I will try to outline the fundamental concepts you should be teaching your kids. I realize that you yourselves may not be familiar with these concepts, so I will explain them to you in very simple terms so that you can easily broach the topics with your kids.

My recommendation is that you point out these principles to your kids as they are running their businesses or as current events in the financial world unfold. For example, if interest rates are going up, you can relate inflation to interest rates. However, as you talk to your kids about these concepts, it is imperative that you keep it simple and fun. The quickest way to turn kids off is to act as if you are giving them a lesson.

SUPPLY AND DEMAND

The best way to describe the dynamics of supply and demand is to go through an example of a lemonade stand operation.

Let's say that a young entrepreneur sets up a lemonade stand in front of her house during the summer. One day she displays five cups filled with cold lemonade on her stand and prices them at 50¢ each. She sells all of the lemonade she displays and has to go inside to make more. She makes a second batch and it ,too, goes in twenty minutes. She thinks to herself, "If these people want my lemonade so much, maybe I can raise my price and make more money." She makes another batch and increases her price to 75¢ per cup. This batch goes in 25 minutes. She makes a fourth batch and increases her price to $1 per cup. At this price, only two customers buy lemonade in the same period of time. She then reduces the price to 75¢ and sells all of the drinks on her stand.

Believe it or not, this simple example illustrates supply and demand. At the price of 50¢ per cup, the demand exceeded the supply and, hence, your daughter sold all of her lemonade. At the price of $1.00 per cup, the supply of lemonade exceeded the demand so she had to lower her price. At the price of 75¢ per cup, supply met demand and, therefore, the lemonade sold at a steady pace. The lesson here is that there is a price at which people will pay for the products or services so that there is neither an excess nor a shortage of the products or services.

THE TIME VALUE OF MONEY

The time value of money is the most basic concept in financial analysis. The application of this concept is what determines your monthly mortgage, car loan, or installment loan payments.

The only thing kids have to understand is that a dollar received today is worth more than a dollar received one month from now because the dollar received now can start earning interest immediately.

A youngster less than 9 years old will probably have a hard time understanding the time value of money because at this age, she may not have quite mastered the concept of time (see Chapter 3). From age 9 on, in the later stages of the concrete Operational stage as outlined by Piaget, kids are capable of understanding that a dollar received today is worth more than a dollar received tomorrow. To explain the time value of money, I will use an example to illustrate how time can affect the growth of money.

Suppose someone told you that you can have $100,000 today or you can have $105,000 a year from now (assuming you have no immediate need for the money). Which would you prefer?

You cannot really answer this question until I supply you with one more piece of information: the current savings rate paid by banks. Assume you can put any money you earn in a savings account paying you 10% each year. Now you can easily answer my question.

For those of you who would rather have the $105,000 one year from now, you have cheated yourself of $5,000. If you collect $100,000 today, you can put it in a savings account and earn 10%, or $10,000, on that money. By year's end, you would have $110,000.

If I told you that you can have $100,000 today or $110,000 one year from now, you would be indifferent because the extra $10,000 I would give you one year from now exactly equals the amount of money you can earn by investing $100,000 for one year.

When your kids are running their own businesses, you can apply the principle of the time value of money to credit terms they give their customers. For example, if your kids receive payment from the customer 60 days after selling them the product or service, you should let them know that they have effectively lost interest on that money because they cannot invest it until they get cash from the customer.

RETURN ON INVESTMENT

Return on investment (ROI) tells business persons the rate of return they earn on their investment. It can help entrepreneurs figure out whether they are better off putting their money in alternative investments such as CDs, stocks, bonds, or yes, even savings accounts.

Once again, I will illustrate ROI using an actual business. Let's suppose your daughter buys 50 plain white T–shirts for $3.00 each. She takes them to a printer who charges her $3.00 apiece to apply a design. Your daughter then sells her T–shirts for $12 each. What is her rate of return on the T–shirts? If she has no other expenses attached to the T–shirts, her rate of return is 100% simply because she invested $6 in each shirt and made $6 profit on each of them.

Now suppose your daughter decides to use better quality T–shirts that cost $5 to purchase and $7 to print for a total production cost of $12. Also suppose that because of market conditions, she can sell the T–shirts for $20. In this case, the rate of return on this use of her money is 66.7%.

Familiarity with ROI can help your daughter see that it is better for her not to invest the extra money in the better quality T–shirts because her rate of return is lower. ROI is perfect for evaluating alternatives when the only consideration is money.

Mathematically, ROI is calculated the following way:

$$[(Revenue/Costs) - 1] \times 100 = \% \ ROI$$

INTEREST CALCULATION AND COMPOUNDING

If your kids are like other young people, they are probably fascinated that the money they deposit in bank accounts actually grows. To help your kids understand interest calculations and compounding, you can help them open up their own passbook savings accounts. Show them how the bank calculates interest and compounding. If you are not sure how it is done, here is a quick lesson.

Suppose you have $1,000 in the bank that earns 10% simple interest per year (or 0.833% per month). Here is how your money stacks up each month for 12 months:

	Monthly Interest	Principal Balance	Interest Earned on Principal
1.	0.833%	$1,000.00	$8.33
2.	0.833%	$1,000.00	$8.33
3.	0.833%	$1,000.00	$8.33
4.	0.833%	$1,000.00	$8.33
5.	0.833%	$1,000.00	$8.33
6.	0.833%	$1,000.00	$8.33
7.	0.833%	$1,000.00	$8.33
8.	0.833%	$1,000.00	$8.33
9.	0.833%	$1,000.00	$8.33
10.	0.833%	$1,000.00	$8.33
11.	0.833%	$1,000.00	$8.33
12.	0.833%	$1,000.00	$8.33
			$99.96

As you can see, the total amount of interest earned is nearly $100. We calculated this amount by applying the monthly interest of 0.833% to the principal outstanding each month. Of course, you will get back your initial principal balance of $1,000 to make the total cash you will receive at the end of one year almost $1,100.

If the bank tells you that you will earn 10% on your money and that the interest will be compounded monthly, you will have more money than in the simple interest situation. Once again, on a monthly basis, you will be earning 0.833%. Here is how your money stacks up each month:

	Monthly Interest	Principal Balance	Interest Earned on Principal
1.	0.833%	$1,000.00	$8.33
2.	0.833%	$1,008.33	$8.40
3.	0.833%	$1,016.73	$8.47
4.	0.833%	$1,025.20	$8.54
5.	0.833%	$1,033.74	$8.61

6.	0.833%	$1,042.35	$8.69
7.	0.833%	$1,051.04	$8.76
8.	0.833%	$1,059.80	$8.83
9.	0.833%	$1,068.63	$8.90
10.	0.833%	$1,077.53	$8.98
11.	0.833%	$1,086.51	$9.05
12.	0.833%	$1,095.56	$9.13
			$104.69

As you can see, with monthly compounding, the interest earned in one year will be $104.69. Adding your initial principal balance, you will receive $1,104.69 at the end of one year. Unlike the simple interest calculation, the monthly interest rate of 0.833% is applied to both initial principal and the interest earned up to that point.

If you want to find out how much money you will have with daily compounding, you can apply the daily interest rate, 10%/365 to the daily outstanding balance (making sure that you apply the rate to the cumulative interest amount as well as the initial principal).

If your kids are 12 years old or older, you can give them the following formula to calculate interest earned regardless of the compounding period:

$$[(1 + R/C) \char`^C - 1] \times 100 = \% \text{ Interest}$$

where R = interest rate in decimal form (i.e., 0.10 for 10%)

C = the compounding period in a year (i.e., 12 compounding periods for monthly com–pounding, 365 compounding periods for daily compounding)

STOCKS AND BONDS

Stocks are essentially shares of a company. Anyone who has the rights to the profits of a company is a stockholder. He or she risks capital in hopes of getting a reasonable return. Of course, there are no guarantees that these investors will make any money or that they will get the principal amount they invested back. If a company goes bankrupt, the stockholders are the ones who lose their investments.

Your kids should be aware that they are the sole stockholders of the businesses they start unless they have partners, in which case their partners are also stockholders of their companies.

Bonds are, of course, loans to businesses. Bondholders typically get interest payments every six months from the companies to whom they lend money. In the event of business failures, the bondholders usually get their money back before stockholders.

If your kids borrow money from you for their businesses, make sure they are aware that you are in fact their company's bondholder and that if they go out of business, they must pay you first.

INFLATION

Inflation is the phenomenon of general price increases. As inflation increases, the amount of goods a person can buy with each dollar decreases.

There are several types of inflation:

1. Inflation caused by an increase in the demand for a product. For example, in an extraordinarily cold winter, heating oil will be in demand, and this may cause a temporary inflation in the price of oil.

2. Inflation caused by companies raising prices in response to increased production costs. For example, car prices went up slightly when automobile companies included air bags in cars.

3. Inflation caused by planned shortages. For example, in the early 1970s and 1980s, boycotts of the Organization

of Petroleum Exporting Countries increased the price of oil.

4. Inflation caused by fear of shortages. For example, at the beginning of the Gulf Crisis, fear of oil shortages drove spot oil prices upward. By the end of the crisis, there was actually a world oil glut, and this indicated that fear of oil shortages may have been unfounded.

You can point out inflation to your kids by comparing prices of items you used to buy when you were their ages with the costs of those items now. For example, a movie ticket may have cost you $1.00 when you were a child. A movie ticket in your neighborhood today probably costs between five and seven times that much.

If you have the opportunity to discuss inflation with your kids, try to relate it to interest rates. Make them aware of the fact that inflation affects the interest you pay on secured loans such as long–term mortgages or even on credit card debt.

If your kids have their own businesses, knowledge of inflation will make them cognizant of increases in the costs of the products or services they are offering their customers. Naturally, when the costs of these products or services increase, they should adjust their prices accordingly.

BREAK–EVEN ANALYSIS

I discussed this topic thoroughly in Chapter 9. The break–even concept can tell a business owner the minimum number of units he or she needs to sell to break even or to make a specified amount of money. It is a tool that can also be used to price products or services (although I think it should not be used for pricing).

OPPORTUNITY COST

Opportunity cost is the value of what one forgoes to choose some other action. To use a very simple example, let's suppose your son decides to go to the movies with his friends instead of mowing the neighbor's lawn for $15. In this case, the opportunity cost to your son for going to the movies is $15 because that is what he would have made had he stayed home to mow the neighbor's lawn.

When your kids understand the concept behind opportunity cost, your kids can make a decision based upon the desirability of taking one action over another. When your son decided to go to the movies instead of mowing the neighbor's lawn, he obviously reasoned that the pleasure he would get from going to the movies outweighed the $15 he would collect for mowing the lawn. This case was clear cut. However, suppose the neighbor offered $20, $30, or $40? He may very well have decided to mow the lawn.

In the business world, entrepreneurs have to constantly make choices in their businesses. Knowing the opportunity cost of each decision will help the entrepreneur decide whether the choice was really worth it.

14

TEACHING YOUR KIDS
BUSINESS ETHICS

By the time he was 16 years old, Barry Minkow had already started his own carpet–cleaning business, ZZZZ Best. By age 18, he was a flashy Ferrari–driving millionaire living in a big house in California's San Fernando Valley. By his twenty–third birthday, he was serving a 25–year sentence in a federal prison for 57 counts of fraud and conspiracy for billing insurance customers for bogus carpet restoration work. Barry was released from prison in 1995.

Barry seemed to embody the worst of the 1980s. He was arrogant, flashy, greedy and unscrupulous. Minkow started out his business like any other young entrepreneur. But when he found financing hard to secure for his overly ambitious business goals, he turned to loan sharks. He also fraudulently overcharged his credit–card customers for work he never did.

The most incredible part of the Barry Minkow story is that he even managed to hoodwink jaded Wall Street investment bankers. By the time he was caught in 1987, Barry had swindled $100 million from investors and had used a good portion of this money to finance his lifestyle.

I tell this story because I think you should be aware of what can happen when ambition goes haywire. In addition, I want to point out to you that young entrepreneurs are also susceptible to the lure of the good life just like those Wall Street tycoons that were falling like flies in the 1980s and early 1990s. Yes, indeed, kids can be crooked, too. However, I also believe that kids can be taught business ethics at an early age before problems manifest themselves.

When I first started to write this book, I was concerned about how parents can teach their kids business ethics. As I did more research, it became obvious to me that ethics in business cannot be separated from ethics in life. That is, if people have been brought up with warped moral values, these values will carry through to other parts of their lives, whether they be entrepreneurs or professionals. I discovered that one of the keys to teaching kids about business ethics is to show them how to apply the values they have learned at home to their entrepreneurial ventures.

BUSINESS ETHICS—THE EARLIER THE BETTER

Webster's dictionary defines ethics as "a set of moral principles or values." Business ethics is simply the same belief system transferred to an enterprise.

Years ago, when I was still at the University of Pennsylvania's Wharton School of Business, it was suggested that all MBAs be required to take an ethics class before graduating. At the time, the average age of MBA candidates was about 27, and I felt that it was probably too late to teach them business ethics. If they hadn't already acquired a sense of right and wrong, they wouldn't get it at graduate school. Just about all that can be done for adults is to alert them to the fact that unethical behavior in business can land them in jail. However, with kids, business ethics taught in conjunction with moral values can indeed help them lead ethically sound entrepreneurial lives.

The moral values you have been teaching your kids should carry through all aspects of their lives—even their business ventures. However, as all parents know, kids sometimes stray from what they know to be morally correct behavior. When they stray at home, you can easily get them back in line by talking to them, reprimanding them, or by meting out the appropriate punishment. However, when they are running their own businesses, you may never find out if they have engaged in behavior that is counter to what you have tried to teach them all of their lives. Fortunately, there are steps you can take to further encourage ethical behavior while they run their businesses.

STEPS YOU CAN TAKE TO TEACH YOUR KIDS BUSINESS ETHICS

Sensitizing them to ethical behavior

Your kids should know that the moral values you try to instill in them are applicable in both social and business environments. If they decide to start their own business, you should make it clear that you expect them to uphold these moral standards and values in their new enterprise.

In an overwhelming majority of cases, kids know when they are engaging in wrongful behavior. But occasionally, they may do something unethical without realizing it. For example, a friend of mine has a daughter, Susan, who works at a doughnut shop at the local mall. Occasionally, Susan's friends would visit her at the shop and Susan gave them free doughnuts. When Susan's mother found out that her daughter was passing out free doughnuts, she firmly reprimanded her and told her that her actions were akin to stealing from her employer. Susan hadn't considered that she was doing anything wrong until her mother talked to her. True, she knew that her manager wouldn't have liked the fact that she was passing out free food, but somehow she felt that because she was working in a business establishment she was not really stealing.

Susan's attitude is quite common among young people. Parents should force their kids to examine their behavior in the context of established moral values and principles. However, in trying to sensitize your kids to ethical business practices, you may have to change your own behavior. There may be things you do that break your own established moral principles. Take for example, a parent who gives his kids notebook paper from work. In a sense, this parent has stolen paper from his employer for his kids just like Susan stole the doughnuts from her employer for her friends.

Letting them know that running a business is hard work

Some young entrepreneurs think that the minute they hang out their shingles, the money will start flowing in their direction with little effort. Your kids should be aware that there are no free lunches in business. The sooner your kids realize that a lot of sweat goes into running businesses, the more likely they are to show patience when working at getting their businesses off the ground. With this philosophy, your kids will be less likely to start their businesses just to make fast money and, hence, will resist the temptation to cheat customers or engage in other unethical behavior. At the Center for Teen Entrepreneurs, I usually advise kids to slow down and think about entrepreneurship as a discipline that will allow them to express their creative independence, help other people, and to make some extra pocket money.

Encouraging them to take pride in their work

Young entrepreneurs should be proud of the services or products they offer. I advocate this philosophy because some young entrepreneurs define good business ethics as the absence of customer complaint. But lack of customer complaint certainly is no indication of ethical business behavior. Take, for example, the baby food manufacturer that recently was caught selling sweetened apple–flavored water as pure apple juice. Thousands of customers fed their kids this fake apple juice without complaining because they had no idea they were being duped. They trusted the manufacturer to deliver what was promised. This is a perfect example of why the absence of complaining customers is not an indication of ethical business behavior. The customer may never know he or she is being cheated. For this reason, the best way to encourage ethical behavior is to encourage your young entrepreneurs to be proud of the products or services they provide. I have found that kids who have pride in what they do, will never even consider giving their customers less than they promised. This should not be surprising. I am sure that you have seen examples of the difference in quality between items or services provided by artisans who have pride in their work versus hackers who just want to make a quick buck.

Consider how 17–year–old Vincent Puzzo discovered that taking pride in his handiwork earned him a good reputation among his customers. Vincent loved to make his own clothes. He picked up the skill from his father, who retired from the haberdashery business after twenty years of running his own business. Vincent discovered that his father's former customers were dissatisfied with their new tailors. They complained that their tailors didn't finish their clothing as well as Vincent's father did. They also complained that their tailors were using nylon threads and that they did too hasty a job on even simple tasks such as hemming pants. Vincent decided to open up his own haberdashery shop, making dresses and suits because he felt that the tailors made inferior clothing. He quickly built a reputation as an excellent tailor who considered his creations to be works of art. His customers knew that he took pride in his work, and they were willing to pay more for his services than they would for the services of other tailors.

Because Vincent enjoyed sewing and was not willing to let any of this creations out the door unless he was satisfied with them, there was no chance that he would cheat his customers or take shortcuts that reduced the quality of his work.

Avoiding talking about punishment for unethical behavior

I once heard a speech given on business ethics to teenage entrepreneurs by a successful businessman. In his speech, this businessman told his audience that it pays to be honest in business because shady business people eventually get caught and ultimately pay for their wrong deeds, either by going to jail or by losing customers. He then went on to give examples of Wall Street insider traders who got their comeuppance. While I agree that, in the long run, honest business people usually outlast the dishonest ones, I am totally against telling young people that they must practice good business ethics for the fear of getting caught and being punished. I am against this for two reasons. For one thing, there is no universal law that guarantees that society will discover and punish all evil deeds swiftly. Your kids need only look at how some politicians carry on to know that not everyone gets his just deserts. I am also against trying to scare kids with the prospect of punishment because they might conclude that, as long as what they are doing is not discovered, their actions are within acceptable boundaries of behavior.

In addition, kids who are afraid of getting caught, might simply try harder not to get caught as opposed to changing their ways.

Instead of trying to scare kids into ethical behavior in their businesses, I recommend that you fall back on the moral code of behavior by which you raised them. Judeo–Christian–Islamic traditions certainly give many parents a basis for reinforcing ethical behavior. Regardless of whether you follow an organized religion or not, you have to depend on the acceptable boundaries of behavior that you have imbued in your children over the years.

Setting realistic goals

When your kids decide to start their own businesses, make sure that their goals are realistic. For example, it is not realistic for your young entrepreneurs to think that their businesses will grow by leaps and bounds in the first few weeks of operations unless they are selling some fantastic product or service. One way to add some realism to their expectations is to take a look at their business plans. Pay particular attention to their volume of sales and profits to see if they make sense. For example, you know that it is not physically or logistically possible for them to make $10,000 mowing lawns in the summer. Ambition is admirable in business, but when an entrepreneur is excessively ambitious, he or she will be inclined to do anything to meet his or her objectives. I know of one young entrepreneur who took on so many lawn–mowing jobs one summer that he did a poor job with all of them. He started cheating his customers by neglecting to cut the grass behind shrubs and other areas not visible to the naked eye. This kid took on too many jobs because he set an unrealistic financial goal for himself for the summer.

If meeting their goals drives your young entrepreneurs to do unethical things while running their businesses, their goals are probably unrealistic. This is one of the reasons a coherent business plan is important.

Letting them know that the end does not justify the means

We are bombarded with stories of rugged entrepreneurs who tirelessly strive for excellence in their businesses. The media even seem to laud the not–so–desirable qualities of these entrepreneurs.

It never ceases to infuriate me when entrepreneurs who are excessively arrogant treat everyone with contempt, or when those who have stepped on people all their lives are raised to near godlike stature. No, I don't expect entrepreneurs to be angels. They generally do demand excellence from the people around them. But I do not agree that they have to be so hard–nosed that they treat other human beings like dirt. The media try to get us to forget the warts that these people have. Take Donald Trump, for example. True, he is a successful entrepreneur. You can even say that for most of the 1980s, he was an expert deal maker. However, the media coverage about him seemed to laud not only his good entrepreneurial qualities but also his excessive flamboyance and arrogance.

Arrogance and nastiness should not be viewed as prerequisites for becoming a successful entrepreneur. In fact, as businesses become increasingly internationalized, Americans will find that these qualities can hinder their ability to do business with foreigners. Simply put, the characteristics that we admire or tolerate in entrepreneurs may not be universally acceptable.

I strongly believe that how a person becomes successful, whether he is an entrepreneur or a professional, matters very much. When we as adults ignore the means through which a person achieves his goals, we send a message to our kids that results are the only things that matter.

Things are beginning to change slowly due to the insider trading cases on Wall Street. People are beginning to look beyond the bottom line to ask how entrepreneurs and other business people are making their money. A *Business Week* article sums it up:

> *During the heyday of Reagan capitalism, Americans were too busy reveling in prosperity to ask how so many were getting so rich, so fast. But such disquieting thoughts are becoming harder to avoid these days. After nearly three years of revelations of insider trading on Wall Street, . . . anger in Washington is rising over a financial system that seems riddled with abuses.*

The only way you can help your kids realize that the ends do not justify the means is to explore with them how our so–called entrepreneurial heroes made their money. If the moral behavior of these heroes does not conform to your own code of ethics, you should point this out to your kids.

MONITORING YOUR CHILDREN'S BUSINESSES

When your kids are dealing with their customers, you have no way of knowing the quality of products or services they are providing. You must, however, find a way to monitor what they are doing outside of the house.

One way to keep an eye on your children's business activities is to speak to their customers. If, for example, your children's customers are in the neighborhood, give them a call to chat about how they feel your kids are doing in their businesses. Ask them whether they feel they received the products or services that your kids promised. One parent periodically visited some of his son's customers to chat about his son's performance in his business. "I like to know how well Matthew is doing in his window–cleaning business so I talk to some of his customers in the neighborhood. They have nothing but good things to say about the service."

If your children's customers are far away, you should ask for the phone numbers of a few of them in order to find out what these customers think about your children's businesses. At first you might feel awkward about doing this. You may even feel that you are interfering in your children's affairs. I think, however, that you will agree with me that this small intrusion into your children's businesses is worth it when you consider that the sooner problems are discovered, the easier they are to head off. In addition, remember that when your kids are doing something unethical in their businesses, it reflects on them and on you since you are their legal guardian. As your children's guardian, you have the right and the obligation to look at how they are running their businesses.

Another way parents can watch their children's businesses is to order the products or services their kids are selling. Parents can put themselves in the customers' shoes and ask themselves, "Am I getting my money's worth?" "Have I received what was advertised?"

One sure way of making sure that your kids provide the products or services they promise is to suggest that they offer a money–back guarantee. Right away you may be thinking to yourself that customers will take advantage of your children's hard labor by asking for a refund after benefiting from the products or services. I have found that an overwhelming majority of customers are quite honest. If your kids are truly providing the products or services they promise, the number of customers who will demand refunds will be minimal. If, on the other hand, lots of customers want their money back, then you can assume that your kids are not delivering on what they promised.

POINTING OUT EXAMPLES OF UNETHICAL AND ETHICAL BEHAVIOR BY BUSINESSES

One of the best ways to help your kids understand the ethical issues of running businesses is to point out real–life examples to them. There are plenty of examples of corporations behaving unethically by purposely continuing to sell items they know to be defective. For example, one big defense contractor was making and selling airplane bolts that it knew were defective. Another company continued to sell birth control devices even after they were determined to cause birth defects in the children of women who used them. You can talk to your kids about such cases and explore the consequences of such unethical behavior. At the same time, you can also talk about companies that behave ethically in moments of crisis. For example, one major drug company pulled all of its analgesics off the shelf as soon as it found out that someone had laced the medicine in several cities with a poison.

Another item you can target in teaching your kids about ethics in business is advertising. Advertising is any form of expression in which the goal is to make a person buy the product or service. However, there is a fine line between advertising a product and lying about a product. I say this because any advertising executive knows that to get someone to buy a product, you don't sell the features of the product, you sell the perceived benefits of the product. And sometimes the truth is bent in touting the benefits of the product or service. Consider some of the beer commercials you see on television. These commercials often feature young men surrounded by sexy women wearing skimpy outfits. What commercials like these are really saying is that, if you buy the product, you too can be surrounded by beautiful women. This, of course, is a big lie.

Children's commercials are even more insidious because kids are more susceptible to the lies of advertising agencies. This is why Congress is passing laws that restrict the number of commercials allowed during children's shows.

You should make your kids aware of the unethical practices in commercials. Point out to them when they are being manipulated into believing that they will actually benefit the way the advertisers are claiming. Sensitizing your children to such unethical behavior by advertisers will help them to understand that they too need to be careful when it comes to telling their customers what products and services they are going to provide. If your kids are under 12 years old, you could make a game of watching commercials to see who can come up with the most number of unrealistic benefits or lies that the company is pushing. For older kids, casual conversation while watching the commercials is sufficient.

WHAT TO DO IF YOUR KIDS ARE RUNNING THEIR BUSINESSES UNETHICALLY

Suppose you found out that your children are not giving their customers what they promised, or that they are somehow cheating their customers. What would you do in this situation?

I believe that when you do discover that your kids are doing unethical things in their own businesses, you should evaluate the nature of the misconduct to see how grave it is. Kids may do things that they do not consider to be unethical. For example, when kids do a hasty job, they may not realize that chances are, they are not giving their customers full value for their money. One young entrepreneur who paints murals on walls usually uses several coats of paint for his paintings. On one of his many jobs, he decided to use only one coat of paint. His customer did not really know the difference. While this artist/entrepreneur felt that his customer was satisfied, his behavior was unethical because it is likely that the mural painted with one coat of paint will fade faster than other works done with two coats of paint.

Back to the question of what to do if your kids do something unethical. Your actions, of course, should depend on the seriousness of the case. If, for example, your kids are billing customers for phony credit–card charges, as Barry Minkow did, I expect you to pull the plug on the business for this blatantly criminal activity. Remember that you are still their legal guardian, so you can exercise this option. In my opinion, stealing from customers is such a heinous crime that you cannot allow your kids to continue with business as usual.

A more subtle form of unethical behavior, such as not providing the products or services promised or advertised, is more common among young entrepreneurs. In this case, you have to tell your kids that they are, in essence, lying to their customers, and that you won't tolerate it. Give them a stern warning. In addition, you must insist that they give refunds to anyone who is not satisfied. Most of all, always remember that you have the right to shut your children's businesses down if they continue to behave in ways you do not approve.

WHAT KIDS HAVE TO SAY ABOUT BUSINESS ETHICS

The survey I conducted of 160 participants of EntreCon, the three–day high school conference on entrepreneurship held at the University of Pennsylvania's Wharton School of Business, revealed how some young people feel about business ethics. One of the questions in the survey attempted to ascertain how the kids felt about the Wall Street insider–trading scandals. Thirty–five percent of the kids surveyed responded that the scandals made them more suspicious of Wall Street and of business in general. Thirty percent felt that the scandal was not really that widespread and that a few greedy individuals were caught with their hands in the cookie jar. Some of the respondents wrote down their own feelings about the scandals instead of selecting one of the choices given to them.

The four quotes below are typical of what the kids had to say about honesty.

"White–collar crime is just as punishable as any other group of crime and not policed enough . . . . It is discomforting to think of the business person's reputation in general as crafty and crooked."

"I understand that in the real world, corruption exists in all areas. I am not surprised that insider trading or any other illegal business practices exist."

"It speaks of a much broader trend of lying, cheating, and stealing in America, not just Wall Street."

"There are going to be scandals all over business; you have to expect, but not condone it."

These responses, as well as the general impression I got from the participants of EntreCon, showed me that kids are aware of the significance of maintaining high business ethics. Many of these kids, even after having witnessed the low ethical standards in Wall Street in the late 1980s, still feel that honest businesses can be run successfully and that they can prove it.

Another part of the survey asked the kids what they felt a parent should do if the parent caught his kids doing something unethical in their businesses. Over 70% of the students felt that the parent should interfere in the business by, either pulling the plug on the business, or monitoring the business more carefully.

In my conversation with some of the respondents, most of them felt that parents had a right to watch their children's businesses to make sure that they were running their businesses honestly. A minority of about 15% of the respondents felt that parents should not interfere at all in their children's businesses. The following four statements by some of the respondents summarize the opinions of the kids.

"The parents should force the child to rectify the situation by restructuring the business and providing some form of compensation for the cheated customer."

"Give a parable—not a direct speech—to tell them about their unethical practices."

"Once again, this shows bad morals were learned at home or school—can you really change 'home training?'"

"Influence their child as to making the correct decision. However, leave it up to the individual to make the correct ethical decision."

Before I close this chapter, I would like to relate a story concerning business ethics from EntreCon. One segment of the conference featured a peer panel of young entrepreneurs. There were nine entrepreneurs on the panel from ages fourteen to twenty. Each of them stood up and talked about his or her business and what motivated them to pursue entrepreneurship. One of the young entrepreneurs sold T–shirts on his college campus, and he had his wares prominently displayed on the blackboard behind him. One of his T–shirt designs had a drawing of what was obviously a marijuana leaf and a slogan meant to appeal to college students. This one shirt provided one of the most heated discussions I had heard in the conference and it gave me a glimpse of how these kids feel about business ethics.

During the question–and–answer period, the high school students in the audience asked this young entrepreneur about the ethics of selling a product with a picture of an illegal drug. One students asked him bluntly, "By selling the T–shirt with the marijuana leaf on it, aren't you condoning drug use?" The entrepreneur responded that his T–shirt was for customers who could relate to the subject on the T–shirt. He continued by stating that he was merely satisfying a demand for that type of T–shirt. When he said this, many of the kids in the audience were obviously appalled. One kid asked why he did not have a picture of a crack vial (purified cocaine) on his shirts since that too may be in demand. This young entrepreneur then had to back off from his assertion that he will sell a product without applying his own moral judgment on the type of message it sends to the potential customers.

As the ethics debate raged on, some kids seemed to say that there had to be some ethical principle that should apply to people no matter what type of businesses they run. There was even a discussion about paying taxes. Some of the kids on the panel were candid enough to admit that, when they started their businesses (many of them started when they were between 12 and 15),they did not report their income. However, all said that they now do. Some felt that the income they were making at the time they started was so small that it was not worth reporting (even though they knew they probably should have). Some of the kids just did not know about tax regulations.

The ethics debate revealed that the kids at the conference were keenly aware of the issues regarding ethical standards in business. It is my opinion that recent business scandals had sensitized some of them to the importance of holding high ethical standards when running their own businesses.

15

GETTING YOUR KIDS INTERESTED IN THE FAMILY BUSINESS

Family businesses run the gamut from owning the local hardware store to owning an automobile company such as the Ford Motor Company. In a *Nation's Business* article, John Ward of Loyola University of Chicago and Craig Aronoff of Kennesaw State College in Georgia defined family businesses in the following way:

> *Most simply stated, a family firm is one that includes two or more members of a family that has financial control of the company. Sometimes, all family members are in the same generation: siblings, husband–wife teams, occasionally cousins. More often, businesses recognize themselves as family businesses when at least two generations are involved: an entrepreneur parent and his or her children or occasionally a nephew or niece. By this definition, family members could be included in ownership, management, or employee roles.*

While it is difficult to get a handle on the number of family businesses in the United States, Ward and Aronoff say that as many as 75% to 95% of all business can be categorized as family businesses and that 33% of the *Fortune 500* companies can also be classified as such. Moreover, they say that an analysis of data from the Small Business Administration indicates that "80% to 90% of all entrepreneurs who have children in their late teens hope—usually quietly—that their kids will someday join them in business."

PREPARING FOR THE TRANSITION

Family business owners don't usually think about preparing their offspring to take over the business until their kids are in their late teens. However, this preparation should begin as soon as the kids can perform tasks in the company. This means that even at age 8, if they can sweep the floor in the family business, they should be given that responsibility to prepare them for increasingly more important responsibilities in the company.

The earlier you teach your kids what the family business is all about, the easier it will be for you to get them interested in eventually running it. One retired family business owner recounts how he gradually eased his son into the family industrial soap business:

> *Each week, it was his job to mop the kitchen floor. I had him use different soaps on the floor each time he mopped it. One week he would use Mr. Clean, the next, Spic and Span. I then had him try our own cleanser. After he found that it took less effort to clean the floor [with cleanser], he started asking questions about what makes cleansers good. His interest was sparked because he saw our product in action.*

This parent recommends that, if possible, parents should have their kids use the products they sell or make to get them interested in the business.

Getting your kids interested in the family business at an early age is also important because it can help you gauge if your kids have the drive to eventually lead the business. It used to be that the heads of family businesses chose their eldest son as the successor and then groomed him to lead the business. These days, the daughters of owners of businesses are increasingly taking over the reigns of the family business. One example is Linda Johnson Rice, heir to a media empire created by her father, John Johnson of Johnson Publishing, which earned $307 million in revenues in 1994.

The only way that a parent can gauge who should rightfully lead the company in the future is to initially give all the kids an equal chance to prove themselves. Give all of your kids the same opportunities and hope that one of them stands out as a clear leader. Often this leader will be the oldest child in the family because in many cases, older children are typically more disciplined than their siblings. In addition, the oldest child typically has a head start on his brothers or sisters when it comes to learning the family business and proving himself or herself. For example, a family business owner who has two kids that are five years apart clearly will start getting his older child interested in the family business before the younger child.

GRADUALLY GETTING YOUR KIDS INVOLVED

As I mentioned earlier, it is important for family business owners to gradually ease kids into the family businesses. I have found that forcing kids to take part in the business generally backfires. When I was in business school, one of my classmates, whose father owned several hotels, resented his father's efforts to force him into the family business. In fact, his father did not want him to go far away for his undergraduate education because he wanted his son to stay close to the business. This student and I were taking the same entrepreneurial management class, so I naturally assumed that he was going to join his family's hotel business. But in a conversation with him one day after class he said to me: "I have no interest in my family's hotel business. I have been around it all my life and the more my father tries to get me to come back and join the management staff, the further I want to get away from it." I suspect that he had developed an aversion to the business as a part of his rebellion against parental authority. In situations like this, it is better to encourage your kids to go out and work at other companies. If after having worked at another company for a few years, they still want nothing to do with the family business, then so be it.

For younger family members who are still living at home, however, there are steps you should take to encourage their entrepreneurial behavior and get them interested in the family business.

To get your kids into the family business, start them off by giving them responsibility for simple tasks in the business. If your family has a manufacturing company, get them involved in the manufacturing process. One business owner got his kids involved in his logging business in Canada by having them do some of the physical work involved in moving lumber. Another business owner, who had a profitable janitorial cleaning service, had his son and daughter go on cleaning assignments with one of his 30 workers. He said of this hands–on training: "I figured that I'd show them the hard work involved in this business. They went on cleaning trips the whole summer just so they could get an idea about the fundamentals of this business. Of course, they got the financial rewards that came along with it too."

As long as the business is not dangerous, hands–on experience is the best way to get your kids involved. If your business involves manufacturing a product that can be easily taken apart, perhaps your kids can take it apart and put it back together. If you have a service business, let them get involved in offering the service.

While introducing them to the business, you shouldn't just focus on the hard work involved in running the business. No matter how enthusiastic your kids are about getting involved, if you constantly harp on the hard work without letting them know the rewards of the business, you will surely turn them off.

I recommend that you don't take the responsibility of personally teaching your kids the ropes. The reason for this is simple: highly motivated parents are generally more critical of their children's accomplishment than outsiders are. To show them the ropes, hand them over to a trusted employee. This employee should report back to you on how your kids are doing. They should also tell you their strengths and weaknesses in the different areas of the business.

You should allow your kids to take responsibility for a particular area in the business. For example, one entrepreneur put his 14–year–old daughter in charge of ordering office supplies. You should also hold them accountable when they do not meet their responsibilities or when they make decisions that are not in the best interest of the business. For example, the girl who was responsible for ordering office supplies once forgot to order paper for the printer. The father had her go out and buy the paper from the local stationery store on her way back from school the next day. He later said: "I had a spare ream of paper in my office in case of a paper shortage. I did not tell my daughter about it because I wanted her to know that I was holding her responsible for the lack of paper in the office. Since then, she has been ordering supplies way in advance."

The first tasks you give your children should not be critical to running your business. Give them tasks that will not harm your business in case they don't come through for you. You might start off with some menial tasks, then gradually move up to tasks that require increasingly more planning and thinking. This process could take several years depending on when you start your kids in the business. If you introduce your kids to your business at age 10, for example, it will probably take four years or so before they can start making any real financial decisions in the company.

Giving your kids responsibilities in the family business also means that you should allow them to solve their own problems. Sure, they can consult you or other people in the business for advice, but make sure that in the end they make their own decisions. Of course, if the decision is going to adversely affect your business, you have to step in to explain to your kids why the decisions they want to make will not be in the best interest of the business. If you have an anecdote that explains your experience in the past after having made the decision they would like to make, tell it. One girl who took orders over the phone on Saturdays for her family's extermination business decided to close at 4:00 p.m. instead of the customary 5:00 p.m. closing, for no reason other than that business was generally slow in the last hour of her weekend shift. When her father told her that she should tend to the phones until 5:00 p.m. on the dot, she replied: "Dad, only one or two customers call in the last hour." The father replied, "If I add up the business in that last hour for one whole year, it can pay for your brother's college tuition for one semester." Sometimes, young people don't understand the economic impact of their actions. Holding them responsible for their decisions involves making them aware that their actions have financial consequences.

As your kids mature, you must give them more important responsibilities. In addition, you also have to let them inject more creativity into the tasks they do for the business. They may have suggestions that can improve the family business. I know of a case where the 16–year–old daughter of one entrepreneur kept pushing for her father to buy a few personal computers for the office. This man was terrified of computers, but he wouldn't admit this to his daughter. Finally, she borrowed a portable computer from her friend's father and started creating spreadsheets on it.

When her father saw the electronic spreadsheets replace the ledgers that were manually filled in, he went out and bought two personal computers for the office.

As your kids get older, you have to treat them less and less like little kids. One common complaint that young people have about joining the family business is that their parents are not treating them any differently than when they were kids.

Even when I was 19 years old, my father insisted that he ring up the daily cash register totals. I almost felt that he didn't think I was responsible enough to do such a simple thing. For Pete's sake, I had been helping him out in the store since I was 12 years old.

PARENTAL ATTITUDES AND HABITS

Parents who own family businesses must be careful that they do not inadvertently turn their kids off to their business. Quite often, parents might say things or do things that tell their kids "this family business of ours stinks. I wish we all had regular jobs."

Arguments are a necessary part of life, but when it constantly centers on the family business, kids start associating negative feelings with the business. Why should a kid want to involve himself in the family business when he sees the unhappiness it is bringing you and your spouse? Kids witnessing such unhappiness will want nothing to do with it.

Kids are also turned off by the family business when all they hear from their parents is how much heartache the business is causing them. There is nothing wrong with letting off a little steam about how difficult a business is. However, you should also counterbalance these complaints with the good points about the business.

Many of the entrepreneurs I know who have family businesses would not give up their businesses even if they were promised higher salaries. This tells me that their business is giving them psychic income—fulfillment that money can't buy. Next time you castigate your business in front of your kids, remember to also present them with reasons why you stick to your business and why you will not give it up for anything in the world.

Another thing that turns kids away from the family business is that they see the negative effects of the hard work on the family's relationship. Now 20 years old, a son whose wealthy entrepreneur father divorced his mother when he was 10 years old gives his analysis as to why he was never interested in following his father's footsteps:

When my parents got divorced, I was devastated. Now that I look back, I know why it happened. My father was never around. I give my mother a lot of credit for enduring his 70–hour work weeks. For me, I rarely spent time with him because of his business. If that's what being an entrepreneur means, you can count me out.

This son obviously associates negative feelings toward his father with the family business.

Every entrepreneur has had the problem of occasionally neglecting the family because of the amount of the time the business demands. The best solution, of course, is to simply cut down the amount of time spent on the business. This is easier said than done, however, because some businesses simply require a lot of time. Many entrepreneurs simply make more of an effort to get their family members more involved in the business. Sure, the entrepreneur still spends a lot of time in his business but at least his family is around to help him out and be closer to him.

If you find yourself in the situation where you do not have enough time to spend with your family, the long–term solution has to delegate some responsibility to other people who can help you. If you are like most entrepreneurs, you probably feel compelled to do everything in your business just to make sure it is done right. In time, you will find that the little pesky tasks you have to do take up all of your time. Sometimes it is better to pay people to do these tasks for you. For example, if you have to mail out lots of form letters, perhaps you can hire some kids or even your own children to fold the letters and stuff envelopes for you. If you sit down and think about your business, I am sure that you can come up with ways to cut down on the amount of time you spend working in your office.

Another turnoff for kids when it comes to family businesses is that these businesses, like giant corporations, feel the effects of a bad economy. When there is a recession, your family business income will go down and it will affect your standard of living. Children, however, relate the family's financial difficulties to the family business without recognizing that the business problems stem from a poor economy. Once again, the children may grow up with no desire to have anything to do with the feast–or–famine realities of the family business. Having grown up in a financially unstable environment, they may only seek a more secure career as a professional. A daughter of one entrepreneur put it this way: "Give me a steady paycheck any day. I can't go through what my father went through in his business."

If your family business occasionally has financial troubles, you should put it in perspective for your kids You should let them know that other industries may be having the same troubles your business is having. Tell them also that in times of economic downturn even big corporations have to lay people off.

16

TODAY'S YOUNG ENTREPRENEURS: AMERICA'S FUTURE

This chapter contains essays written by kids who are actually running their own businesses. In reading these statements, you will find some similarities among the young entrepreneurs. For one thing, all of them are hard workers who really enjoy what they are doing. Second, they all value the idea of being their own bosses and controlling their own destinies.

In presenting these pieces by young entrepreneurs, I tried to respect their privacy. Some of the kids chose to divulge how much money they were making, but most of them understandably were reluctant to give financial details of their businesses. However, I chose these kids for this chapter not because of the amount of money they were making, but for the creative, entrepreneurial qualities I feel they possess. In addition, I chose young people that other kids can relate to.

Reading these statements will help you in figuring out your role in helping your kids become entrepreneurs. In addition, you should pass these inspirational examples to your kids so that they can see that other kids like themselves are starting and running their own businesses.

STATEMENTS BY YOUNG ENTREPRENEURS AND PARENTS

Entrepreneur:	Mark Alexander (name changed to protect privacy)
Business:	Alexander's Bakery (name changed to protect privacy)
Years in Business:	4
Age While Running Business:	17

The following young entrepreneur started his bread–baking business because he was simply too young to get a regular job. He took an idea he saw somewhere else and modified it for his purposes. He is also a good example of how creative young entrepreneurs can be.

In the summer of 1987, my family and I visited Hawaii. During the visit, we came across a small chain of shops called Cindy's Cinnamon Buns. They baked and sold cinnamon buns and people seemed to really like them. Because of my age (I was thirteen at the time), I wanted to find a job. I thought that when I got home, I might try baking cinnamon buns and selling them to friends. It then occurred to me that bread would be more likely to sell.

Two days before I started my freshman year of high school, I baked a few loaves of white bread and sold them to neighbors. I continued doing this every weekend and people continued to buy my bread. By the time the next summer came along, I decided to increase my production to six types of bread. I currently make white, whole wheat, cracked wheat, oatmeal, anadama (corn meal and molasses), and cinnamon–raisin. I found a wholesaler to buy bulk ingredients. I buy 50–lb. bags of flour, 2–lb. bags of yeast, etc. I bought a spreadsheet program for my computer to keep track of all my costs and sales records.

The business basically grew by word of mouth. My income was good enough to support my needs, so I decided not to get an additional job. As of now, I usually bake between 50 and 60 loaves of bread each week. Cinnamon–raisin accounts for about 30% of my sales. I wake up early (usually on Sunday) and spend seven or eight hours baking and then two or three hours delivering. The other work includes making calls and buying ingredients.

One-Year Figures

Loaves Baked	1,443
Income	$3,582.50
Costs	$794.48 or $ .551 per loaf
Profit	$2,788.02 or $1.932 per loaf

Cumulative Figures

Loaves Baked	4,033
Income	$9,428.25
Costs	$2,790.12 or $ .692 per loaf
Profit	$6,638.13 or $1.646 per loaf

My costs are lower for this past year because I have increased production and found ways to buy ingredients at lower prices.

My parents have been very supportive of my business. Just before I started, they did not really like the idea that I would be starting a business just as I was beginning high school, but I did start and they were supportive. They have never charged me for utilities or use of the car. They did not otherwise help me financially, but they drove me around everywhere until I got my license and my mother gives up the kitchen every Sunday. They never discouraged me about anything.

In college, I plan to study business administration or management. After college, I hope to continue with my bread–baking business or some other venture.

Entrepreneur:	Zakia Ericka Andrews
Business:	Simple Pleasures
Years in Business:	2
Age While Running Business:	17

This entrepreneur has always been encouraged by her parents to think of being her own boss. She is also a good example of how organizations can help young people start and run their own businesses.

Before I became an entrepreneur, I was always interested in businesses and how they were operated. Even as a little girl, my mother talked about being "your own boss." She never once told me to go

to school just so I could get a good job. She always wanted me to be independent and self–reliant.

When I heard about the two–week summer program (the Young Entrepreneurs Program) that the Wharton School was offering, I couldn't refuse. My mother encouraged me to enroll.

During the two weeks I learned about the stock market, how it works, and how to start a business and run it successfully. After the two weeks, I came up with my own business idea. I believed it would be very successful although I was a little skeptical about telling my mother that her daughter would be selling lingerie. To my surprise, she was very supportive. A few months later the students from the program received Wharton MBA students as mentors. With the help of my mentor, Patricia Im, I presented a business plan to a venture capital board and I received a grant for $500.

Soon after, I started my business of selling lingerie with the help of my family and friends. I gave lingerie parties where I exhibited my products. (Zakia did not model the lingerie.)

On average I would have two parties per month. My income per month would average between $400 and $500.

My philosophy towards life is that if you believe in yourself and work hard you can achieve your highest goals. Through hard work and determination, I achieved my goal of being an entrepreneur.

I am uncertain of what my future career goals are. I do know, however, that I am going to college. Whatever I choose to do in the future, it will lead me down the path of entrepreneurship. Being an entrepreneur enables you to have control over your own life and destiny.

Entrepreneur: Morris D. Beyda

Business: Computers Simplified

Years in Business: 2

Age While Running Business: 16

This young entrepreneur credits his family for giving him the support necessary to run his business successfully. He also says that he grew up in an entrepreneurial environment in which his father was always involved in one business venture or another.

My interest in business began at a young age, probably somewhere around the age of ten. My parents established from early in my childhood that they would not buy me things just because I wanted them. Instead, I had to either wait for a special occasion or buy them myself. As I accumulated money on these occasions from my grandparents, my parents would reinforce that the money was mine. I could buy whatever I pleased with my money, regardless of their opinion of its actual value and importance (but not their feelings on safety). They allowed me to make my own decisions and make my own mistakes. Again and again I would hear them telling me, "It is your money, do whatever you want with it."

At the same time I was learning the value of money, my father played a large role in contributing to my knowledge of business, even from my younger years. Without a doubt, the single most important thing he ever did for me was to talk to me. He was constantly getting involved in new business ventures, coming up with new ideas, and investing in new stocks in the market. Every time there was something new on his mind he would tell me and would explain things until I understood. At the age of ten, I had already made my first independent investment in a stock called Up John and had tripled my investment in a short period of time. As in the past, I was told that I could do whatever I pleased with this money, and after putting half of it in the bank, I came to a decision. I went out with my parents to the local bicycle store and bought myself the sleekest new Mongoose dirt bike made. Despite the fact that all of my friends had them, my parents had refused to buy me one for the simple reason that I already had a bike that worked fine. Buying that Mongoose was the first time that I realized that I liked having money to spend and that I wanted to make more.

I was eight when my father bought our first home computer, and from then on I have spent countless hours working with them. Over the years I have had opportunities to work with every major brand of computer, and as a result I have built an immense knowledge base for myself as well as a fundamental understanding of how they work. I actually got started in the computer business about four years ago when friends of my parents began asking me to come to their houses to help them out with basic problems that they had with either programs or their actual computers. I found that most of the time the only problem was a lack of common sense on the part of the customer. There have been countless times when I would receive a call from a panicked neighbor screaming about how their computer was dead or permanently damaged, only to find simply that a plug was not totally in an outlet. Occasionally, a problem would require that I dismantle an entire system and check one piece at a time until the problematic device was found. This also was mostly common sense (although, at times it required some basic knowledge of the system). In addition, I began giving advice on what type of system to buy, and this was naturally followed by requests that I make purchases on commission. The entire time that this was going on both of my parents allowed me to conduct my own affairs, watching as I made mistakes and learned from my mistakes. I was always encouraged to use my own judgment and thus formed my own opinions on what I should be doing. Inevitably, having seen so many fresh business ventures begun in my house, Computers Simplified was created, giving me a name and a reason to professionalize.

Since its inception, my computer business has continued growing. Currently Computers Simplified offers a number of services that I have found to appeal to the average computer user. My most common request is over–the–phone consultation, whether it be on purchasing or problem analysis. I now have the ability to accommodate any purchasing request, no matter how large or small for a customer, and from this I receive a commission. As far as problem situations are concerned, my policy is to only offer a minimal amount of advice over the phone with average clients, and for anything more complex, I usually suggest a personal visit. In addition, I provide publishing services, which often include community newsletters.

When I first started helping individuals, I would usually ask for a token payment of five dollars, regardless of the time or effort involved, but I have been able to steadily raise my rates without complaint ever since. I now operate at a base salary of between $25 and $35 per hour, which when compared to other similar professional computer services, is rather inexpensive. It is always interesting to have a customer meet me for the first time after a phone conversation and realize that I am only sixteen. Often I have to prove myself before people will trust me and consequently pay me. My most common request is for individual lessons, which I give to people of all ages on the topic of their choice, including store–bought programs and the basic concepts of using computer equipment. The only area that I usually do not get involved in is programming, mainly because of the simple fact that it is boring and time consuming. But as far as everything else goes, my policy is that if I am not familiar with something or do not understand it, I will learn and then teach it. The extent and variety of services that Computers Simplified now encompasses keep me busy during most of my spare time, while the only forms of advertising that I have utilized are referrals and business cards. My parents still encourage me to make my own decisions, as far as how much I charge and how I balance my business and school. Being that I work out of my house, no initial capital was necessary, and through profits I currently have a net worth approaching $10,000. Perhaps the biggest improvement in my business will be when I receive my full New York State driver's license on my 17th birthday, because having to depend on alternate transportation can be crippling.

My parents stay very aware of what I am doing with my business and are always there to offer moral support. They realize that even though my knowledge with respect to computers is superior, that I am still a teenager that needs help every once in a while. They have yet to squander money away without good reason for me, but this is what has driven me to really work. I have acquired a very selective preference in how I spend my free time, and whether it be my stereo system or my computer, I always seem to have something that I want to buy, which directly affects my productivity. I feel that I will have a large advantage over others my age when I finally reach the real world as a result of my experiences.

My father, while nurturing my understanding of business and success, has not been afraid to admit mistakes. It is from hearing both the good and the bad sides of the business world that I make most of my decisions. As I get older I am finding that I am better able to assess situations and the likelihood of their success, as a direct result of hearing my father's experiences. Computers Simplified is a product of a indirect influence of my parents and the direct result of my willingness to work for what I want.

Entrepreneur: Stan Bush

Business: Wooden Falls Poultry Farms

Years in Business: 4

Age While Running Business: 19

This young entrepreneur is unique among the other kids in this chapter because he has already graduated from high school, and he is trying to raise enough money to expand his business. Currently, he has a job and he invests the money he makes on his job into his business. He says that he will eventually go to college but first he wants to get his business off the ground.

When I was in grade 8, I had to pick a high school to go to. I had many options, but I chose a vocational agricultural school because I always wanted to be a farmer.

When I started high school, I knew little or nothing about poultry or any other agricultural field. To get credits for my Vo–Ag class, I needed a project related to agriculture. At first, I chose landscaping, but soon changed to poultry. I started with 30 pullets, a small chicken coop, and some knowledge about the production of eggs. My second year in high school I really got involved with starting a poultry farm with my friend, Charlie Olmstead. I started raising capons, ducks, geese, guineas, turkeys and some pheasants for the next two years. After exploring the fields of the poultry business, I decided on what type of poultry I was going to raise for my business.

I now have more customers than I can supply. My business is growing, and in a few years I will have no problem supplying customers. I'd have to say that it was the vocational agricultural teachers from Nonnewaug High School that gave me the most motivation to pursue my dreams. My father pushed me to do more work in the poultry area and it wasn't until after he passed away, during my senior year in high school, that I finally realized what he was saying. Sometimes when I need to make a decision in my business, I stop and think, "What would Dad do?"

Right now my business consists of 50 laying hens. I just sold my geese and ducks and traded for young birds in the spring. I have over 200 baby chicks on order for both meat and egg production. In the spring, I have plans to get turkeys and capons since they were requested again for this year. For my first two years in the poultry business, I made a good but small profit. After that, I explored different types of poultry and lost money. The way I see it, though, you have to spend some money now and invest to make some money later.

I now own the poultry farm by myself and have decided to keep the name Wooden Falls Poultry Farms, because everybody knows that it means farm fresh eggs and meat products.

Entrepreneurs:	Keemya Dickerson
	Nayo Francis
	Aliya Francis

Business:	Just 3!
Years in Business:	1
Ages While Running Business:	16

These young entrepreneurs have also benefited from an entrepreneurship program that helped them start their business. They are especially grateful for their mentor's help in giving them the support they needed to put their business ideas into action.

Just 3! is a partnership consisting of three motivated young ladies. Together we plan to sell stylish hosiery. Considering the fact that we all attend an all–girls school, St. Jean Baptiste High School, it is necessary to wear leg accessories with the uniform skirt. Therefore we have an edge on our competitors because Just 3! will be there firsthand to satisfy the customers' needs. In addition, our hosiery will be purchased at a lower price than at department or retail stores. Besides in school, we plan to sell our merchandise to our friends and neighbors who reside in our buildings and to the congregation members of our church. Between those two target audiences, our main objective is to acquire at least 60% of the people to be loyal customers.

Although starting a business is a lot of hard work, Just 3! decided starting one would be a good experience. The group knew time and effort had to be put in. The group had to realize all aspects of the business field as possible. The help from the program [Young Entrepreneurs Program at the Columbia University Business School] the three of us successfully completed made our job easier. Determination was the key to our desire to start our own business. We also have the love and support of our friends at the business school, especially our mentor Janet Roles.

Our parents have also had a significant role in our business. They encourage us to do the best we can in any situation. Just 3!'s parents are totally behind them in the decisions they make. Although our parents do not give us any financial support.

Entrepreneur: David Leopold

Business: D & L Collectibles

Years in Business: 2

Age While Running Business: 17

This entrepreneur started his business because of his love of sports. One unexpected twist in his business is that he and his stepfather are actually closer to each other now because they both have a keen interest in anything related to sports. I have include both his statement and a statement from his stepfather to give you an idea of the parental role from a parent's perspective.

I am a sports fanatic. For as long as I can remember, I've always read the sports pages in the newspaper everyday. Like most preteens who loved sports, I collected baseball cards. I would go to supermarkets and baseball card stores to buy packs of cards. By 1986, I had accumulated several thousand cards, which cost me approximately $100. My mother told me to get rid of them because they were taking up room in my closet. I had always replied that they would be worth something one day. Finally, I decided to take these cards to a nearby baseball card store. Much to my surprise, they were worth about $350, which to a 13 year old is like winning the lottery. Because I'm such a sports enthusiast and love, follow, and play baseball, I decided to start a little business.

My parents have always tried to support what I wanted to do, and this was no exception. They allowed me to use the money I had made from selling my cards to start my business and were also always willing to help me out financially if I needed the aid. They provided me with transportation and always gave me encouragement and praise.

Today, my business, D & L Collectibles, has between 400,000 and 500,000 cards with an annual budget of about $6,500. The sports card hobby—basketball, football, baseball, golf, and hockey cards—has grown in popularity and profitability. It has become a market with sales of over $1 billion annually. More and more card producing companies enter the market every year in a constant attempt to provide the collector with a better and more valuable card. A card's value is determined by its scarcity, the player's popularity, and the player's talent and statistics. Usually a player's rookie card is the most valuable unless scarcity becomes an issue.

Although it remains a business, I'm not involved in this business just to make a profit. I simply love all sports as well as my business. Not only do I run my business, but I, along with my step-father, have accumulated an individual collection outside of my business. This, combined with my business, helps fulfill my love for baseball and other sports. It provides me the facts and statistics I've followed and studied for years. My business should not be confused with a scheme just to make money.

My business is comprised of buying, holding, and selling sports cards, especially baseball cards. I do this by advertising in hobby magazines and by purchasing and selling cards through mail order. I do the bulk of my business at card shows. At these shows, I rent a table on which to display my cards. These shows are held in gymnasiums, hotel ballrooms, and expo centers. Usually organized by another dealer, the shows charge an admission fee for collectors to look at and purchase cards that are displayed by the dealers. Profits can be made by buying old or new cards and holding them for a few years thus allowing them to appreciate in value. Some cards' values can grow as much as 30% to 40% annually. Once these cards increase in value, they are resold at a healthy profit to a collector. Profits can also be made by buying new cards in large quantities from wholesalers and producers and reselling them within a matter of weeks to collectors in smaller quantities for a 10% to 20% profit.

This year, my parents have helped me create a budget. Once I presented it to them, they lent me the money for the year that is to be used for my business. This money, $5,000, along with my remaining profits from the previous year, $1,500, has become my budget for this year. After the first six moths of this year, June 15 to November 15, I have spent about $3,600 of the money in my budget. In the first six months I have gross sales of about $7,300 and made a gross profit of about $1,700 before taking out a salary. I've put about $8,000 into my current inventory over the past three years. This inventory has appreciated to a value of about $12,000. My inventory and my profits have been attained by purchasing some old and mostly more recent cards. The cards that have been sold have resulted in my profits for this year while the cards that have appreciated in my inventory will provide me with future profits.

My business has been an incredible learning experience. It has shown me a lot about gross profit margins, net income, cost of sales, and fixed overheads. It has also taught me how to relate to people in a business sense as well as the importance of trust and respect in business.

Lawrence J. Ansin (David Leopold's Stepfather)

David and I share a mutual love of sports and we found that through this interest, a deep bond developed between us.

Since early childhood, David has been a collector of baseball cards. I found that to be educational, rewarding, and exciting. In reading financial investment advisors' recommendations for the 1990s, baseball cards had appreciated as a collectible during the 1980s at a 30% compound growth rate. I quickly realized that not only would this be a bonding, but it would be a good opportunity for David to learn business and entrepreneurship with very little investment.

Since the inception of David's company, D&L Collectibles, a year and a half ago, I have functioned in the capacity of coach, not owner or boss. I have tried to teach him the art of determining gross profit margin, fixed overhead, and strategies in merchandising and purchasing. He is a quick learner. It is wonderful to see the progress he has made and I feel that throughout his business career, he will stay involved in this entrepreneurial enterprise and, more than likely, will pass his business and knowledge in the sports collectibles area on to his son.

Entrepreneur: Kim McCombs

Business: Kim's T–Shirts

Years in Business: 1

Age While Running Business: 16

Kim is one on the growing number of young entrepreneurs who have benefited from programs that teach inner–city kids about the basics of business start–ups. The Young Entrepreneurs Program held at the Walter A. Haas School of Business (UCLA) and funded by the Milken Institute has helped her discover entrepreneurship. The institute also funds similar programs at the Columbia University Business School and the University of Pennsylvania's Wharton School of Business.

I am a 16–year–old sophomore at Berkeley High School. I am also the owner of Kim's T–Shirts. I sell a variety of T–shirts, but I specialize in handmade shirts. At the moment, I do not have a permanent shop because I am still attending school. I sell my shirts at home where my business is currently based. I store and make my shirts here.

I have been in business less than a month and my business has taken off to a great start. I never dreamed it would be this successful so soon. So far, I have been able to make about 50% profit on every sale. Once I get started and am better known I am sure I will be able to raise my prices.

Although I did not gain my interest in entrepreneurship from my parents, they still have a lot to do with my success. They have given me encouragement and supported everything that I have done. They even put up half of my start–up cost. I guess you can say what motivated me to start my own company was my knowledge and interest in business.

About five years ago, I moved to the San Francisco Bay area. The school I attended here offered classes on entrepreneurship. This had been a long–time interest of mine, so I excelled in these classes. The more I learned, the more interested I became. When I heard about the Young Entrepreneur Program, I jumped at the chance to be a part of it. It was one of the best decisions I have made in my life. When you hear the word entrepreneur, the first thing you think is that starting a business is complicated and mysterious. The teacher in the program made it easy and exciting to learn how to go about starting a business. The program has changed my life. It takes inner–city minority children who have been told by society that they would never amount to anything, gives them goals, and the opportunity to make something of themselves.

Entrepreneur: Adam Miller

Business: Baseball Card Dealer

Years in Business: 27

Age While Running Business: 16

Adam and his friend have teamed up to run a baseball card business. I am impressed with how he and his friend have used the resources around them and their connections to make their business work.

I got interested in dealing baseball cards because I was an avid collector myself. The key to this business is figuring out which rookies are going to be hot and to buy up their rookie cards fast. My friend and I got tips from scouts that my friend's dad knew, and we investigated all the minor league teams. We came up with a bunch of players and when the 1987 sets came out, I had about one hundred cards of each of those players bought very cheaply. Jose Canseco, Will Clark, Mark McGwire, and others became real hot. We started to sell them off very slowly at first because I anticipated a boom in the business that year. The stars soared while the flops died. But who cares about the busts anyway? We got them for chump change. Eventually we had enough money to put in a bid for a show. We paid a reasonable fee for the use of the Holiday Inn ballroom for five hours. My friend, who did most of the work as far as organizing the show (I paid a slightly higher fee to compensate him for his effort), got in touch with Brooks Robinson. He agreed to sign autographs for $5,000. After selling all the tables to dealers, we got enough money back to pay for half our original expenses. Fortunately my friend's dad knew someone in radio and we got free advertising over the airwaves. We planned to charge a $3.50 admission fee. I still can't believe how many people we got through that door. The big money, though, was with Brooks. At $8.00 an autograph, he signed enough autographs to completely cover our expenses and gave us each a profit of $1,500. Not bad for a couple of kids.

I believe that entrepreneurship is a game and that those who play their cards right win the pot. I love the challenge of risk, but I'm not a gambling person. If I see a major flaw in an investment, I'll shut it out of my wallet as fast as a Mac machine spews out $20.00 bills.

My parents have always encouraged me to analyze every aspect of a business before getting involved. They would say to me, "Always know what you're getting into." Financially, I invested my own money, not my parents. However, they did buy me a computer.

Many parents tend to stay out of what I'm doing, and I like it that way. Both my parents are in education so I don't know how I got interested in entrepreneurship.

As far as business is concerned, I believe to be successful, one must have several connections in various fields of expertise. I think you also have to have a lot of common sense. Succeeding in school is also a good start to succeeding in business.

Entrepreneur: Viveka Ryn

Business: Grass Catchers Lawn Service

Years in Business: 3

Age While Running Business: 18

This young entrepreneur took traditional lawn mowing and turned it into big business in her community. She showed incredible maturity by managing four employees who handled her forty accounts.

In the last two years I started, built up, and managed "Grass Catchers Lawn Service," my own lawn–mowing and snow–removal company, a sole proprietorship. It grew to the point that I had four employees, one of them full time. I did all the advertising, met with prospective customers, negotiated fees, set efficient schedules for employees, managed accounts receivable, including the preparation of invoices, and generally handled company finances and salaries. That I could perform all of these tasks with ease and self–confidence, and that, through my efforts, the business grew to as many as forty lawns a week, was a source of great satisfaction. I started to acquire a reputation in the local community for running a good and reliable service. People started to make jokes to my parents and myself about the 16–year–old "big entrepreneur." I felt a good deal of pride knowing that I could turn my own ideas into reality and make a substantial profit as a result.

Trying to expand my list of customers, I had for a long time been eyeing a very large lawn close to that of one of my customers. It was one that would be easy to cut but for which I could charge a high fee and still be very competitive. I tried several times to persuade the particular home–owner to change from his lawn service, a large regional company, to Grass–Catchers, which would be less expensive. Finally, he decided to make the change. He would cancel his present contract, and let me take over in a few weeks. I could not have been more pleased. Adding this particular lawn would be very profitable over time.

While I was waiting for this new customer to sign on, I happened to have a conversation with one of my workers, Jimmy. He is a man in his forties, married with four children. By what he had earlier told me and by the way he spoke, dressed, and carried himself, I knew that he was poor and that his circumstances were unsettled. Jimmy had tried on his own to support his family by cutting grass. He hadn't been very successful getting customers, which is how I came to employ him. And yet he was a good worker and an honest, dependable person. What I now learned about him, from a passing remark he made, was that he was having real trouble. He had a chronic health problem but had not been able to afford insurance and could not pay for the medical care he needed. In order to help finance treatment at a clinic he was going to sell his VCR.

I did not really need that new, big profitable lawn. If Jimmy were to take it on himself and not just receive the usual commission from me, he could pocket the whole weekly fee with little extra effort. And I, with little sacrifice, would substantially ease his burden. And so it was arranged.

It was then that I really understand that financial achievement could never be my deepest source of happiness, and that, whatever my life may bring, money will always be secondary. However, I believe that I will always be interested in entrepreneurship.

Entrepreneur:　Christian Sepe

Business:　Disc Jockey Service

Years in Business:　1

Age While Running Business:　16

This young entrepreneur is philosophical about youth entre-preneurship. He has some incredibly perceptive ideas about par-ents' roles in cultivating their children's interest in starting their own businesses. Although he feels that entrepreneurs are born and not made, he nevertheless acknowledges that his father and grand-father, who are both entrepreneurs, may have influenced his pro-pensity towards business.

The primary instincts of an entrepreneur are, in my opinion, inbred. Granted, most human behavior is learned, but there are still certain things that differentiate entrepreneurs from others. First and foremost, is their way of thinking. Entrepreneurs tend to look at things from the standpoint of their effectiveness and efficiency. Second, entrepreneurs have desire to capitalize on situations.

Personally, my entrepreneurial characteristics manifested themselves at a young age. I can remember selling portions of my lunch to classmates. This did not give me substantial amounts of money, but it was enough to allow me to buy an ice cream or a pretzel each day. It is things like this which emphasize the differ-ence between entrepreneurs and others. My parents did not promote or train me to do this type of thing, nor did they in any way encour-age me to become involved with small entrepreneurial ventures. It was something that I just took a liking to. Actually, I think the fact that my grandfather owned his own construction company and that my father began a unique promotional business has had something to do with my desire to become involved in my own venture. Nei-ther my grandfather nor my father has ever really pushed me to-ward entrepreneurship, however.

I believe that the role of parents in the young entrepreneur's venture should not be a leading or a dominating one. Parents should let their children do what they feel is in the best interest of their ventures, and if the child's decisions turn out not to be productive, then that is not necessarily bad. It is important for children to experiment with different ideas and ways of going about things, and failure is an excellent teacher. It shows children that some things just are not effective in certain circumstances. The young entrepreneur would probably tend to analyze why his or her particular decision did not prove beneficial and hence would try to go about improving the venture by other means, and again maybe these other means will fail, but through these failures, much important knowledge is gained. It seems to me that the most successful entrepreneurs are not afraid to fail now and then, and they are not as critical of their employees who experiment with different ideas thereby creating an environment in which creativity is stimulated and often proves successful.

Parents should serve as a resource to their children. They should make themselves available to their children when their children have questions. When a child has a question about the way in which he or she should go about something, however, I suggest that the parent give the child various methods and ideas in response. When a parent gives one definitive answer, a child who may be insecure with his ability to make decisions, will most likely subscribe to that particular solution. Hence, the child does not learn how to make decisions for himself and will begin to rely too heavily on the parent. Again, parents must allow their children to experience failure in order to promote the child's ability to make successful decisions.

I created my own business from a hobby that I had. I was very interested in stereos and music and therefore decided to start my own disc jockey service. My parents in no way dictated how I was to go about this. My father was always willing to offer his time and give me suggestions, but he always left the final decision up to me.

In the beginning, my business was cumbersome, but as time progressed I gained more skills and I became more efficient. After each job, I would analyze what had occurred and how I could go about improving on it. For instance, in the first job I did, it took me about an hour and a half to set up and another hour to break down. This was far from efficient, but as time progressed, I was able to cut this time to about twenty minutes for each step. I cut this time by experimenting. I experimented with different types of set–ups, and, yes, at times my trials failed, but eventually I succeeded in reducing the time. I have learned a lot about how certain things should be done through these failures and the experiences I have had has helped to strengthen my ability to make decisions.

Once entrepreneurial qualities are found in a child, it is important for parents to nurture those qualities. Parents have the responsibility to try and sharpen the abilities of their children and in doing so must follow a few guidelines. The parents must control themselves and not become overly involved with their children's ventures. They must also learn to, at times, allow their children to fail. In the failure, however, it is important to teach the child why he or she has failed.

Entrepreneur: Steve Woyicki

Business: SpecialtyNewspaper/Delivery Service

Years in Business: 3

Age While Running Business: 17

Steve has taken a paper route concept and modified it to offer something a little bit different from his peers. Steve's statement also shows that a parental philosophy that encourages independence and innovation among kids also affects children's entrepreneurial behavior. I follow the statement of this young entrepreneur with a short piece by his parents to give you a glimpse as to how his up-bringing has nurtured his entrepreneurial tendencies.

My parents have always encouraged me to be independent. From the time I was little, they always approved of anything unique or innovative that I did. They urged me to stand out from the crowd and to make my own decisions. They always gave me a great deal of responsibility and stressed how much faith they had in me. Often, they might make a suggestion that I would take and then expand above and beyond the original expectations. Therefore, it was only natural for me to expand on their suggestion of getting a job where I was my own boss, or rather starting my own business.

My business is, in effect, a specialty newspaper route. However, I've never really thought of it as a business, but rather as a service I provide. In addition to delivering papers, I have performed a number of jobs ranging from snow shoveling and lawn mowing to grocery delivery, emergency baby–sitting, and the distribution of missing pet notices. I have acquired all of these jobs as a result of my paper route, although I never sat down and determined what services I was willing to provide. For the most part, my customers have all notified me whenever they wanted something. I never even planned to perform these odd jobs when I started my route, but after I helped out a few people the news spread by word of mouth and the jobs started coming in more frequently.

The paper route itself is a little different than most in the method by which I acquired it. It came to my attention in about March of 1987 that my family and several of our neighbors wanted to receive the Sunday home delivery of some of the larger newspapers such as the New York Times. However, for one reason or another, nobody was receiving these papers. My parents suggested to my younger brother, Randy, and I the idea of starting our own paper route by taking orders, buying these papers at a local store, and then delivering them to our customers for a little more than the newsstand price. I proceeded to approach the owners of a number of stores carrying these papers at a local store, and then delivering them to our customers for a little more than the newsstand price. I proceeded to approach the owners of a number of stores carrying these papers and asked them if they could reserve a certain number of papers for me to pick up early Sunday mornings. Upon hearing of my plan to resell these papers, one owner even offered me a small discount based on the amount of papers I bought. While I was doing this, my brother and I began going door to door asking people if they were interested in receiving these papers and paying slightly more. We found a number of interested parties and I was in business. Every Sunday, my father would drive me down to the store where we purchased the papers, and then I delivered them. Soon I expanded to include the local Pittsburgh Press as a number of customers were having difficulty receiving this, too. During the summer of 1987, I took over the Press route in my neighborhood and expanded further. The other papers eventually became too much trouble on Sundays, so I gradually phased them out. Since then, I have further expanded by taking on a second neighborhood route. To date, I have roughly 120–130 Sunday or daily Pittsburgh Press customers. I would prefer not to mention how much I make in the interest of privacy.

In addition to my business, I am a member of the Canevin Catholic High School's Future Business Leaders of America (FBLA), where I am the chapter public relations director and the Pennsylvania Region 10 president. My duties as regional president include presiding at regional meeting, representing my region and school as a voting delegate to the state leadership conference, speaking at various chapter meetings, and representing my school in the Battle of the Chapters competition at the State leadership workshop.

Margaret and Donald Woyicki (Steve's Parents)

We have always encouraged Steve to be an independent thinker, not necessarily follow the crowd, to take the initiative and be responsible for himself and his actions. Coupled with this, we encouraged him to be pleasant, friendly, and sensitive to others. Thus, he was always an extrovert who made friends and acquaintances very easily.

One of Steve's friends had a daily paper route and would always tell Steve about all the spending money he was making. He was able to purchase somewhat expensive things for himself and was also putting money in the bank awaiting the day he could buy his own sports car. Naturally this spurred the desire in Steve to get a job, but since he was only about 12, his options were limited. After a few brainstorming sessions between us, Steve, and his younger brother the idea of a paper route dealing in out–of–town papers was conceived. Although the papers were available in close proximity, many people were not anxious to go out in inclement weather early on Sunday mornings to purchase their papers.

Because of Steve's outgoing personality and friendliness, he was able to convince a number of people to take a chance and let him deliver their Sunday morning out–of–town papers. When people recognized his maturity and sense of responsibility, they began to ask him to perform other odd jobs. Through word of mouth his business grew and grew until it reached such proportions that he had to begin refusing jobs.

As far as what role we may have played in Steve's business, my husband came up with the idea. He also provided the necessary transportation and initial financing for the first few purchases. Steve began making a profit immediately and quickly repaid the loan. Steve did all of his own bookkeeping and maintains his own checking account. He continues to be very popular with people for the other services he provides, which include baby–sitting, lawn care, dog–sitting, errands, and whatever else one may need. He has recently expanded to include doing banking for some elderly neighbors.

We believe one of the secrets to raising a responsible child is to keep him so occupied doing things he enjoys that he doesn't have the time or the energy to get into trouble. We also believe in encouraging independent thinking, not to let his peers make his decisions for him. And probably most of all, responsibility and independence encourage good self–esteem. We believe all of these attributes contribute to making an entrepreneur, be he child or adult.

17

THE CENTER FOR TEEN
ENTREPRENEURS SURVEY

As I was doing my research for this book, I discovered that there had never been a survey done on teenagers who are either interested in entrepreneurship or who have actually started their own businesses. I came up with my own survey and gave it to the high school students that recently attended EntreCon, the High School Conference on Entrepreneurship held at the University of Pennsylvania's Wharton School. To my knowledge, this is the only survey of its kind ever conducted on young business–minded kids.

My purpose for attending the conference was to find out the character of the future generation of entrepreneurs. What I found were 160 motivated individuals with their own ideas and philosophies. They were all at this three–day conference to find out how they, too, can either start their own businesses or do better at businesses they were already running.

The survey these high school students filled out revealed quite a lot about their character. In this chapter, I would like to go over in detail the results of this survey and connect it to some of the ideas I have already discussed, such as ethics, self–esteem, achievement motivation, and money management.

WHAT MOTIVATED THEM TO CONSIDER ENTREPRENEURSHIP

In the survey, I wanted to find out exactly how the kids at the conference got interested in entrepreneurship. What I discovered was that nearly all of the kids developed an interest in entrepreneurship because at least one of their parents is an entrepreneur, they had entrepreneurial role models outside of the family, or their parents encouraged them to try their hands at starting their own businesses. Others said they wanted to be in business to control their own destinies. (Note: Responses may exceed 100% because students could make more than one choice.) Here are the questions and answers related to their motivation for considering entrepreneurship:

Question
How did you get interested in becoming an entrepreneur? (Choose as many as you like.)

a) We have a family business, so it was only natural.

b) My parent is an entrepreneur, so it was only natural.

c) My parents encouraged me to consider starting my own business.

d) I met an entrepreneur who got me interested in starting my own business.

e) Other (please specify) _____

Responses
a) 8% b) 20% c) 20% d) 40% e) 50%

Comments
As you can see, many of the respondents said that their family, parents, or other entrepreneurs helped them to consider entrepreneurship as an option. Choice (e) provided the kids with an opportunity to elaborate on how they became interested in entrepreneurship. Here are the written responses from the students:

"I believe the best working environment for me would be one that I set up. Fear of restraining my creativity by working for someone else."

"The love of a hobby became a business."

"I have just always been interested in self–employment."

"I like the idea of being in control and having power."

"I saw what corporate life does to family and friends."

"I am a shareholder and officer in some of my father's businesses."

"I have good raw ideas and found that I can refine them and market them into productive businesses through my determination."

"I became interested because of the challenge to make money for yourself rather than have a fixed income working for someone else like my parents."

"Gut instinct."

"I am someone who likes to know that I have control over situations around me, and I don't like to be stifled. I have always felt this way and being an entrepreneur will allow me freedom."

"I saw a good example of an entrepreneurial venture.."

Question

What do you consider most important about becoming an entrepreneur? (Choose one.)

a) Entrepreneurs make lots of money.

b) Entrepreneurs don't have to answer to anyone but themselves.

c) Entrepreneurs can be as creative as they want.

d) Entrepreneurs don't have to work as hard as people who have regular jobs.

e) Other (please specify) _____

Responses

a)15% b) 30% c) 40% d) 0% e) 15%

Comments

The response to this survey question shows that kids who were interested in entrepreneurship were not motivated by the lure of money. Only 15% of the kids wanted to become entrepreneurs because of money. Most of the kids were interested in entrepreneurship because they either wanted their independence or because it would allow them to express their creative talents. Choice (e) provided the kids the opportunity to write in their own answers. Here are some of the things they said:

"Entrepreneurs are organized and creative in all endeavors. Their main goal is to be a success first, then make money."

"They provide employment for others."

"By being an entrepreneur you can help your community."

"Entrepreneurs are responsible for their own success and can determine what that success will be."

"The sky is the limit in entrepreneurship."

"Entrepreneurs have complete freedom of choice."

"A love of the business you start."

"Entrepreneurs may make lots of money and may not have to answer to anyone depending on who financed the business (yourself, other)."

"Entrepreneurs can make money enjoying what they want to do."

"It's exhilarating to plan something, to watch it grow, and to know you made it happen!"

"It is important to me to have my own store and to be creative and to make other people happy."

"While making money, I am setting up a service to benefit the community."

"Security—happiness that I will be doing something I created. As an entrepreneur you don't have limits unless you limit yourself."

"Creativity, risk, exploration, opportunity."

"A personal sense of satisfaction that I have accomplished something that people are pleased to receive (i.e., my lawn—mowing service)."

"I can own my business doing something I enjoy."

"Open—ended opportunities and challenge."

"You get out of it what you put into it. Put a lot in, get a lot out."

"Power, freedom, security, and the desire to help others by helping myself."

"Power, freedom, recognition, and satisfaction."

"Entrepreneurs have control over all decisions."

"The satisfaction of achieving a goal for my own personal benefit."

"Entrepreneurs do everything themselves and that leads to great self–satisfaction."

"You are your own boss: you control your own destiny."

"The sense of self–satisfaction."

BUSINESS ETHICS

Question

Which one of these statements best represents how you feel about the insider–trading scandals in Wall Street over the past few years? (Choose one.)

a) The scandal was not really that widespread. A few individuals were just plain greedy.

b) The scandals made me more suspicious of Wall Street and business in general.

c) I always felt that Wall Street was corrupt, so I wasn't surprised about the scandals.

d) The people who were convicted are all innocent.

e) Other (please specify) _____

Responses
a) 30% b) 35% c) 15% d) 0% e) 20%

Comments
The answers the kids gave to this question indicate that about half of the kids either were more cynical about business after the scandals or had always been suspicious about the ethics of the business community. One–third of the students felt that the scandal was limited to just a few greedy individuals. Here are some of the answers the kids who selected choice (e) wrote:

> *"Some people saw the opportunity and took it even if it was illegal."*

> *"White–collar crime is just as punishable as any other group and not policed enough. With the press primarily reporting about the negative or covert business situation, it is discomforting to think of the business person's reputation, in general, as crafty and crooked. Few people realize that the companies that survive are the reputable ones who aren't established to screw everyone else."*

> *"It happens often. I am not surprised."*

> *"I understand that in the real world, corruption exists in all areas. I am not surprised that insider trading or any other illegal business practices exist."*
> *"People eventually get so greedy, they don't know when to stop. I feel that these people did something very wrong, and they should pay for their mistakes."*

> *"I wasn't surprised, but I don't feel that Wall Street is completely corrupt either."*

> *"There are going to be scandals all over business; you have to expect but not condone it."*

> *"I am not surprised about scandals anymore because they are so prevalent now."*

"It speaks of a much broader trend of lying, cheating, and stealing in America, not just Wall Street."

"It disappoints me when business is dishonest."

"It shows the destitution of morals and ethics in society."

"Some people were able to get an edge in a cut–throat business and are now paying the price for the edge."

Question

If a parent found out that his (her) young entrepreneur was cheating his (her) customers, which one of these actions would you expect the parent to take? (Choose one.)

    a) Temporarily pull the plug on the business to teach a lesson.

    b) Pull the plug on the business for good.

    c) Give a warning and then watch him (her) for signs of further unethical behavior.

    d) Parents should not interfere in their children's businesses.

    e) Other (please specify) _____

Responses

a) 18% b) 6% c) 46% d) 15% e) 15%

Comments

Seventy percent of the kids felt that some parental interference was justified if a young entrepreneur was caught cheating his customers. Fifteen percent of them on the other hand felt that parents should not interfere in their children's businesses even if these kids were cheating their customers. After talking to the respondents, I discovered that many of them felt that a young entrepreneur who cheated customers will eventually fail when he is marked as a cheat. These students who chose (d), felt that kids should learn from their mistakes. That is, business failure will teach them that it does not pay to cheat. Of course, as I indicated in Chapter 12 on business ethics, I disagree with this philosophy. I am happy that most kids also felt that direct parental interference is warranted when kids are unethical. Here are some of the written answers by the kids who chose (e):

"You have to allow them to learn from their own mistakes."

"Discuss the situation with him or her and jointly decide on what needs to be done to change the situation."

"Young entrepreneurs must learn by their mistakes and realize them themselves. There is no such parental supervision in the real world."

"Once again, this shows bad morals were learned at home or school. Can you really change 'home training'?"

"The parents should force the child to rectify the situation by restructuring the business and providing some form of compensation for the cheated customer."

"If the parents are in any way funding or helping the business, they should stop."

"Talk to them to explain how it is wrong."

"Discuss with the entrepreneur that this type of behavior may be proving successful now but it will eventually catch up with them."

"Influence their child as to making the correct decision. However, leave it up to the individual to make the correct ethical decision."

"Warn them and help them do what is right."

"Make the child go back to those customers, explain what he has done, and then settle on a reconciliatory agreement."

"Discuss consequences, pull plug on company until ethical."

"Advise him about it but don't interfere."

"Give a parable—not a direct speech—to tell them about their unethical practices."

SELF–ESTEEM

Question
How would you describe your self–confidence?

a) Extremely high. I feel that I can do anything.

b) Very high. I have a very positive attitude about myself and my ability to accomplish my goals.

c) Moderately high. I have confidence in myself but I occasionally doubt my abilities.

d) Low. I have very little confidence in myself and I often don't feel very good about myself.

e) Other (please specify) _____

Responses
a) 18% b) 48% c) 28% d) 3% e) 3%

Comments
As I discussed in an earlier chapter, most entrepreneurs have a lot of confidence in themselves. This characteristic is particularly obvious among young entrepreneurs. The survey showed that 66% of kids surveyed had either extremely high or very high confidence in their capabilities. Twenty–eight percent had moderately high self–confidence and only 3% had low self–confidence. Here is a representative sample of how most of the kids felt about themselves:

"I feel like I can do anything and shape my own destiny. However, I, as a normal teenager, have moments of self–doubt."

"I have a great amount of self–confidence but I'r.i flexible to changes in time. I feel if you get overconfident, one makes mistakes."

MONEY MANAGEMENT

Question
Which one of the following choices describes how you get money from your parents? (Choose as many as you like.)

    a) I get an allowance from my parents with no strings attached.

    b) My parents pay me for the chores I do around the house.

    c) I get an allowance from my parents and they have control as to how I spend it.

    d) I get money from my parents on an as–needed basis.

    e) Other (please specify) _____

Responses
a) 30% b) 4% c) 1% d) 50% e) 30%

Comments
Thirty percent of the kids got allowances, while 50% of them got money when they needed it for a purchase. As I indicated in Chapter 6 on money management, the best way to teach kids how to handle money is through the allowance method. However, as you can see, many parents still give their kids money on an as–needed basis. Here is a sample of the written responses by the students:

> *"I normally don't ask or receive money from them except for special occasions such as this conference."*

> *"For grades higher than 85%, I get a certain amount of money for each grade. If I get lower than an 85% in anything, I pay them money."*

"I work for the things I want (e.g., movies). My parents buy only the essentials (school clothes)."

"Although they give me money, they don't spoil me. I get money for reasonable purposes."

"I have an expense account with my parents whereas I budget my allowance on clothes and miscellaneous."

"I don't get money from my parents except for special occasions."

"(I get money from my parents) when I get straight A's or win some kind of award."

"My parents pay me money for chores around the house as well as work I do for their business with no string attached. If I need more money, they give it to me but generally I must budget well."

"I have had part–time jobs since I was 11 years old."

"(I get money) for how well I do in school."

"I make my own money."

"I work for all of my spending money for clothes, entertainment, etc. My parents give me money from time to time for various things, but not on a regular basis."

"I get an allowance from my parents according to my 24–hour daily conduct."

Question

At what age did you start thinking about becoming an entrepreneur? (Choose one.)

 a) When I was less than 8.

 b) Between ages 8 and 10.

 c) Between ages 11 and 15.

 d) Between ages 16 and 18.

Responses

a) 13% b) 12% c) 55% d) 20%

Comments

I was surprised to find out that 25% of the young people who responded to the survey had actually thought about entrepreneurship by age 10. Eighty percent of all respondents had thought about entrepreneurship by the time they were 15 years old. Keep in mind that the kids who answered the survey were all juniors or seniors in high school so they were all between 16 and 18.

THE IMPORTANCE OF EDUCATION

Question

If you became successful at a business while still attending high school, which one of these decisions are you most likely to make about college? (Choose one.)

 a) I will forget about college and work on my business.

 b) I will go to college and delegate the responsibility of running my business to someone else until I finish college.

c) I will go to a college nearby and continue with my business at the same time.

d) I will postpone college for a few years while I run my business.

e) Other (please specify) _____

Responses
a) 0% b) 41% c) 42% d) 5% e) 12%

Comments
The responses showed that business–minded young people are aware of the benefits of a good education and have no intention of forsaking it to pursue their business ventures. In talking to the respondents, I found that most of the kids felt that an education will make them well–rounded individuals and that it will help them in running their businesses. Only 5% of the students that responded would consider postponing college if their businesses proved to be successful.

OTHER QUESTIONS

Question
Would you consider a person who starts a charitable organization to be an entrepreneur?

_____ Yes   _____ No

Responses
No: 17% Yes: 83%

Have you ever started your own business?

_____ Yes   _____ No

Responses
No: 69% Yes: 31%

THE CENTER FOR TEEN ENTREPRENEURS SURVEY OF ENTRECON PARTICIPANTS

Here is the survey in its entirety as it was presented to the participants of the High School Conference on Entrepreneurship (Entrecon). Once again, this survey was merely designed to give me a flavor as to the type of kids that are entrepreneurially minded.

At what age did you start thinking about becoming an entrepreneur? (Choose one.)

a) When I was less than 8.

b) Between ages 8 and 10.

c) Between ages 11 and 15.

d) Between ages 16 and 18.

Which one of the following choices describes how you get money from your parents? (Choose as many as you like.)

a) I get an allowance from my parents with no strings attached.

b) My parents pay me for the chores I do around the house.

c) I get an allowance from my parents and they have control as to how I spend it.

d) I get money from my parents on an as–needed basis.

e) Other (please specify) _____

How did you get interested in becoming an entrepreneur? (Choose as many as you like.)

a) We have a family business, so it was only natural.

b) My parent is an entrepreneur, so it was only natural.

c) My parents encouraged me to consider starting my own business.

    d) I met an entrepreneur who got me interested in starting my own business.

    e) Other (please specify) _____

What do you consider most important about becoming an entrepreneur? (Choose one.)

    a) Entrepreneurs make lots of money.

    b) Entrepreneurs don't have to answer to anyone but themselves.

    c) Entrepreneurs can be as creative as they want.

    d) Entrepreneurs don't have to work as hard as people who have regular jobs.

    e) Other (please specify) _____

What business publications do you read regularly? (Choose as many as you like.)

    a) *Entrepreneur*

    b) *Success*

    c) *Business Week*

    d) *Inc.*

    e) *Wall Street Journal*

    f) Other (please specify) _____

What business organizations do you belong to? (Choose as many as you like.)

    a) Junior Achievement

    b) Future Business Leaders Of America

    c) Distributive Education Club Of America

    d) Other (please specify) _____

How would you describe your self–confidence?

a) Extremely high. I feel that I can do anything.

b) Very high. I have a very positive attitude about myself and my ability to accomplish my goals.

c) Moderately high. I have confidence in myself, but I occasionally doubt my abilities.

d) Low. I have very little confidence in myself, and I often don't feel very good about myself.

e) Other (please specify) _____

If you became successful at a business while still attending high school, which one of these decisions are you most likely to make about college? (Choose one.)

a) I will forget about college and work on my business.

b) I will go to college and delegate the responsibility of running my business to someone else until I finish college.

c) I will go to a college nearby and continue with my business at the same time.

d) I will postpone college for a few years while I run my business.

e) Other (please specify) _____

Which one of these statements best represents how you feel about the insider–trading scandals in Wall Street over the past few years? (Choose one.)

a) The scandal was not really that widespread. A few individuals were just plain greedy.

b) The scandals made me more suspicious of Wall Street and business in general.

c) I always felt that Wall Street was corrupt, so I wasn't surprised about the scandals.

d) The people who were convicted are all innocent.

e) Other (please specify) _____

If a parent found out that his (her) young entrepreneur was cheating customers, which one of these actions would you expect the parent to take? (Choose one.)

a) Temporarily pull the plug on the business to teach a lesson.

b) Pull the plug on the business for good.

c) Give a warning and then watch for signs of further unethical behavior.

d) Parents should not interfere in their children's businesses.

e) Other (please specify) _____

Would you like to be a subject for my book entitled *The Lemonade Stand* about young entrepreneurs ?

_____ Yes   _____ No

If you answered yes to this question, please write your address and phone number below:

Address:
Phone:
What is your sex?

_____ Male   _____ Female

What is your race?

_____ White   _____ Hispanic
_____ African–American
_____ Other (please specify) _____

Do you now own a business?

_____ Yes   _____ No

If you answered yes to this question, please tell me what type of business you own.

Have you ever started your own business?

_____ Yes   _____ No

Would you consider a person who starts a charitable organization to be an entrepreneur?

_____ Yes   _____ No

18

ORGANIZATIONS, CAMPS, CONFERENCES, AND PUBLICATIONS TO ENCOURAGE YOUNG ENTREPRENEURS

In 1987, I formed the Center for Teen Entrepreneurs (formerly the Center for Child Entrepreneurs). I started the organization because I felt there was no place young people could turn to for help in starting and running their own businesses. The vast majority of entrepreneurial organizations were geared toward adults and none of the business publications on the market even acknowledged the presence of teen and preteen entrepreneurs. My gut told me that more teenagers in the United States are running their own modest businesses than most people think. As I began researching my hypothesis, I discovered that there were lots of kids running business that had nothing to do with lawn mowing or delivering papers—stereotypical teenage entrepreneur businesses. Furthermore, I found that kids wanted to have a forum to exchange business ideas with other kids and to learn how to start and run their own enterprises.

The Center for Teen Entrepreneurs' sole purpose is to help kids become entrepreneurs. The organization does this primarily through the Teen Business Camp which is a camp held during the summer on the campuses of the New Jersey Institute of Technology and Rutgers University in Newark, New Jersey. Rutgers University will be the site of a year round entrepreneurship program for young people to be run by CTE in the near future. Young people can turn to CTE for assistance in developing their business ideas and running their enterprises.

For more information on CTE's activities and new initiatives, write to:

Center for Teen Entrepreneurs
P.O. Box 3967
New York, New York 10163–6027L
Phone: 800–438–8336

Here are some other organizations, conferences, camps, and competitions that can help introduce kids to the world of entrepreneurship. Some of the organizations actually have programs that teach kids about entrepreneurship while others advocate better economic education for kids in schools. In addition, some of the organizations focus on at–promise kids (sometimes called at–risk kids)—economically disadvantaged kids enrolled in uninspiring schools—while others target the general population. Although I spoke to senior managers of many of these organizations, in some cases, the information in this chapter comes from their promotional brochures.

ORGANIZATIONS TEACHING THE MECHANICS OF ENTREPRENEURSHIP

An Income of Her Own

The mission of An Income of Her Own (AIOHO) is to give girls and young women the tools, knowledge, and experience to help them for independence and economic well being. To create a social and economic web for young women, AIOHO partners with such organizations as Girls Inc., Girl Scouts of the USA, the National Association of Women Business Owners, as well as with school systems, and foundations which have as their common concern the economic future of young women.

AIOHO sponsors a teen business plan competition, holds conferences, runs a business camp for teen women, publishes a newsletter of teen women, and provides business resources and a support network for its members.

For more information, write to:

An Income of Her Own
P.O. Box 987
Santa Barbara, CA 93102
Phone: 805–646–1215 or 800–350–2987

Administration for Native Americans

This organization can provide information on youth entrepreneurship programs on American Indian reservations. Examples of youth entrepreneurship projects funded by the Administration for Native Americans are: the Native Hawaiian Youth Entrepreneurship Project, the Nez Perce Youth Equitation and Entrepreneur Project, Going For Self (a two–year training program in entrepreneurial skills for 15 to 17 year olds), Unity Inc. (a hands–on youth entrepreneurship project), and the Bering Strait Regional Native Youth Entrepreneurial Project.

For more information, write:

Administration for Native Americans
200 Independent Ave., S.W
Washington, D.C. 20201
Phone: 202–690–7776

Business Kids

Business Kids is an organization that introduces kids to the free enterprise system. It does so by providing kids with the Business Kit: a kit that takes kids through the step–by–step process of starting their own businesses.

For more information, write to:

Business Kids
1 Alhambra Plaza #1400
Coral Gables, FL 33134
Phone: 305–445–8869 or 800–282–5437.

Cities in Schools

Cities in Schools is an organization that endeavors to reduce the high school dropout rate nationwide. The organization is piloting a program to teach kids about entrepreneurship in its affiliates around the country.

For more information, write to:

Cities in Schools
1199N. Fairfax Street #300
Alexandria, VA 22314–1436
Phone: 703–519–8999

Do Something

Do something is a nonprofit organization that provides training, guidance, and financial resources to emerging young leaders of all backgrounds so they can help build their communities.

As I have mentioned earlier in this book, a person can be an entrepreneur even if he or she engages in an activity where he or she expects to make no money. Community organizations like Do

Something encourage young people to apply entrepreneurial skills to find innovative solutions to the things they see that are wrong in their communities. Here are some notable activities of the Do Something organization:

1. *Local Grants Program.* One of the ways that Do Something encourages creative problem–solving in the communities in which it operates is to off local grants of $500 to give young people the opportunity to transform their community building ideas into action.

2. *Sponsorship of Community Coaches.* Do Something sponsors "community coaches"—teachers in schools who work with students to improve their community both inside the school and in the surrounding neighborhood.

3. *Leadership Courses.* Each local fund offers a series of leadership courses which enables participants to work with their peers and established community leaders, learn management theories and practice leadership skills.

To find out more about Do Something, contact:

Do Something
P.O. Box 2409 JAF
New York, NY 10116
Phone: 212–978–7777

Distributive Education Clubs of America

The Distributive Education Clubs of America (DECA) is a nonprofit organization that prepares high school students for rewarding careers in marketing and management, and that encourages entrepreneurship among kids. It provides marketing–related activities and leadership development based on classroom study. DECA's activities focus on competition at the local, state, and national levels. The events related to entrepreneurship involve high school students presenting and submitting business plans for their business ideas. The kids are judged for their business idea and their marketing, finance, and management plans for their businesses.

DECA activities also teach kids the principles of economics and the free enterprise system through classroom instruction. DECA has branches in every state and in Canada.

I have been a finance judge at the DECA entrepreneurship competition in New Jersey. The high school entrepreneurs I judged had unbelievably well–developed business plans.

For more information, write:

Distributive Education Clubs of America
1908 Association Drive
Reston, VA 22091
Phone: 703–860–5000

Educational Designs that Generate Excellence

Educational Designs that Generate Excellence (EDGE) uses entrepreneurship as a catalyst to prepare young people as well as adults for economic success as heads of their own businesses or as valued employees.

EDGE offers a wide range of hands–on entrepreneurship programs for children and adults that includes classroom training, seminars, teacher training, and a business camp.

For more information, write to:

EDGE Inc.
Cabrini Boulevard #21
New York, NY 10033
Phone: 212–978–0262

Educational, Training and Enterprise Center

The Educational, Training and Enterprise Center (EDTEC) is an organization that encourages kids to become entrepreneurs. It does this through classroom instruction and workbooks. EDTEC's workbooks (or units as they call them) take kids through the step–by–step process of starting a business. EDTEC's specific goals are to:

- Prepare kids for independence.

- Teach kids about their parents' economic values in a form they can swallow.

- Teach kids responsibility without preaching.

- Show kids alternative employment options.

- Teach kids the value of a dollar.

EDTEC also offers staff training and technical assistance to schools and other organizations interested in youth entrepreneurship.

For more information, write:

EDTEC
309 Market Street
Camden, NJ 08102
Phone: 609–342–8277

The Entrepreneurial Development Institute

The Entrepreneurial Development Institute (TEDI) is a nonprofit organization that seeks to empower disadvantaged youth, ages 7–21, by teaching them how to develop their own small businesses, avoid drugs, sharpen academic skills, and form positive attitudes about themselves and their communities.

TEDI's program includes basic entrepreneurship training, case study analysis, and hands–on entrepreneurial projects.

For more information write to:

The Entrepreneurial Development Institute
2025 I Street, NW Suite 905
Washington, DC 20006
Phone: 202–822–8334

First Nations Development Institute

The First Nations Development Institute is a nonprofit organization whose objective is to encourage economic development on Indian reservations. Sherry Salway Black, the First Nations vice president was quoted in the New York Times as saying, "Our belief is that there are tremendous resources on the reservations that they need to develop from within."

The organization has a development fund called the Eagle Staff Fund designed to help native people control their economic future. In the past, this fund has provided seed money for young American Indians to start and run their own businesses.

For more information, write:

First Nations Development Institute
The Stores Building
11917 Main Street
Fredericksburg, VA 22408

Future Business Leaders of America

The Future Business Leaders of America (FBLA) is a non-profit organization whose stated goal is to help high school students (grades 7–12) become entrepreneurs or seek careers in business. The organization helps members nationwide turn their ambitions and abilities into financial successes. FBLA also has entrepreneurship competitions.

For more information, contact:

Future Business Leaders of America
1912 Association Drive
Reston, VA 22091
Phone: 703–860–3334

Hugh O'Brian Youth Foundation

The Hugh O'Brian Youth Foundation (HOBY) is a nonprofit organization that exposes kids to the American economic incentive system and its democratic process. HOBY programs are for high–school sophomores who have demonstrated some leadership potential. Each year, 20,000 high school sophomores attend HOBY leadership seminars. Because each school can send only one student to a HOBY seminar each year, the participants are usually very highly motivated. They are not always the best academically in their respective schools, but they are high achievers. All the participants have been designated as having great leadership potential. Barry Whitmer, senior vice president for field operations, says that the leadership workshops "attract students who display many of the characteristics attributed to entrepreneurship, such as high motivation and self–esteem." Whitmer emphasizes the point that HOBY teaches kids how to think.

The HOBY leadership workshops typically cover five topics, all of which are relevant to entrepreneurship:

1. The American incentive system.

2. Education.

3. Entrepreneurship.

4. Media/communications.

5. The future of the United States as a world leader.

HOBY does not ignore business ethics either. The organization feels that it is important to show kids that not all business people are crooks, and to show them the importance of ethics in business.

For more information, write:

Hugh O'Brian Youth Foundation
10880 Wilshire Boulevard, Suite 900
Los Angeles, CA 90024
Phone: 310–474–4370

Inventors Workshop International

The Inventors Workshop is a nonprofit organization formed by inventors to help other inventors profit from their creativity. The organization accepts all inventors—including grade school, high school, and collegiate inventors. Inventors Workshop also co–sponsors the Young Creators and Inventors program.

For more information, write to:

Inventors Workshop International
7332 Mason Avenue
Canoga Park, CA 91306–2822
Phone: 818–340–4268

Institute for Youth Entrepreneurship

The Institute of Youth Entrepreneurship (IYE) is a community–owned initiative that provides a rigorous, supervised, comprehensive set of classroom and work–related experiences for program participants. IYE serves young people from ages 12 through 18. The program model consists of two basic areas: the classroom and the living business—each of which is simultaneously linked to a mentoring component.

IYE is a project spearheaded by the One to One Partnership and operated in collaboration with community based organizations such as Alianza Dominicana, The Harbor for Boys & Girls, and The Valley.

For more information write:

Institute for Youth Entrepreneurship
310 Lenox Avenue
New York, NY 10027
Phone: 212–369–3900

For information on IYEs in other cities, contact the One to One Partnership using the address in the description of the organization found below.

Junior Achievement

Junior Achievement is the largest, oldest, and fastest–growing, nonprofit economic education organization in the world. Through partnerships with the business and education communities, Junior Achievement currently reaches over 2.5 million elementary, middle and high school students in the United States and in over 80 countries. Junior Achievement is financed by over 100,000 businesses, foundations and individuals. By utilizing classroom volunteers, Junior Achievement educates and inspires young people to value free enterprise, understand business and economics and be workforce ready. In the United States, over 57,000 volunteers present Junior Achievement programs in almost 14,000 schools each year.

Since its founding in 1919 by Horace A. Moses, president of Strathmore Paper Company, Junior Achievement has contributed to the business and economic education of almost 18 million young people.

Junior Achievement programs for kindergarten through grade 12 include:

- Applied Economics—an in–school, one semester course that uses a text book and special computer software to teach high school sophomores, juniors, and seniors basic economics.

- The Company Program—the original Junior Achievement program, which provides high school students with practical business experience through the organization and operation of an after school business enterprise.

- The Middle Grades Program—an in–school, economics and business curriculum for seventh, eighth, and ninth grade students. It is organized around three major themes: Personal Economics, Enterprise in Action and The International Marketplace.

- The Elementary School Program—an in–school course where kindergarten through sixth graders learn about the roles they play as individuals, workers, and consumers.

In addition, Junior Achievement hosts the annual International Student Forum for students all over the world. This extended learning experience for Junior Achievement students consists of educational workshops, group discussions with top business leaders and leadership development activities.

However it is the unfailing leadership and dedication of Junior Achievement contributors and volunteers which have kept the dream of economic education alive for millions of young people.

There are currently over 200 local Junior Achievement offices throughout the United States and 85 member nations.

Please check your local phone book or write to:

Junior Achievement Inc.
One Education Way
Colorado Springs, CO 80906
Phone: 719–540–8000

I have been personally involved with some of Junior Achievement's programs. For example, I volunteered my time for a 4–month period as a consultant for Applied Economics in New York City. In addition, I have conducted a workshop for the International Student Forum held annually at the University of Indiana. My experience with the organization has been very pleasant and I came away feeling that I had contributed to the intellectual growth of the young people with whom I came in contact.

Minority Youth Entrepreneurship Program

The Minority Youth Entrepreneurship Program at Washington University in St. Louis, Missouri, is designed to expose high school minorities to the prospects of self–employment and at the same time encourage them to pursue higher education. The program is offered to a select group of about 40 local St. Louis high school students. Gary Hockberg, associate dean for undergraduate studies at Washington University, stresses that "nearly 100% of the kids that are chosen for the program are college bound."

The Minority Youth Entrepreneurship Program has three components:

1. *Educational Component.* The kids are taught basic business skills in accounting, finance, and economics.

2. *Entrepreneurship Component.* Owners of local minority businesses give speeches and hold sessions meant to inspire kids to consider entrepreneurship.

3. *Personal Skills Component.* The kids are taught presentation skills, writing, and research skills.

At the end of the program, the students are expected to write and present their own business plans.

For more information, write:

Minority Youth Entrepreneurship Program
John M. Olin School of Business
Campus Box 1133
1 Brooking Drive
Washington University
St. Louis, MO 63130
Phone: 314–935–6380

The National Center for American Indian Enterprise Development

The National Center for American Indian Enterprise Development serves as a management consulting firm and chamber of commerce to American Indians in starting and running their own businesses. The organization is headquartered in Mesa, Arizona, and it has regional offices in Seattle, Washington; El Monte and Los Angeles, California. The organization works with all American Indian entrepreneurs, including high school and junior high school students. The organization's work with high school and junior high school students focuses on entrepreneurial education and provides young American Indians with an opportunity to interface with American Indian business people. The organization publishes its own newsletter and holds an annual conference.

For more information, write:

The National Center for American Indian
Enterprise Development
953 East Juanita Avenue
Mesa, Arizona 82054
Phone: 602–545–1298

The National Foundation for Teaching Entrepreneurship

The National Foundation for Teaching Entrepreneurship (NFTE) is a nonprofit organization whose mission is to bring basic business knowledge and entrepreneurial literacy to the economically disadvantaged youth of America's inner cities. The organization is also committed to encouraging entrepreneurship among kids with disabilities.

NFTE aims to give young people the tools with which to turn around the economic devastation of their neighborhoods and to give them a positive vision for the future.

Each participant in the NFTE program can expect to learn:

- Basic math and communications skills.
- The importance of business ethics and personal values.
- How to utilize economic and financial concepts.
- How to recognize business opportunities.
- How to write memos and business letters.
- How to research potential markets.
- How to draw up basic contracts.
- How to open a bank account.
- How to legally register a business.

The founder of the organization, Steve Mariotti, says that the lessons that the kids learn go beyond the mechanics of starting businesses. "True, the kids learn about business" says Steve. "But they also get a heightened sense of accomplishment and self–worth when they realize that they are capable of running their own businesses and forging their own destinies."

For more information, write:

The National Foundation for Teaching Entrepreneurship
64 Fulton Street #700
New York, NY 10038
Phone: 212–233–1777

National 4–H Council

The National 4–H Council has local and national programs designed to help young people consider entrepreneurship as career objectives. Here are a few of the programs:

- Youth Entrepreneurial Seminar (Minnesota).

- 4–H Youth Enterprise Program (New York).

- 4–H Entrepreneurship (Indiana).

- 4–H Teenpreneur Program (Ohio).

- 4–H Learn to Earn Program (national).

If the regional programs are not in your state, you can call 4–H to find out how you can have the program introduced in your area.

The National 4–H Council has a program called Revitalizing Rural America in which it holds various programs designed to help young people start businesses in rural areas.

For more information, write:

National 4–H Council
7100 Connecticut Avenue
Chevy Chase, Maryland 20815
Phone: 301–961–2818

The One to One Partnership

The One to One Partnership is a nonprofit organization established in 1989 by leading philanthropists, business people, educators, social activists and entrepreneurs. One to One is dedicated to bringing more mentoring to more children—mentoring to help them develop to their fullest potential as individuals, and as productive, financially responsible individuals. The organization has affiliates in eleven major metropolitan communities.

One to One sponsors the Institute for Youth Entrepreneurship (as described in a previous page) in some of the cities in which it operates.

For more information on the One to One organization and on its Institutes for Youth Entrepreneurships write to:

One to One Partnership, Inc.
2801 M Street, NW
Washington, DC 20007
Phone: 202–338–3844

Operation Enterprise

Operation Enterprise, a program of the American Management Association (AMA), is a 10–day session for high school students 16 years of age or older. Operations Enterprise focuses on issues such as entrepreneurship, personal growth, professional success, and self–motivation. The core curriculum includes:

- Planning and setting objectives.

- Organizational skills.

- Motivation.

- Life and career planning.

- Computerized business simulation:

- Challenge to leadership.

For more information, write to:

Operation Enterprise
American Management Association
Box 88
Hamilton, NY 13346
Phone: 315–824–2000 or 800–634–4262

Ready Program

Ready is a comprehensive, sustained and broad intervention program that is designed to help a cross–section of Newark youth realize their full potential. The organization does so by working with about 600 students in the Newark school system. Among the organization's activities is an entrepreneurship program, during the academic year, to teach high school students the basics of starting and running a business. The students, all of whom received stock at a minority owned bank in Newark, also learn money and banking basics.

Ready also has a mentoring program designed to provide it's students with stable caring adults who can give them guidance and support.

For more information, contact:

Ready Inc.
240 MLK Boulevard
Newark, NJ 07102
Phone: 201–624–0455

Rural Entrepreneurship Through Action Learning (REAL)

REAL Enterprises is an experiential entrepreneurship program offered in over 100 high schools and post–secondary institutions in 17 states designed to link rural education and development through student entrepreneurship.

Through the program, rural young people get their first exposure to the option of entrepreneurship and the opportunity to be job creators instead of job applicants. In the REAL course, which is taught for credit, students assess their entrepreneurial abilities, analyze their local community, and research and write business plans for businesses or nonprofit community services that fill a local need. Students with feasible ideas are encouraged to start microenterprises that "graduate" with them to become a part of the local economy. REAL students have started businesses providing products and services ranging from computer hardware to pressure washing, and from furniture to small engine repair.

For more information, write to:

REAL Enterprises, Inc.
115 Market Street #320
Durham, NC 27701–3221
Phone: 919–688–7325 or 800–798–0643

Small Business Development Centers

Small Business Development Centers (SBDC) offer seminars and other training designed to help small businesses. Says Brenda Hopper, State Director of the New Jersey SBDC, "the core of what we do is one on one counseling and training".

SBDC's are usually based on college campuses and are funded by both the state and federal governments, as well as private institutions.

One of the many goals of the SBDCs is to focus its support on "special groups" which includes young entrepreneurs. Each SBDC offers its own programs in order to meet this goal. For example, SBDC of Iowa has the Young Entrepreneur Seminars designed to expose young people to business start–ups. The SBDC of Georgia has the Black Youth Entrepreneurship Program designed to encourage African–American juniors and seniors to consider entrepreneurship, and the New Jersey SBDC at Rutgers University in Newark provides teachers and in–kind services to Teen Business Camp, a two–week youth entrepreneurship camp.

There are probably many programs like the three I have just mentioned in the 50 or so SBDCs around the country. To get information on the location on.

To find the location of the SBDC near you, contact:

The Association of SBDC
1300 Chain Bridge Road –Suite 201
McLean, VA 22101–3967
Phone: 703–448–6124

Service Corps of Retired Executives

The Service Corps of Retired Executives (SCORE) is an organization set up by the Small Business Administration (SBA)—a government agency, whose sole purpose is to give small businesses free business advice. SCORE is made up of over 13,000 retired and semi–retired business executives scattered in 750 counseling locations all over the country.

If your kids need advice on how to run their businesses, they should contact SCORE and set up an appointment with one of the business counselors for a one–on–one session.

For more information call the SBA Answer Desk at 1–800–827–5722.

Trickle Up Program

The Trickle Up Program is an independent, nonprofit organization dedicated to creating new opportunities for employment and economic and social well–being among low–income populations of the world. Now in 108 countries, Trickle Up has helped more than a quarter of a million entrepreneurs start 40,000 small businesses.

Trickle Up also helps high school students in inner–city neighborhoods start businesses. It offers small start–up capital to these students and a simple business training program.

Trickle Up works with volunteer coordinators. Most of its coordinators are employees of grass–roots community development agencies, in addition to Peace Corps volunteers, United Nations volunteers, governmental extension offices, and international organizations (such as CARE, and the Christian Children's Fund). In the United States, Trickle–Up works through youth organizations and high schools.

For more information, write:

Trickle–Up Program
54 Riverside Drive
New York, NY 10024–6509
Phone: 212–362–7958

The University–Community Outreach Program

The University–Community Outreach Program is sponsored by the Milken Institute for Job and Capital Formation. It is the mother institution for the Wharton West Philadelphia Project, East Bay Outreach Project, and the Columbia Business School Community Collaboration (all listed in this chapter). It hopes to oversee similar programs at different institutions all over the country.

The University–Community Outreach Program also sponsors other programs such as the Technical Assistance Program (TAP); Skills, Training and Employment Preparation (STEP); and BRIDGES—a personal support and recreation program.

For more information, write:

Milken Institute
401 City Avenue, Suite 204
Bala Cynwyd, PA 19004
Phone: 610–668–5330

Volunteers of America—Midas Touch Program

Volunteers of America's Midas Touch Program is designed to help teach young people the fundamentals of the free enterprise system and the social responsibilities of business. The program targets kids who wouldn't otherwise consider the entrepreneurial alternative to making a living.

Midas Touch pairs each young person in the program with mentors who can help guide them to start and run their businesses successfully.

Mark Cossman, president of the Friends of Volunteers Of America, tells me that the Midas Touch Program has attracted the attention of a group of psychologists from the Kirov Institute of Advanced Medical Studies in St. Petersburgh, Russia:

> *The Kirov Institute asked us to replicate the Midas Touch Program in Russia. As you know, they are trying to make a transition to a market economy and they are starting with their young people. I went there to set up a committee that will implement the program.*

For more information, write:

Volunteers of America
Midas Touch Program
3600 Wilshire Blvd., #1500
Los Angeles, CA 90010
Phone: 213–389–1500

Wharton West Philadelphia Project, Columbia Business School Community Collaboration and East Bay Outreach Project

The Wharton West Philadelphia Project runs a program called the Young Entrepreneurs at Wharton (YEW). The goal of the program is to teach kids how to start and run their own businesses. YEW is a two–part program. In the summer, the high–school participants attend a two–week session of instructions and activities at the University of Pennsylvania's Wharton School. During the school year, each of these same students is paired off with a Wharton Business School mentor and participates in activities at the university.

Each high–school participant in the program can look forward to:

- Creating a business based on their talents and interests.

- Working individually with Wharton School graduate students who will counsel them on how to implement their business ideas, help them with schoolwork, and help them establish long–term educational and career goals.

- Participating in monthly activities focused on education, careers, and sometimes just fun.

- Designing and creating their own business cards and advertisements, and making videotaped sales presentations.

- Meeting successful entrepreneurs.

The program is for motivated high school students (entering the tenth, eleventh, and twelfth grades) interested in learning about the world of business. To qualify for the program, each student must fill out an application and convince the directors that they will make a year–long commitment to it. Priority is given to residents of West Philadelphia.

What I like about this program is that in addition to training young entrepreneurs, it also encourages the participants to go to college. Mentor Laura Bisset says that the program gives some of the kids more of an incentive to attend college. "One girl was so intimidated by the prospect of going to college that she wasn't even going to apply. YEW gave her a lot of confidence in herself. Confidence that sprang out of the fact that she saw there was nothing to be intimidated about in college and in the business world."

The Columbia Business School Community Collaboration, and the East Bay Outreach operate the same way as the Wharton West Philadelphia Project except that they recruit students from New York City, and Berkley, California, respectively. All three organizations are funded by the Miliken Institute's University–Community Outreach Program. In addition, they all focus on entrepreneurship for minority youth.

For more information, write:

The Wharton West Philadelphia Project
325 Vance Hall
3733 Spruce Street
Philadelphia, PA 19104–6301
Phone: 215–898–2490

Columbia Business School Community Collaboration
Columbia University
Central Mail Room
Box 1373
New York, New York 10027
Phone: 212–870–3543

East Bay Outreach Project
University of California School of Business
350 Barrows Hall
Berkeley, CA 94720
Phone: 510–642–7880

Young Americans Education Foundation

The Young Americans Education Foundation is a nonprofit organization dedicated to advocating financial education for kids. Its mission is to teach kids how to handle finances responsibly, and to grow and prosper in the free enterprise system. Young Ameri-Towne, the hands–on lesson in free enterprise with a highly interactive curriculum that incorporates both academic and interpersonal skills, is the flagship program of Young Americans Education Foundation. At AmeriTowne, kids from 10 to 13 years old experience the hands–on approach to running the economy of a simulated town set up by the students themselves. This town is set up on the campus of the University of Denver and it is complete with a government, shops, consumers, and other components of a real town.

The Young Americans Education Foundation also offers seminars related to youth entrepreneurship, basic banking and finance, personal financial planning, investments, college financial planning, and careers in banking. In addition, the organization runs the Young Americans Bank which is open to young people under the age of twenty–two. The bank has over 18,000 depositors and offers credit cards (with a $200 credit line) and small personal loans to its young customers.

For more information, write:

Young Americans Education Foundation
311 Steele Street
Denver, CO 80206
Phone: 303–321–2954

ECONOMIC AND CREATIVITY EDUCATION

The Academy for Economic Education

The Academy for Economic Education is a nonprofit organization dedicated to providing young citizens with an understanding of our nation's economic system, their role in this system now, and in the future as workers, consumers, and voters of the 21st century. The academy accomplishes its objectives by providing graduate–level economics education programs for K–12 teachers and by developing and distributing educational materials to these teachers and their students.

For more information, write:

The Academy for Economic Education
125 NationsBank Center
Richmond, VA 23277
Phone: 804–643–0071

American Institute of Small Business

The American Institute of Small Business is a publisher of educational materials, video and books on small business, entrepreneurship, and free enterprise. In addition, the institute holds business training workshops and seminars for educators and students.

Some of the materials sold by the institute tell young people how to start their own small businesses and how to write their own business plans.

For more information, write:

American Institute of Small Business
7515 Wayzata Blvd., Suite 201
Minneapolis, MN 55426
Phone: 612–545–7001 or 800–328–2906

Creative Education Foundation

The Creative Education Foundation is a nonprofit organization that promotes creativity, innovation, and entrepreneurship through publications and programs. The CPSI Youth Program offered by the foundation is designed to unleash and challenge the natural creativity of young people between the ages of 8 and 16.

For more information, write:

Creative Education Foundation
1050 Union Road
Buffalo, NY 14224
Phone: 716–675–3181

Ewing Marion Kaufman Foundation

The programs of the Ewing Marion Kaufman Foundation focus on teaching kindergarten to post–secondary students economics and entrepreneurship basics. The organization has such programs as Mother and Daughter Entrepreneurs in Teams (for seventh graders), and EntrePrep Institute (for high school students).

For more information write to:

Ewing Marion Kauffman Foundation
4900 Oak Street
Kansas City, MO 64112–2776
Phone: 816–932–1000

Inventors Bookshop

This book shop sells information about how develop, market, and cash in on inventions. It has quite a few publications for aspiring young inventors. The organization that runs the book shop, M&M Associates, also works with inventors to get inventions to the market.

For more information, contact:

Inventors Bookshop
M&M Associates
12424 Main Street
Fort Jones, CA 96032
Phone: 916–468–2282

National Council on Economic Education

The National Council on Economic Education (NCEE) is a nonprofit organization whose goal is to increase the quantity and enhance the quality of economic education in the nation's schools.

The NCEE trains teachers and develops curriculum material. Through training programs, the NCEE helps educators at all levels develop a better understanding of basic economic concepts and the operation of the American economic system.

Through a national cooperative effort with school districts, the NCEE influences the level of economic understanding of students, kindergarten to twelfth grade.

Other programs offered by NCEE are the Entrepreneurship In the U.S. Economy Program, and the Choices and Changes Program (CC). These programs are designed to empower young people with the skills, knowledge, and attitudes that will enable them to think entrepreneurially and perhaps become entrepreneurs.

For more information, write:

National Council On Economic Education
1400 Avenue of The Americas
New York, NY 10036
Phone: 212–730–7007

The National Center for Financial Education

The National Center for Financial Education (NCFE) is a nonprofit organization that encourages both adults and children to plan their financial future. The organization offers publications and programs designed to help children understand money management and it also offers a list of educational resources for young people.

For a catalog, send $1 to:

The National Center for Financial Education
P.O. Box 3914
San Diego, CA 92163
Phone: 619–232–8811

National Schools Committee for Economic Education, Inc.

The National Schools Committee for Economic Education (NSCEE) is a nonprofit organization dedicated to researching, developing, and disseminating classroom materials that will help teach young people (up to 8th grade) the basics of the American economic system.

For more information, write:

National Schools Committee for Economic Education P.O. Box 295, 86 Valley Road
Cos Cob, CT 06807
Phone: 203–869–1706

The National Entrepreneurship Education Consortium

The National Entrepreneurship Education Consortium is committed to helping youngsters and adults pursue their dreams, create their own jobs, and find success in small businesses. The consortium is a good source for material on small–business development and economic education.

For more information, write:

Center on Education and Training for Employment
Ohio State University
1900 Kenny Road
Columbus, OH 43210–1090
Phone: 800–848–4815

Project XL

Project XL is a program of the U.S. Patent and Trademark Office designed to encourage the development of inventive thinking and problem–solving skills through:

- Designing national and regional workshops which "teach teachers to teach" creative thinking.

- Creating special teaching materials and lecture kits on creativity and problem–solving.

- Partnerships with other organizations to promote creative thinking, problem–solving, and the inventing process throughout America's public and private schools.

For more information write to:

Project XL
Public Affairs Office
US Patent and Trade Office
2121 Crystal Drive — Suite 100
Arlington, VA 22202
Phone: 703–305–8341

The Stock Market Game

The Stock Market Game is a public school program designed to teach kids grades 4 to 12 about basic economics and investments. The game is sponsored by the Securities Industry.

For more information, write:

The Securities Industry Association
120 Broadway, 35th Floor
New York, NY 10271
Phone: 212–608–1500 (they prefer that you write)

CAMPS/CONFERENCES

Camp Entrepreneur

Camp Entrepreneur is run by the National Education Center for Women in Business (NECWB), a nonprofit organization established to promote women in business ownership on the national level. The camp is for teens ages 10–19 and it is designed to introduce budding entrepreneurs to the idea of business ownership.

For more information write to:

The National Education Center For Women In Business
Seton Hill College
Seton Hill Drive
Greensburg, PA 15601
Phone: 800–NECWB–4–U

Camp Start–Up

Camp Start–Up is an entrepreneurial summer camp for teen women which is held on both the east coast and the west coast. The camp is run by An Income of Her Own.

Camp Start–Up provides opportunities for girls around the country to experience entrepreneurial skill building.

For more information, write to:

An Income of Her Own
P.O. Box 987
Santa Barbara, CA 93102
Phone: 805–646–1215 or 800–350–2987

Creativity In America

Creativity in America is a national showcase of expositions and conferences at Universal Studios Hollywood, for and about creative people, inventors, designers, artists, songwriters, performers, entrepreneurs, and scientists. This expo is co–sponsored by organizations such as: Project XL (of the U.S. Patent and Trademark Office), U.S. Small Business Administration, Inventors Workshop International, and other organizations.

For more information, contact:

Inventors Workshop International
7332 Mason Avenue
Canoga Park, CA 91306–2822
Phone: 818–340–4268

EntreCon

EntreCon, a high–school conference on entrepreneurship, brings together outstanding high school junior and seniors from across the country for an intensive four–day study of entrepreneurship. It is run by the Sol C. Snider Entrepreneurial Center at the University of Pennsylvania's Wharton School of Business. Entre-Con focuses on two areas:

- The basics of business and educational career opportunities available to students interested in business.

- The specifics of the entrepreneurial process, and the various methods and strategies employed in starting and running businesses.

The conference was not held in 1994 or 1995 because the student who started it graduated and retained the trademark rights on the name "Entrecon". I have no doubt that the conference will be resurrected in the near future.

For more information, write:

EntreCon—High School Conference on Entrepreneurship
Director of Undergraduate Education
Wharton Undergraduate Division, Suite 1100
Steinberg–Dietrich Hall
Philadelphia, PA 19104
Phone: 215–898–7607

Loyola College Money Management Camp for Young People and Camp Lemonade Stand

The Loyola College Money Management Camp for Young People teaches kids (ages 12 to 16) how to do just that—manage money. In addition, it delves a bit into entrepreneurship by training kids how to write and present business plans. Camp Lemonade Stand is an entrepreneurship camp for kids 12 years old or younger.

For more information, write:

Loyola College Money Management Camp
for Young People
Loyola College School of Professional Development
Sellinger School of Business and Management
4501 North Charles Street
Baltimore, MD 21210–2699
Phone: 410–617–5061

Money Management Camp for Kids

The Money Management Camp for Kids is designed to be a fun and informative method of introducing children ages 12–15 to the stock market, investments, and the value of savings. Workshops covered during the camp include the following: Bulls, Bears, and Broncos (How the Stock Market is Like Professional Sports); Creating a Budget You Can Live With; Enough Is Enough (How

Much Risk You Can Take); Spending, Saving and Strategic Investing; Picking Winning Stocks, Bonds, and Mutual Funds; and more.

The Money Management Camp is held annually at the Breakers Hotel in Palm Beach, Florida. The Breakers requires that a parent or guardian accompany the child since regulations don't allow minors to stay in a hotel room by themselves.

For more information, write:

Money Management Camp for Kids
The Breakers
Palm Beach, FL 33480
Phone: 407–655–6611

Teen Business Camp

Teen Business Camp (TBC), a two–week overnight entrepreneurship camp for teenagers is held during the summer at college campuses in Newark, New Jersey. TBC is run by the Center For Teen Entrepreneurs in Newark, New Jersey. The purpose of the camp is to introduce teenagers (ages 14 to 17) to the concept of entrepreneurship and to help them start and run their own businesses. These objectives are achieved through entrepreneurship and business workshops, hands–on business training, and through discussions with entrepreneurial role models who help camp participants understand the ups and downs of running a business. Examples of the type of workshops offered are:

- Business Plan Basics (a series of 9 workshops on writing a business plan)
- Setting Up Your Own Company
- Stocks & Bonds
- Creating Your Own Resume
- Basic Business Concepts You Should Know
- Giving Back To Your Community
- Presentation Skills and other business–related workshops.

Teen Business Camp
Center for Teen Entrepreneurs
P.O. Box 3967
New York, New York 10163–6027L
Phone: 800–438–8336

Youth Entrepreneurial Camp

The Youth Entrepreneurial Camp (YEC) is a program offered through the North Idaho College Small Business Development Center. This program consists of a week–long agenda designed for the "young hopeful" entrepreneur.

During the camp, Junior and Senior aged high school students engage in challenging hands–on skill building projects. These projects include group exercises, market research projects, and the opportunity to witness business environments first hand.

For more information write to:

Youth Entrepreneurial Camp
North Idaho College Small Business Development Center
525 W. Clearwater Loop
Post Falls, ID 83854–9400
Phone: 208–769–3444

A similar camp is also run by the Small Business Development Center in Portland, Oregon.

For more information write to:

Youth Entrepreneurial Camp
Small Business Development Center
Portland Community College
123 N.W. Second Avenue #321
Portland, OR 97209
Phone: 503–414–2828

Youth Entrepreneurship Business Camp

The Youth Entrepreneurship Business Camp (YESBC) is a two week intensive business camp designed to teach elementary through high school aged students about owning and operating small businesses. Topics explored during the camp include: how to develop a business idea, economics, goal setting, marketing planning, market research, pricing, legal structures, and other relevant business topics.

For more information, write to:

YESBC
EDGE Inc.
Cabrini Boulevard #21
New York, NY 10033
Phone: 212–978–0262

COMPETITIONS

Great Idea Contest

This international contest is co–sponsored by Inventors Workshop International, *PopSci for Kids* magazine (by the publishers of *Popular Science* magazine) and other organizations. Aspiring young Thomas Edisons can enter this contest and win three cash prizes in age categories 8–10, 11–13, 14–16.

For more information, write:

Inventors Workshop International
7332 Mason Avenue
Canoga Park, CA 91306–2822
Phone: 818–340–4268

Invent America

Invent America is a national nonprofit educational program and student invention competition designed to help kindergarten through eighth–graders develop and exercise their analytical and problem–solving skills. Children learn by creating their own inventions to solve everyday problems.

Invent America, the most prestigious invention competition in the United States, was launched by then–Vice President George Bush in 1987 to help develop the creative talents of school–age children.

The specific goals of Invent America are to:

- Raise self–esteem.

- Increase parental involvement.

- Increase student motivation.

- Develop problem–solving skills.

Hundreds of thousand of students participate yearly in state and regional Invent America competitions held for each grade level.

The competition is endorsed by the U.S. Department of Education, Department of Commerce, and the National Science Foundation.

For more information, write:

Invent America
510 King Street, Suite 420
Alexandria, VA 22314
Phone: 703–684–1836

National Teen Business Plan Competition

This competition is designed to encourage the entrepreneurial spirit of teenagers. It is run by An Income of Her Own (see earlier description). Entrants to this competition get access to An Income of Her Owns resources for support, coaching, and information.

For more information, write to:

An Income of Her Own
P.O. Box 987
Santa Barbara, CA 93102
Phone: 805–646–1215 or 800–350–2987

Outstanding High School Entrepreneur

The Outstanding High School Entrepreneur Contest is sponsored by Center for Entrepreneurial Studies at Johnson & Wales University in Providence, Rhode Island. Contestants make presentations to a panel of judges—mostly entrepreneurs themselves—who then score them on their business plans, financial strategies, and marketing approaches. Over $100,000 is awarded in scholarship to contestants.

For more information write to:

Outstanding High School Entrepreneur
Public Relations Department
Johnson & Wales University
8 Abbott Park Place
Providence, RI 02903
Phone: 401–598–1848

Outstanding Young Business Owner

A competition open to entrepreneurs who start businesses by age 21. The top prize is $1,000. Second–place and third–place finishers receive $500 and $250 respectively. The following is a list of the award criteria:

- Description of the business, including products sold or services rendered, number of employees, and the location.

- Explanation of the creativity involved in starting and operating business.

- Evidence of business success.

- Explanation of why the young business owner believes he or she has been a successful entrepreneur.

For more information, write:

National Federation of Independent Business Education
        Foundation #700
Maryland Avenue, S.W.
Washington, DC 20024
Phone: 202–554–9000

CANADIAN ORGANIZATIONS

Association of Collegiate Entrepreneurs

The Association of Collegiate Entrepreneurs (ACE) is a non-profit organization dedicated to encouraging young people to learn about the free enterprise system..

For more information, write to:

ACE
Renfrew Drive #200
Markham, Ontario L3R 7B8
Phone: 905–470–5193

Federal Business Development Bank

The Federal Business Development Bank (FBDP) is a Crown corporation that promotes the development and expansion of small and medium–sized businesses in Canada. It offers specialized financing for commercially–viable businesses including loans, and venture capital, as well as a wide range of business counseling, training and mentoring services.

The FBDP sponsors a program in which high school students apply for, and if qualified receive seed loans up to $3,000 to start businesses during the summer.

For more information, call your local FBDB or write to the main office at:

FBDB
Head Office
Victoria Square
Box 335
Montreal, Quebec H4Z 1L4
Phone: 514–283–5904

The phone numbers of other regional offices are as follows: Prairie & Northern Regional Office (204–983–7811), Atlantic Regional Office (902–426–7860), Ontario Regional Office (416–973–1144), and the B.C. & Yukon Regional Office (604–666–7800).

I Want To Be A Millionaire

Developed by the Cumberland Development Authority in Amherst, Nova Scotia, the I Want To Be a Millionaire Program serves as an employment alternative for school aged youth. The intent of this program is to award each successful participant $100 seed money to start their own small business after the submission of a one page application and a business plan.

Over the course of the summer, each youth must participate in each of the following training sessions:

- Student workbook orientation

- Basic financial record keeping

- Marketing, promotion, and display

- Customer service and quality

- Millionaire market

The emphasis of this program is on both the financial and social benefits of entrepreneurship.

For more information write to:

West Yellowhead Community Futures Development Corp.
221 Pembina Avenue
Box 6682
Hinton, Alberta T7V 1X8
Phone: 403–865–1224

YM–YWCA Enterprise Center

The Enterprise Center is a national program sponsored by Employment and Immigration Canada and the National YM–YWCA. There are nine centers operating across Canada designed to help people of all ages create self–employment through small–business development. Contact the YM–YWCAs in the following cities for more information:

- Saint John's, Newfoundland.
- Glace Bay, Nova Scotia.
- Saint John, New Brunswick.
- Montreal, Quebec.
- Toronto, Ontario.
- Ottawa, Ontario.
- Winnipeg, Manitoba.
- Edmonton, Alberta.
- Vancouver, British Columbia.

Fondation de L'Entrepreneurship

Fondation de L'Entrepreneurship is a nonprofit organization whose purpose is to encourage entrepreneurship among the Quebec population. The foundation has traditionally supported Jeunes Entreprises (the Quebec version of Junior Achievement), but it is considering a more realistic approach to entrepreneurship by mimicking real start–up businesses.

Fondation de L'Entrepreneurship has also sponsored the Cascade Contest: A province–wide contest for grade 5 students in economic education. All material provided by this organization is in French.

For more information, write:

Fondation de L'Entrepreneurship
160, 76 rue Est, bureau 250
Charlesbourg, Quebec G1H 7H6, Canada
Phone: 418–6461994

Junior Achievement

Junior Achievement (JA) is a nonprofit organization that encourages youth entrepreneurship and economic literacy. The organization operates the same way in Canada as it does in the United States. (See description of JA programs.)

For more information, write:

Junior Achievement, Inc.
1 Education Way
45 East Clubhouse Drive
Colorado Springs, CO 80906
Phone: 719–540–8000

Kiwanis Enterprise Center

The Kiwanis Enterprise Center (KEC) is a nonprofit organization that provides a business incubator for high school students. The incubator gives these kids an office from which they can conduct their business activities. Mac Taylor of KEC stresses that the organization firmly believes that "young people should learn about business by actually starting and operating them."

The students who use KEC's facilities are given course credits by their high schools. KEC also teaches sessions on finding business opportunities, writing business plans, and obtaining money for businesses. Each student that participates in KEC's program must operate their own businesses by their senior year.

For more information, write:

Kiwanis Enterprise Center
10805 14th Street
Dawson Creek, BC V1G 4V6, Canada
Phone: 604–782–5745

There are other Enterprise Centers that you should know about. One is in Beaver Lodge, Alberta, and others are under construction in Swift Current, Saskatchewan and Brandon, Manitoba.

Projet Entrepreneurship Project

Projet Entrepreneurship Project (PEP) was developed by the Universite de Moncton and Mount Allison University. PEP's mandate is to conduct research on the values and beliefs concerning entrepreneurship that currently exists in the school system, analyze how entrepreneurship is presented in daily school studies, investigate what the business community expects from the school system, and discover how entrepreneurship can be developed in teacher–training institutions.

PEP's main goal is to enhance the vitality of Atlantic Canada. To reach this objective, it must come up with answers on how to cultivate the spirit of enterprise in the students of the region and how to produce students who are fully aware of the entrepreneurial opportunities in a global economy.

PEP is essentially a research venture, so your kids cannot join it. However, the results of the organizations research may affect the availability of entrepreneurial education for your kids in your area. The principal co–researcher of PEP, Basil Favaro, told me that "PEP will play a role in moving beyond entrepreneurship to the implementation of enterprise education across all the grade levels."

PEP's research is the most ambitious work related to youth entrepreneurship that I have seen. Thus far, the project has gone through two phases —the research phase and the developmental phase (which is currently underway throughout the Province of New Brunswick). The first phase was funded by the Atlantic Canada Opportunities Agency (ACOA) and the second phase is being funded by the Cooperation Agreement on Entrepreneurship and Human Resource Development. The Department of Education is evaluating the PEP initiative for possible implementation in other provinces.

For more information, write:

The Coordinator
PEP, Mount Allison University
Sackville, New Brunswick EOA 3CO
Phone:506–364–2528

The Provincial Ministries of Education
In many cases, your Provincial Ministry of Education has programs designed to teach kids about entrepreneurship. For example, Ontario recently established a curriculum guideline for entrepreneurship studies. This guideline authorizes credit courses in grades 11 and 12. In addition, the province has developed an entrepreneurship awareness program, Vision, for use in grades 7 and 8. Write to your Ministry of Education and ask them about their pro-

grams for entrepreneurship education. If they don't have such programs, perhaps you can suggest that they contact the Ministry of Education of other provinces for help in establishing one.

Shad Valley

Shad Valley is a four–week residential program in technology and entrepreneurship for outstanding students in grades 11 and 12 (sec. V and CEGEP I). The program is offered by the Canadian Centre for Creative Technology, a charitable organization. Shad Valley runs at eight universities across Canada. Each of the host universities—British Columbia, Calgary, Manitoba, Waterloo, Carleton, Sherbrooke, New Brunswick, and Acadia—welcomes 50 of Canada's best senior high school students. A few spots are available to international students. The program administrators are looking for the following qualities among the candidates: academic achievement (especially in math and science), creativity, initiative and drive, and good interpersonal skills.

For more information, write:

Shad Valley
Canadian Center for Creative Technology
8 Young Street East
Waterloo, Ontario N2J 2L3, Canada
Phone: 519–884–8844

PUBLICATIONS

Books for Parents

1. *Piggy Bank to Credit Card—Teach Your Child the Financial Facts of Life,* by Linda Barbanel. This books tells parents how they can teach their kids how to use money and how to avoid abusing it.

2. *Money–Smart Kids,* by Janet Bodnar. This book helps parents turn their kids into wise financial consumers by teaching them how to save, shop and use credit properly.

3. *Your Child's Self–Esteem,* by Dorothy Corkille Briggs. This book tells parents how to help their kids acquire strong feelings of self–worth.

4. *Teach Your Child Decision Making,* by John F. Clabby and Maurice J. Elias. This book provides an eight–step program for parents to teach kids how to solve everyday problems and make decisions.

5. *Activities to Teach Your Child About Money,* by Bonnie Drew. This book shows parents how to use fun activities to teach their preschool to junior high school kids about money.

6. *Kids Who Succeed,* by Dr. Beverly Neuer Feldman. This book gives parents advice on how to raise happy, successful, and well–adjusted kids.

7. *Raising Self–Reliant Children (In a Self–indulgent World),* by H. Stephen Glenn and Jane Nelsen. This book tells parents about the seven building blocks for developing capable young people.

8. *No More Frogs to Kiss: 99 Ways to Give Economic Power to Girls,* by Joline Godfrey. This book offers parents concrete ideas, games, and strategies to teach their daughters the basics of business and finance.

9. *Money Doesn't Grow on Trees—A Parent's Guide to Raising Financially Responsible Children,* by Neale S. Godfrey and Carolina Edwards.This book is filled with age–appropriate ways to teach kids money management skills.

10. *Smarter Kids,* by Lawrence J. Green. This book tells parents how to help their kids manage time more effectively, analyze the consequences of their actions, learn from their mistakes, bounce back from setbacks, and many other life skills.

11. *Developing Positive Self–Images and Discipline in Black Children,* by Jawanza Kunjufu. This book outlines a

home program African–American parents can follow to increase their children's self–esteem.

12. *Teach Your Child the Value of Money,* by Harold and Sandy Moe. This book gives parents the tools to help their kids understand the value of money.

13. *How to Understand Economics in 1 Hour,* by Marshall Payne. This book teaches kids as young as 12 years old about economics basics.

14. *It Doesn't Grow on Trees,* by Jean Ross Peterson. This book advises parents on how to teach their children about money.

15. *Your Family Business,* by Arthur Pine. This book gives people in family businesses advice of how to anticipate and solve potential conflicts.

16. *Teaching Your Child About Money,* by Chris Snyder. This book tells parents how to teach their kids about managing and investing money.

17. *Children and Money: A Parent's Guide,* by Grace Weinstein. This book is a guide for teaching children about money.

18. *Raising Positive Kids in a Negative World,* by Zig Ziglar. This book is for parents who want to raise positive and successful kids.

Books for Kids

1. *The Totally Awesome Money Book for Kids and Their Parents,* by Adriane Berg and Arthur Berg Bochner. This book tells 10–17 year olds about the fundamentals of saving, investing, borrowing, taxes, and the American workforce. It is complete with puzzles, riddles, forms, games and other fun devices to make it easy to read.

2. *Better Than a Lemonade Stand,* by Daryl Bernstein. This book is by a then–15 years old Daryl who describes 51 of

his favorite small enterprises. The book also gives kids tips on starting and running their own business.

3. *Every Kid's Guide to Making and Managing Money,* by Joy Berry. This book teaches kids, from ages 6 and up, how to get money and how to spend it wisely. The book goes well with another book by Joy Berry called *Every Kid's Guide To Intelligent Spending.*

4. *The Kids' Money Book*, by Neale S. Godfrey. This book tells kids ages 8 and up everything they ever want to know about money and the economy. It discusses everything from the history of money to becoming a wise consumer.

5. *Fast Cash for Kids*, by Bonnie Drew and Noel Drew. This book is full of 101 money–making ideas for kids.

6. *Capitalism for Kids*, by Karl Hess. This book tells kids about capitalism and the free enterprise system.

7. *The Monster Money Book,* by Loreen Leedy. This book is for kids in grades K–4. It is a story book that incorporates basic elements of money management such as budgeting, shopping, and saving.

8. *A Teen's Guide to Business* by Linda Menzies, Oren S. Jenkins, and Rickell R. Fisher. This book shows teenager how to become entrepreneurs.

9. *The Teenage Entrepreneur's Guide*, by Sarah Riehm. This book is a collection of fifty business ideas for teenagers.

10. *Smart Spending,* by Lois Schmitt. This book shows the young consumer how to budget, spend wisely, read warranties, avoid consumer fraud, and become a well informed buyer.

11. *Making Cents* by Elizabeth Wilkinson. This book shows kids, ages 6–12, how they can earn money by providing goods and services to their neighbors and friends.

Form 1040 Department of the Treasury—Internal Revenue Service

U.S. Individual Income Tax Return ⊗ **1994** | IRS Use Only—Do not write or staple in this space.

For the year Jan. 1–Dec. 31, 1994, or other tax year beginning , 1994, ending , 19 | OMB No. 1545-0074

Label
(See instructions on page 12.)
Use the IRS label. Otherwise, please print or type.

Your first name and initial	Last name	Your social security number
If a joint return, spouse's first name and initial	Last name	Spouse's social security number
Home address (number and street). If you have a P.O. box, see page 12.	Apt. no.	For Privacy Act and Paperwork Reduction Act Notice, see page 4.
City, town or post office, state, and ZIP code. If you have a foreign address, see page 12.		

Presidential Election Campaign (See page 12.)
Do you want $3 to go to this fund? . . . .
If a joint return, does your spouse want $3 to go to this fund? . . . . .
Yes No | Note: Checking "Yes" will not change your tax or reduce your refund.

Filing Status (See page 12.)
Check only one box.
1 Single
2 Married filing joint return (even if only one had income)
3 Married filing separate return. Enter spouse's social security no. above and full name here. ►
4 Head of household (with qualifying person). (See page 13.) If the qualifying person is a child but not your dependent, enter this child's name here. ►
5 Qualifying widow(er) with dependent child (year spouse died ► 19). (See page 13.)

Exemptions (See page 13.)
If more than six dependents, see page 14.

6a ☐ Yourself. If your parent (or someone else) can claim you as a dependent on his or her tax return, do not check box 6a. But be sure to check the box on line 33b on page 2 .
b ☐ Spouse . . . .
c Dependents:
(1) Name (first, initial, and last name) | (2) Check if under age 1 | (3) If age 1 or older, dependent's social security number | (4) Dependent's relationship to you | (5) No. of months lived in your home in 1994

No. of boxes checked on 6a and 6b ___
No. of your children on 6c who:
• lived with you ___
• didn't live with you due to divorce or separation (see page 14) ___
Dependents on 6c not entered above ___
Add numbers entered on lines above ► ☐

d If your child didn't live with you but is claimed as your dependent under a pre-1985 agreement, check here ► ☐
e Total number of exemptions claimed . . . .

Income
Attach Copy B of your Forms W-2, W-2G, and 1099-R here.
If you did not get a W-2, see page 15.
Enclose, but do not attach, any payment with your return.

7 Wages, salaries, tips, etc. Attach Form(s) W-2 . . . . | 7
8a Taxable interest income (see page 15). Attach Schedule B if over $400 . . . . | 8a
b Tax-exempt interest (see page 16). DON'T include on line 8a | 8b |
9 Dividend income. Attach Schedule B if over $400 . . . . | 9
10 Taxable refunds, credits, or offsets of state and local income taxes (see page 16) . | 10
11 Alimony received . . . . | 11
12 Business income or (loss). Attach Schedule C or C-EZ . . . . . . | 12
13 Capital gain or (loss). If required, attach Schedule D (see page 16) . . . | 13
14 Other gains or (losses). Attach Form 4797 . . . . | 14
15a Total IRA distributions . | 15a | b Taxable amount (see page 17) | 15b
16a Total pensions and annuities | 16a | b Taxable amount (see page 17) | 16b
17 Rental real estate, royalties, partnerships, S corporations, trusts, etc. Attach Schedule E | 17
18 Farm income or (loss). Attach Schedule F . . . . | 18
19 Unemployment compensation (see page 18) . . . . | 19
20a Social security benefits | 20a | b Taxable amount (see page 18) | 20b
21 Other income. List type and amount—see page 18 . . . . | 21
22 Add the amounts in the far right column for lines 7 through 21. This is your total income ► | 22

Adjustments to Income
Caution: See instructions . . ►

23a Your IRA deduction (see page 19) . . . . | 23a
b Spouse's IRA deduction (see page 19) . . . . . . | 23b
24 Moving expenses. Attach Form 3903 or 3903-F . . . | 24
25 One-half of self-employment tax . . . . . . | 25
26 Self-employed health insurance deduction (see page 21) | 26
27 Keogh retirement plan and self-employed SEP deduction | 27
28 Penalty on early withdrawal of savings . . . . | 28
29 Alimony paid. Recipient's SSN ► | 29
30 Add lines 23a through 29. These are your total adjustments . . . . ► | 30

Adjusted Gross Income
31 Subtract line 30 from line 22. This is your adjusted gross income. If less than $25,296 and a child lived with you (less than $9,000 if a child didn't live with you), see "Earned Income Credit" on page 27 ► | 31

Cat. No. 11320B   Form **1040** (1994)

Form 1040 (1994)   Page 2

Tax Computation (See page 23.)	32	Amount from line 31 (adjusted gross income)	32	
	33a	Check if: ☐ You were 65 or older, ☐ Blind; ☐ Spouse was 65 or older, ☐ Blind. Add the number of boxes checked above and enter the total here . . . . . ▶ 33a		
	b	If your parent (or someone else) can claim you as a dependent, check here . ▶ 33b ☐		
	c	If you are married filing separately and your spouse itemizes deductions or you are a dual-status alien, see page 23 and check here . . . . ▶ 33c ☐		
	34	Enter the larger of your: { Itemized deductions from Schedule A, line 29, OR Standard deduction shown below for your filing status. But if you checked any box on line 33a or b, go to page 23 to find your standard deduction. If you checked box 33c, your standard deduction is zero. • Single—$3,800 • Head of household—$5,600 • Married filing jointly or Qualifying widow(er)—$6,350 • Married filing separately—$3,175 }	34	

(See page 23.)

If you want the IRS to figure your tax, see page 24.	35	Subtract line 34 from line 32	35	
	36	If line 32 is $83,850 or less, multiply $2,450 by the total number of exemptions claimed on line 6e. If line 32 is over $83,850, see the worksheet on page 24 for the amount to enter .	36	
	37	**Taxable income.** Subtract line 36 from line 35. If line 36 is more than line 35, enter -0-.	37	
	38	Tax. Check if from a ☐ Tax Table, b ☐ Tax Rate Schedules, c ☐ Capital Gain Tax Work- sheet, or d ☐ Form 8615 (see page 24). Amount from Form(s) 8814 ▶ e ⎹	38	
	39	Additional taxes. Check if from a ☐ Form 4970 b ☐ Form 4972 . . . . . ▶	39	
	40	Add lines 38 and 39 . . . . ▶	40	

Credits (See page 24.)	41	Credit for child and dependent care expenses. Attach Form 2441	41		
	42	Credit for the elderly or the disabled. Attach Schedule R . .	42		
	43	Foreign tax credit. Attach Form 1116	43		
	44	Other credits (see page 25). Check if from a ☐ Form 3800 b ☐ Form 8396 c ☐ Form 8801 d ☐ Form (specify)_____	44		
	45	Add lines 41 through 44	45		
	46	Subtract line 45 from line 40. If line 45 is more than line 40, enter -0-. . . . ▶	46		

Other Taxes (See page 25.)	47	Self-employment tax. Attach Schedule SE	47	
	48	Alternative minimum tax. Attach Form 6251	48	
	49	Recapture taxes. Check if from a ☐ Form 4255 b ☐ Form 8611 c ☐ Form 8828	49	
	50	Social security and Medicare tax on tip income not reported to employer. Attach Form 4137	50	
	51	Tax on qualified retirement plans, including IRAs. If required, attach Form 5329 . . .	51	
	52	Advance earned income credit payments from Form W-2	52	
	53	Add lines 46 through 52. This is your **total tax** . . . . ▶	53	

Payments Attach Forms W-2, W-2G, and 1099-R on the front.	54	Federal income tax withheld. If any is from Form(s) 1099, check ▶ ☐	54		
	55	1994 estimated tax payments and amount applied from 1993 return .	55		
	56	Earned income credit. If required, attach Schedule EIC (see page 27). Nontaxable earned income: amount ▶ ⎹ ⎹ and type ▶	56		
	57	Amount paid with Form 4868 (extension request)	57		
	58	Excess social security and RRTA tax withheld (see page 32) .	58		
	59	Other payments. Check if from a ☐ Form 2439 b ☐ Form 4136	59		
	60	Add lines 54 through 59. These are your **total payments** . . . . . . ▶	60		

Refund or Amount You Owe	61	If line 60 is more than line 53, subtract line 53 from line 60. This is the amount you **OVERPAID**. . ▶	61	
	62	Amount of line 61 you want **REFUNDED TO YOU.** . . . . ▶	62	
	63	Amount of line 61 you want **APPLIED TO YOUR 1995 ESTIMATED TAX** ▶ 63		
	64	If line 53 is more than line 60, subtract line 60 from line 53. This is the **AMOUNT YOU OWE.** For details on how to pay, including what to write on your payment, see page 32 . . . ▶	64	
	65	Estimated tax penalty (see page 33). Also include on line 64 65 ⎹		

Sign Here Keep a copy of this return for your records.	Under penalties of perjury, I declare that I have examined this return and accompanying schedules and statements, and to the best of my knowledge and belief, they are true, correct, and complete. Declaration of preparer (other than taxpayer) is based on all information of which preparer has any knowledge.		
	▶ Your signature	Date	Your occupation
	▶ Spouse's signature. If a joint return, BOTH must sign.	Date	Spouse's occupation

Paid Preparer's Use Only	Preparer's ▶ signature	Date	Check if self-employed ☐	Preparer's social security no. ⎹ ⎹
	Firm's name (or yours if self-employed) and address ▶		E.I. No.	
			ZIP code	

SCHEDULE C
(Form 1040)

Department of the Treasury
Internal Revenue Service (00)

Profit or Loss From Business
(Sole Proprietorship)

▶ Partnerships, joint ventures, etc., must file Form 1065.

▶ Attach to Form 1040 or Form 1041. ▶ See Instructions for Schedule C (Form 1040).

OMB No. 1545-0074

19 94

Attachment
Sequence No. **09**

Name of proprietor | Social security number (SSN)

A Principal business or profession, including product or service (see page C-1) | **B** Enter principal business code (see page C-6) ▶

C Business name. If no separate business name, leave blank. | **D** Employer ID number (EIN), if any

E Business address (including suite or room no.) ▶
City, town or post office, state, and ZIP code

F Accounting method: (1) ☐ Cash (2) ☐ Accrual (3) ☐ Other (specify) ▶

G Method(s) used to value closing inventory: (1) ☐ Cost (2) ☐ Lower of cost or market (3) ☐ Other (attach explanation) (4) ☐ Does not apply (if checked, skip line H) | Yes | No

H Was there any change in determining quantities, costs, or valuations between opening and closing inventory? If "Yes," attach explanation . . . .

I Did you "materially participate" in the operation of this business during 1994? If "No," see page C-2 for limit on losses. . . . ▶ ☐

J If you started or acquired this business during 1994, check here . . . . ▶ ☐

Part I   Income

1	Gross receipts or sales. Caution: If this income was reported to you on Form W-2 and the "Statutory employee" box on that form was checked, see page C-2 and check here . . . . ▶ ☐	1	
2	Returns and allowances	2	
3	Subtract line 2 from line 1	3	
4	Cost of goods sold (from line 40 on page 2)	4	
5	Gross profit. Subtract line 4 from line 3	5	
6	Other income, including Federal and state gasoline or fuel tax credit or refund (see page C-2) . . . ▶	6	
7	Gross income. Add lines 5 and 6 . . . . ▶	7	

Part II   Expenses. Enter expenses for business use of your home **only on line 30.**

8	Advertising	8		19 Pension and profit-sharing plans	19	
9	Bad debts from sales or services (see page C-3) . .	9		20 Rent or lease (see page C-4):	
				a Vehicles, machinery, and equipment .	20a	
10	Car and truck expenses (see page C-3) . .	10		b Other business property . .	20b	
11	Commissions and fees. . .	11		21 Repairs and maintenance . .	21	
12	Depletion.	12		22 Supplies (not included in Part III) .	22	
13	Depreciation and section 179 expense deduction (not included in Part III) (see page C-3) . .	13		23 Taxes and licenses	23	
				24 Travel, meals, and entertainment:	
14	Employee benefit programs (other than on line 19) . .	14		a Travel	24a	
15	Insurance (other than health) .	15		b Meals and entertainment .	
16	Interest:			c Enter 50% of line 24b subject to limitations (see page C-4) .	
a	Mortgage (paid to banks, etc.) .	16a			
b	Other	16b		d Subtract line 24c from line 24b .	24d	
17	Legal and professional services	17		25 Utilities	25	
				26 Wages (less employment credits) .	26	
18	Office expense	18		27 Other expenses (from line 46 on page 2)	27	

28	Total expenses before expenses for business use of home. Add lines 8 through 27 in columns. . ▶	28	
29	Tentative profit (loss). Subtract line 28 from line 7	29	
30	Expenses for business use of your home. Attach **Form 8829**	30	
31	Net profit or (loss). Subtract line 30 from line 29. • If a profit, enter on **Form 1040, line 12,** and ALSO on **Schedule SE, line 2** (statutory employees, see page C-5). Estates and trusts, enter on Form 1041, line 3. • If a loss, you MUST go on to line 32.	31	
32	If you have a loss, check the box that describes your investment in this activity (see page C-5). • If you checked 32a, enter the loss on **Form 1040, line 12,** and ALSO on **Schedule SE, line 2** (statutory employees, see page C-5). Estates and trusts, enter on Form 1041, line 3. • If you checked 32b, you MUST attach **Form 6198.**	32a ☐ All investment is at risk. 32b ☐ Some investment is not at risk.	

For Paperwork Reduction Act Notice, see Form 1040 instructions.   Cat. No. 11334P   **Schedule C (Form 1040) 1994**

Schedule C (Form 1040) 1994

Part III   Cost of Goods Sold (see page C-5)

33	Inventory at beginning of year. If different from last year's closing inventory, attach explanation . .	**33**	
34	Purchases less cost of items withdrawn for personal use	**34**	
35	Cost of labor. Do not include salary paid to yourself	**35**	
36	Materials and supplies	**36**	
37	Other costs	**37**	
38	Add lines 33 through 37	**38**	
39	Inventory at end of year	**39**	
40	**Cost of goods sold.** Subtract line 39 from line 38. Enter the result here and on page 1, line 4 . .	**40**	

Part IV   **Information on Your Vehicle. Complete this part ONLY if you are claiming car or truck expenses on line 10 and are not required to file Form 4562 for this business. See the instructions for line 13 on page C-3 to find out if you must file.**

41   When did you place your vehicle in service for business purposes? (month, day, year) ▶ ..../......../....... .

42   Of the total number of miles you drove your vehicle during 1994, enter the number of miles you used your vehicle for:

a   Business .... b   Commuting c   Other ....

43   Do you (or your spouse) have another vehicle available for personal use?. . . . . ☐ Yes   ☐ No

44   Was your vehicle available for use during off-duty hours? . . . . ☐ Yes   ☐ No

45a   Do you have evidence to support your deduction? . . . . ☐ Yes   ☐ No
   b   If "Yes," is the evidence written?. . . . . ☐ Yes   ☐ No

Part V   **Other Expenses. List below business expenses not included on lines 8–26 or line 30.**

....		
....		
....		
....		
....		
....		
....		
....		
....		
46 **Total other expenses.** Enter here and on page 1, line 27	**46**	

SCHEDULE SE (Form 1040) Department of the Treasury Internal Revenue Service (X)	**Self-Employment Tax** ▶ See Instructions for Schedule SE (Form 1040). ▶ Attach to Form 1040.	OMB No. 1545-0074 **1994** Attachment Sequence No. **17**
Name of person with **self-employment** income (as shown on Form 1040)	Social security number of person with **self-employment** income ▶	: :

Who Must File Schedule SE

You must file Schedule SE if:

- You had net earnings from self-employment from other than church employee income (line 4 of Short Schedule SE or line 4c of Long Schedule SE) of $400 or more, **OR**
- You had church employee income of $108.28 or more. Income from services you performed as a minister or a member of a religious order **is not** church employee income. See page SE-1.

Note: *Even if you have a loss or a small amount of income from self-employment, it may be to your benefit to file Schedule SE and use either "optional method" in Part II of Long Schedule SE. See page SE-2.*

Exception. If your only self-employment income was from earnings as a minister, member of a religious order, or Christian Science practitioner, **and** you filed Form 4361 and received IRS approval not to be taxed on those earnings, **do not** file Schedule SE. Instead, write "Exempt–Form 4361" on Form 1040, line 47.

May I Use Short Schedule SE or MUST I Use Long Schedule SE?

```
                    ┌─────────────────────────────────────────┐
                    │   Did you receive wages or tips in 1994? │
                    └─────────────────────────────────────────┘
              No │                                        │ Yes

 ┌──────────────────────────────────┐        ┌──────────────────────────────────────┐
 │ Are you a minister, member of a  │        │ Was the total of your wages and tips  │  Yes
 │ religious order, or Christian    │ Yes    │ subject to social security or railroad├────▶
 │ Science practitioner who received│───▶    │ retirement tax plus your net earnings │
 │ IRS approval not to be taxed on  │        │ from self-employment more than $60,600?│
 │ earnings from these sources, but │        └──────────────────────────────────────┘
 │ you owe self-employment tax on   │                          │ No
 │ other earnings?                  │                          │
 └──────────────────────────────────┘                          │
              No │                                              │
 ┌──────────────────────────────────┐        ┌──────────────────────────────────────┐
 │ Are you using one of the optional│ Yes     No │ Did you receive tips subject to       │ Yes
 │ methods to figure your net       │───▶  ◀────│ social security or Medicare tax that  ├───▶
 │ earnings (see page SE-2)?        │           │ you did not report to your employer?  │
 └──────────────────────────────────┘          └──────────────────────────────────────┘
              No │
 ┌──────────────────────────────────┐
 │ Did you receive church employee  │ Yes
 │ income reported on Form W-2 of   │───▶
 │ $108.28 or more?                 │
 └──────────────────────────────────┘
              No │

 ┌──────────────────────────────────┐        ┌──────────────────────────────────────┐
 │ YOU MAY USE SHORT SCHEDULE SE    │        │ YOU MUST USE LONG SCHEDULE SE ON THE  │
 │ BELOW                            │   ◀────│ BACK                                  │
 └──────────────────────────────────┘        └──────────────────────────────────────┘
```

Section A—Short Schedule SE. Caution: *Read above to see if you can use Short Schedule SE.*

1	Net farm profit or (loss) from Schedule F, line 36, and farm partnerships, Schedule K-1 (Form 1065), line 15a	**1**	
2	Net profit or (loss) from Schedule C, line 31; Schedule C-EZ, line 3; and Schedule K-1 (Form 1065), line 15a (other than farming). Ministers and members of religious orders see page SE-1 for amounts to report on this line. See page SE-2 for other income to report	**2**	
3	Combine lines 1 and 2	**3**	
4	**Net earnings from self-employment.** Multiply line 3 by 92.35% (.9235). If less than $400, do not file this schedule; you do not owe self-employment tax . . . . ▶	**4**	
5	**Self-employment tax.** If the amount on line 4 is: • $60,600 or less, multiply line 4 by 15.3% (.153). Enter the result here and on **Form 1040, line 47.** • More than $60,600, multiply line 4 by 2.9% (.029). Then, add $7,514.40 to the result. Enter the total here and on **Form 1040, line 47.**	**5**	
6	**Deduction for one-half of self-employment tax.** Multiply line 5 by 50% (.5). Enter the result here and on **Form 1040, line 25**	**6**	

For Paperwork Reduction Act Notice, see Form 1040 instructions.   Cat. No. 11358Z   Schedule SE (Form 1040) 1994

Schedule SE (Form 1040) 1994

	Attachment Sequence No. **17**	Page **2**
Name of person with **self-employment** income (as shown on Form 1040)	Social security number of person with **self-employment** income ▶	┊ ┊

Section B—Long Schedule SE

Part I   Self-Employment Tax

Note: *If your only income subject to self-employment tax is church employee income, skip lines 1 through 4b. Enter -0- on line 4c and go to line 5a. Income from services you performed as a minister or a member of a religious order is not church employee income. See page SE-1.*

A If you are a minister, member of a religious order, or Christian Science practitioner **and** you filed Form 4361, but you had $400 or more of **other** net earnings from self-employment, check here and continue with Part I . . . . . ▶ ☐

1	Net farm profit or (loss) from Schedule F, line 36, and farm partnerships, Schedule K-1 (Form 1065), line 15a. **Note:** *Skip this line if you use the farm optional method. See page SE-3* . .	**1**	
2	Net profit or (loss) from Schedule C, line 31; Schedule C-EZ, line 3; and Schedule K-1 (Form 1065), line 15a (other than farming). Ministers and members of religious orders see page SE-1 for amounts to report on this line. See page SE-2 for other income to report. **Note:** *Skip this line if you use the nonfarm optional method. See page SE-3.*	**2**	
3	Combine lines 1 and 2	**3**	
4a	If line 3 is more than zero, multiply line 3 by 92.35% (.9235). Otherwise, enter amount from line 3	**4a**	
b	If you elected one or both of the optional methods, enter the total of lines 15 and 17 here . .	**4b**	
c	Combine lines 4a and 4b. If less than $400, **do not** file this schedule; you do not owe self-employment tax. **Exception.** If less than $400 and you had church employee income, enter -0- and continue . ▶	**4c**	
5a	Enter your church employee income from Form W-2. **Caution:** *See page SE-1 for definition of church employee income*	**5a**		
b	Multiply line 5a by 92.35% (.9235). If less than $100, enter -0-	**5b**	
6	**Net earnings from self-employment.** Add lines 4c and 5b	**6**	
7	Maximum amount of combined wages and self-employment earnings subject to social security tax or the 6.2% portion of the 7.65% railroad retirement (tier 1) tax for 1994	**7**	60,600	00
8a	Total social security wages and tips (total of boxes 3 and 7 on Form(s) W-2) and railroad retirement (tier 1) compensation	**8a**		
b	Unreported tips subject to social security tax (from Form 4137, line 9)	**8b**		
c	Add lines 8a and 8b	**8c**	
9	Subtract line 8c from line 7. If zero or less, enter -0- here and on line 10 and go to line 11 . ▶	**9**	
10	Multiply the **smaller** of line 6 or line 9 by 12.4% (.124)	**10**	
11	Multiply line 6 by 2.9% (.029)	**11**	
12	**Self-employment tax.** Add lines 10 and 11. Enter here and on Form 1040, **line 47**	**12**	
13	**Deduction for one-half of self-employment tax.** Multiply line 12 by 50% (.5). Enter the result here and on **Form 1040, line 25**	**13**		

Part II   Optional Methods To Figure Net Earnings (See page SE-2.)

Farm Optional Method. You may use this method **only** if:
- Your gross farm income[1] was not more than $2,400, **or**
- Your gross farm income[1] was more than $2,400 and your net farm profits[2] were less than $1,733.

14	Maximum income for optional methods	**14**	1,600	00
15	Enter the **smaller** of: two-thirds (⅔) of gross farm income[1] (not less than zero) **or** $1,600. Also, include this amount on line 4b above	**15**	

Nonfarm Optional Method. You may use this method **only** if:
- Your net nonfarm profits[3] were less than $1,733 and also less than 72.189% of your gross nonfarm income,[4] **and**
- You had net earnings from self-employment of at least $400 in 2 of the prior 3 years.

Caution: *You may use this method no more than five times.*

16	Subtract line 15 from line 14	**16**	
17	Enter the **smaller** of: two-thirds (⅔) of gross nonfarm income[4] (not less than zero) **or** the amount on line 16. Also, include this amount on line 4b above	**17**	

[1]From Schedule F, line 11, and Schedule K-1 (Form 1065), line 15b.   [3]From Schedule C, line 31; Schedule C-EZ, line 3; and Schedule K-1 (Form 1065), line 15a.
[2]From Schedule F, line 36, and Schedule K-1 (Form 1065), line 15a.   [4]From Schedule C, line 7; Schedule C-EZ, line 1; and Schedule K-1 (Form 1065), line 15c.

INDEX

ORDERING FROM GATEWAY PUBLISHERS

The Lemonade Stand: *A Guide To Encouraging The Entrepreneur In Your Child* is available from Gateway Publishers at special discounts for bulk purchases for sales promotions, premiums, fund–raising, or educational use.

To order individual copies, please send $19.50 plus $3.75 shipping and handling to the address on the bottom of this page. Checks should be made out to Gateway Publishers.

The Following Books Can Also Be Ordered Through Gateway Publishers:

1. **Piggy Bank To Credit Card**: *Teach Your Child the Financial Facts of Life*, by Linda Barnabel. (For parents).

2. **Better Than A Lemonade Stand**: *Small Business Ideas for Kids*, by Daryl Bernstein. (For kids).

3. **Money Skills**: *101 Activities to Teach Your Child About Money*, by Bonnie and Noel Drew. (For parents).

4. **Fast Cash For Kids**: *101 Money-Making Projects for Young Entrepreneurs*, by Bonnie Drew. (For kids).

5. **No More Frogs To Kiss**: *99 Ways to Give Economic Power to Girls*, by Joline Godfrey.(For parents).

6. **Money Doesn't Grow on Trees**: *A Parent's Guide To Raising Financially Responsible Children*, by Neale S. Godfrey. (For parents).

7. **The Kid's Money Book**, by Neale S. Godfrey. (For kids).

8. **Smart Spending**: *A Young Consumer's Guide*, by Lois Schmitt. (For kids).

For a full description and price list for each of these books, contact:

Gateway Publishers
P.O. Box 1749
Newark, NJ 07101
1-800-438-8336

DEAR READER

Do you know any:

- young entrepreneurs or inventors?
- young people who are making a difference in their communities through volunteerism?
- organizations that encourage youth entrepreneurship?

If so, please contact me so that I can include them in the next edition of *The Lemonade Stand*. Please send the information to:

Emmanuel Modu
c/o Gateway Publishers
P.O. Box 1749
Newark, NJ 07101

I can also be reached via E-Mail at:

modu@ix.netcom.com